Mesas & Cosmologies in Mesoamerica

With Contributions by

James E. Brady

Roberto Campos-Navarro

Allen J. Christenson

James W. Dow

Judith Green

Matthew G. Looper

Bruce Love

John Monaghan

H. B. Nicholson

Alan R. Sandstrom

Stacy B. Schaefer

Douglas Sharon

Mesas & Cosmologies in Mesoamerica

Edited by Douglas Sharon

San Diego Museum Papers 42
2003

Mesas & Cosmologies in Mesoamerica
Edited by Douglas Sharon
San Diego Museum Papers 42

Copyright © 2003
San Diego Museum of Man
1350 El Prado
San Diego, California 92101

www.museumofman.org

Lithographed in the United States of America
by Thomson-Shore, Inc., Dexter, Michigan

ISBN 0-937808-80-6

Cover photograph by Roberto Campos-Navarro
"In a close-up, we observe the protective cross with a plastic toy representing a little sorceress beside it."
(See paper beginning on page 19)

Cover Design by Suzan Peterson

Contents

vii   Preface
Douglas Sharon

Introduction

1   Shamanism, Mesas, & Cosmologies in Middle America
Douglas Sharon

Central and Northern Mexico

19   Curanderos' Altar-*Mesas* in Mexico City
Roberto Campos-Navarro

25   Sierra Otomí Religious Symbolism:
Mankind Responding to the Natural World
James W. Dow

33   The Annual "Royal Ceremony" on Mt. Tlaloc:
Mountain Fertility Ritualism in the Late Pre-Hispanic Basin of Mexico
H. B. Nicholson

51   Sacred Mountains and Miniature Worlds:
Altar Design Among the Nahua of Northern Veracruz, Mexico
Alan R. Sandstrom

71   The Wixárika (Huichol) Altar:
Place of the Souls, Stairway of the Sun
Stacy B. Schaefer

Southern Mexico and Guatemala

83   In My Hill, In My Valley:
The Importance of Place in Ancient Maya Ritual
James E. Brady

93   Manipulating the Cosmos:
Shamanic Tables Among the Highland Maya
Allen J. Christenson

105   Altars for Ancestors:
Maya Altars for the Days of the Dead in Yucatán
Judith Green

119   Wind, Rain, and Stone:
Ancient and Contemporary Maya Meteorology
Matthew G. Looper

131   Shamanic *Mesas* of Yucatán and Their Historical Roots
Bruce Love

141   Shamanism, Colonialism, and the *Mesa* in Mesoamerican Religious Discourse
John Monaghan

Mesas & Cosmologies in Mesoamerica
is a collection of papers presented at the
11th Latin American Symposium
San Diego Museum of Man
March 16, 2002

Preface*

Douglas Sharon

In his classic ethnography on the Tepehua of Veracruz, Roberto Williams Garcia (1960:145-146) clearly defined the subject matter of the Museum of Man's 11th Latin American Symposium held on March 16, 2002.

> The lay-outs on the ground before which the diviners and midwives act are considered *mesas* and at times they employ boxes and when possible real tables. The idea is to signify that they are serving the tables where, in imagination, the deities eat; therefore when they talk of *levantar la mesa* [raising the table] they mean that the offering placed on the lay-out of *muñecos* or *muñecas* [dolls] has been delivered.

The cosmological link is made clear in the following:

> The Hill of Gold is the solar mansion where the *antiguas* [ancients] and other divinized human beings live…In the mythical Hill music plays without interruption, continual processions arrive preceded by musicians and followed by midwives swinging censers, four of them bearing a tablecloth with offerings. The deputies of the *antiguas* come out to receive the offering which they deliver before a large table…. The solar mansion is shared by autochthonous deities and those of the Catholic cult.
>
> The diviners collect archaeological pieces, including sculptures, obsidian knives, and spindle whorls. They keep these objects exposed on their altars. As a whole, they are called *antiguas* since they represent the old deities The diviners also keep a diverse variety of crystals and glass objects which they say are their companions, so that *on their altars they reconstruct the situation of the sacred mansion* [emphases mine]; they also overload their altars with lithographs and images of the Catholic cult, expressing the conjunction of the two religions. On these altars the diviner lights the candle brought by the client for consultation, signifying the contact established with the deities [ibid.:144-145].

Among the Totonac of northern Puebla, pre-Columbian *mesa* objects called *antiguas* (or *tawilanas*) representing the ancient deities (Ichon 1973:219-229) are laid out on the ground (ibid.: Lám. 10.1) or on boxes (ibid.:Lám 11.2) or household altars (ibid.:Lám. 12.1) for divination, curing, or fertility rituals (ibid.:39, 41, 227-228, 258-259, 261, 293, 295, 346, 352-353). *La Mesa de las Ofrendas* replicates *La Mesa divina* in the east where the sun rises and where the gods receive offerings from the human realm (ibid.:47, 103, 105, 157, 233). According to Ichon (ibid.:221), the *antiguas* "contain the soul, the spirit of those gods; they are, therefore, deities in their own right and not simple intermediaries." *Mesas*—as well as the home, the sweat bath, and the village—take the form of the Universe conceived of as a sacred rectangle sustained at the vertices by four saints (ibid.:43-44).

Corn kernel divination traceable to the original divine couple of the Aztecs is a common prac-

Douglas Sharon, ed., *Mesas & Cosmologies in Mesoamerica*. San Diego Museum Papers 42, 2003.

tice of the Nahua of northern Veracruz (Sandstrom 1991:235-237, Color Plate 11). The kernels are cast on a white embroidered cloth draped over a box. Other *mesa* objects include crystals, coins, and archaeological artifacts. Regarding Nahua altar symbolism, Sandstrom (ibid.:286) says that "Offerings are dedicated to the sky, earth, water, and underworld realms as symbolized respectively by the food-laden altar table with its arch, the floor array, the altar set up at the spring, and the initial offering to the spirits of the dead."

Among the Guatemalan Maya, one of the main methods of divination is the "table and beans" complex which is "almost a symbol of the shaman-priest" (Wagley 1969:64). Tedlock (1982:153-171, including Illustration 11) provides a detailed analysis of this method as applied by highland K'iche' Maya priest-shamans of Momostenango, who use the sacred bundle (*baraj*) containing crystals and *tz'ite* seeds (*Erythrina corallodendrum*), tools of the Mayan first couple. Betts and Libbey (1993) document the use of *los frijolitos* among the Kaqchikel. Oakes (1954) provides a photo of the medicine bag and *mixes* used by Mam *chimanes* along with quartz, marbles, and dice.

Among the Yukatek Maya, the sacred crystal (*sastum*) is the divination instrument par excellence, but corn grains are also used (Redfield and Villa Rojas 1934:170, Plate 14a); cleansing of evil winds (*santiguar*) is often performed at a small table (ibid.:Plate 14b). (For altars elsewhere in Middle America see the *Handbook of Middle American Indians*, Ethnology, 1969, Part 1, Vol. 7, and Part 2, Vol. 8—p. 92, Figure 14 for K'iche'; p. 140, Fig. 7 for Pokoman; p. 618, Fig. 13b for Nahua; p. 658, Fig. 15 and p. 677, Fig. 20 for Totonac of Veracruz; and p. 862, Fig. 18 for Tarahumara; for Huichol, see Schaefer and Furst 1996:10.)

Considerable information on altars is contained in two articles in the anthology, *Mesoamerican Healers* (Huber and Sandstrom 2001). James Dow's survey, "Central and North Mexican Shamans" makes the point that "the presence of the supernatural is constantly brought to mind through hundreds of small altars in houses, on the roadside, and in public transportation" (Dow 2001:77). He points out that there are innumerable outdoor shrines—especially at caves, mountains, and lakes—where native deities manifest their powers. The Otomi and Nahua worship the sun god on mountaintops while caves are the haunts of rain, earth, and mountain gods. Lakes and springs often are the abodes of the goddess of fresh waters (ibid.:80). Dow (ibid.:81-82, Fig. 4.2) provides a photo of an Otomi curing altar, indicating that each place where curing occurs should have an altar. He adds that shamans also conduct rituals in oratories or special temples serving an extended family, neighborhood, or village. In addition, they may use the church. Their altars are complex spaces where supernaturals are addressed through the medium of wands, arrows, crystals, paper, tubes, feathers, stones, eggs, etc., utilizing tobacco and white cane alcohol as curing and purifying agents.

Frank Lipp's article, "A Comparative Analysis of Southern Mexican and Guatemalan Shamans" contains examples of table-altars drawn from the ethnographic literature, i.e., the divining table received at the end of training among the Kaqchikel, Mochó, Mam, Ixil, K'iche', and Mazatec (Lipp 2001:102, 106-109).

Alcorn (1984:198-201) provides a wealth of information on Teenek (Huastec) medicine and ethnobotany of Veracruz and San Luis Potosí. She relates how ceremonial offerings are a necessary part of life, being used to assure the deities' protection of infants, dancers, musicians, marriages, families, and farmlands, and to insure the rains. She describes how "Offerings are placed on a cloth-covered table in front of the household altar (if done inside the house), on a table outside, or on a cloth on the ground in the field or cave." Offerings include candles, copal, aguardiente, tobacco, soft drinks or beer, coffee, "new" water, bread, *bolims* (chile-dipped meat in maize dough), eggs, flowers, money, etc. Archaeological objects and crystals facilitate ceremonies, which include adorned arches during *Todos Santos*.

Ceremonies open by addressing the Creator, followed by the Earth and the deities of the four cardinal directions and center. During the ceremony, aguardiente is repeatedly poured at the four corners and midpoint of the offering. After prayers and supplication, the *bolims* are offered to the deities, food and drink are quietly shared, cigarettes and alcohol are finished, the cloth is "lifted," and the ceremony concludes with a ritual "sweeping" and oral spraying of alcohol for all present. With regard to ritual speech, Alcorn (ibid:199) indicates that "The temporal structure of the speech dictates the interval of pulsed repetition of formulaic actions. It is speech that drives the movement of the offering, taps the god-powers, and argues the supplicants' case."

Regarding cosmology, Greenberg's (1981:83-85) description of the Chatino cosmos of Yaitepec, Oaxaca, correlates well with indigenous concepts found elsewhere in Middle America—it is:

> conceived as an ecological system in which human beings, animals, spirits, ancestors, and geographical places reciprocate with and interact with one another to maintain equilibrium in the universe.... The universe, like a cosmic egg, is composed of three major layers...[T]he sun's circuit through heaven and the underworld delimits the universe.... The sky and the underworld are further subdivided into layers [ibid.:83].

The cosmic layers are connected by "doors" used by specific gods, e.g., with the sea shared by the sun and moon, two nostril-like holes used by the wind god, springs for the rain god, and caves for the use of mountain and forest gods.

"Doors" lead to "houses" which constitute a key Chatino metaphor basic to spatial orientation. The house icon represents the human body such that parts of the house have the same names as parts of the body. The "house" to "body" equation maps the Chatino pantheon onto nature, making them identical. Thus the mountaintop house of the rain god *is* the rain god. Also, the house is replicated on each level of the social and cosmological order. This world view is made explicit and reinforced by ritual:

> To understand the role of the house in ritual, we first must appreciate that every house…(whether it be an individual, a house…a church, a graveyard, the village, etc.) has for the purposes of ritual a door, a housecross, a patron saint, and a heart in its center.… The house of the rain god has its door in a spring, and its housecross, altar, and its center or heart on a mountaintop. The "house" of the rain god…serves as a temple for the non-Christian deities… but it has its patron saints, the Santa Cruz and the Virgin of Rosario [ibid.:85].

Crosses mark boundaries, passages between worlds, and kinship relations. Thus for each birth into a household, two crosses are made: one is placed underneath the altar of the home while the other is "planted" in one of the five sacred sites visited on ritual circuits to the mountains around the village (ibid.:86), such that "crosses chart a mortal's path from cradle to grave (ibid.:87).

Candles have an iconic quality; their flames are like the human spirit:

> A basic component of all Chatino rites is the placing of candles for houses, saints and crosses…[following] a formula that applies to every religious rite…[and marking] the transition from the world of men to the universe of the supernatural. The formula requires two or three sets of thirteen candles.… When prayers are offered to the mountain, rain, wind, forest or sun gods, candles are also left on mountains and in springs. On such occasions, continuing from the cemetery, the villagers proceed to the "house of the rain god." Candles are placed in his "corral"—a mountaintop; at his "door"—a spring; and before his altar and the cross of his house—another mountaintop [ibid.:88-89].

Greenberg (ibid.:118) sees ceremonial circuits as "symbolically multivocal," representing "cycles of birth and death, relations of reciprocity, marriage connubiums, and the passage of the seasons which they mark." He refers to Gossen's (1974:29-44) suggestion that in Chamula ritual these circuits represent the path of the sun through heaven and the underworld. Once projected onto the horizontal plane, the solar path yields a counterclockwise circuit with the conceptual east as the beginning of all ritual circuits.

With regard to content, from the initial call for papers every effort has been made to maintain a focused and empirical approach to the symposium topic. To that end, early drafts of Sharon's introductory paper were sent to a diverse cross-section of Mesoamerican scholars who have considerable first-hand knowledge and expertise gained over many years of fieldwork. We believe that this has resulted in a balanced overview of the roots and continuities of shamanism, *mesas*, and cosmologies in the Middle American cultural sphere of influence.

Following the lead provided by *Mesoamerican Healers*, papers are organized into two sections, "Central and Northern Mexico" and "Southern Mexico and Guatemala." Within these sections individual articles are ordered by alphabetized authors' surnames.

For Central and Northern Mexico, the first

paper by Roberto Campos discusses the *mesa* of Doña Marina, a *curandera* living in Mexico City, briefly comparing it with the altars of other healers in the metropolitan area. An interesting aspect of *curandero* world view is the growth of the cult of Holy Death, which may have pre-Hispanic roots.

James Dow's paper on Sierra Otomi symbolism emphasizes the manner in which oratory rituals have evolved in maintaining an animistic link between mankind and nature.

H.B. Nicholson transmits excerpts from early colonial period documents describing Aztec mountain and lake fertility rituals at Mt. Tlaloc and Pantitlán, syncretized versions of which are practiced by contemporary *graniceros*.

Alan Sandstrom describes the three basic altars used by the Nahua of Northern Veracruz, showing how, collectively, they represent miniaturized versions of the four levels of the Nahua universe. He also documents a pilgrimage to the most sacred mountain of the area, which is a model of the cosmos.

Stacy Schaefer provides ethnographic descriptions of four versions of the Huichol *niwetari* or *mesa*, describing the contexts in which they are used to link humans to their gods, ancestors, and the cosmos.

For Southern Mexico and Guatemala, James Brady leads off with archaeological documentation of dry-cave "benches," which he links to contemporary Maya "Earth Lord" beliefs and practices.

Allen Christenson cites the Popul Vuh to demonstrate how contemporary Maya shamans' sacred ancestral vision is a gift from the gods. He shows how highland Guatemalan shamans manipulate the three layers of the cosmos through the agency of their microcosmic *mesas*.

Judith Green analyzes Day of the Dead *mesas* among the Yukatek Maya, characterizing them as sacred spaces constructed to communicate with ancestors and the supernatural realm. She demonstrates the pre-Hispanic roots of this tradition.

Mathew Looper draws upon archaeological examples from Copán and Quiriguá, comparing the meteorological significance of ancient Maya monumental sculpture to the rituals of the contemporary Ch'orti' Maya of Southern Guatemala.

Bruce Love documents six Yukatek Maya rituals—ranging from simple to complex—as practiced by shamans *(hmeen'ob)* using one or more *mesas*. He delves into the similarities and differences between *mesas* in order to distinguish which aspects are invariable and which are subject to change.

John Monaghan combines Oaxacan Mixtec ethnography and ethnohistory to determine the status of the *mesa* in Mesoamerican theology, and to learn how this loan word came to be used, even in isolated, monolingual communities, to express alimentary idioms of power.

In the final analysis, it is hoped that these papers will contribute to an early chapter on the development of an ethnology of popular religion in Middle America.

* For references please see Sharon's "Shamanism, Mesas, & Cosmologies in Middle America" (page 1).

Introduction

Shamanism, Mesas, & Cosmologies in Middle America

Douglas Sharon

Introduction

In Latin American countries, shamanism is deeply rooted in pre-Hispanic culture, practiced extensively by indigenous groups, and frequently used by a broad cross-section of the larger society. Medicinal plant lore is a major component of shamanism. Knowledge is preserved and transmitted by traditional healers, shamans or *curanderos*, and has survived the rigors of the Spanish conquest, extensive *mestizaje* or racial intermixing, and the industrial revolution. Shamanism is, however, a dynamic phenomenon in constant evolution and additional knowledge has been acquired by natural selection over the centuries.

Since the 1930s, ethnographers working in Latin America have been documenting the use of the *mesa*, or altarlike arrangement of power objects serving as the focus of curing and fertility rituals conducted by native shamans. In spite of syncretism with Christianity, the *mesa* with its associated beliefs and practices appears to reflect an ancient and remarkably similar indigenous world view.

Regarding the antiquity and continuity of Native American world view, American anthropologist Peter Furst is one of the most prolific scholars active today. In his seminal article, "The Roots and Continuities of Shamanism," published in *artscanada*, he demonstrated that, wherever New World shamanism manifests itself today, it does so with a "similar fundamental *Weltanschauung* and cosmology" (Furst 1973-74:37). This world view perceives the universe as multi-layed and quartered, but ultimately divisible into a celestial Upperworld and a chthonic Underworld. Connecting these levels is a central pivot or *axis mundi*. Recently, pre-Contact expressions of this Amerindian world view have been insightfully interpreted by scholars using the concept of *ritual landscapes* or *sacred geography* adopted by Richard Townsend (1992) from David Carrasco (1990, 1991) while Alcina Franch (1997) has compared Andean and Mesoamerican "*cosmovisión*" defined by Broda (1982:81) as "the structured view in which the ancient Mesoamericans combined their notions of cosmology into a systematic whole," and refined by Carrasco (1990:xvii) as "the way in which Mesoamericans *combined their cosmological notions relating to time and space into a structured and systematic worldview.*"

In the introduction to the anthology on Siberian and New World shamanism, edited in conjunction with the exhibit *Nomads: Masters of the Eurasian Steppe* (Denver Museum of Natural History, 1989), Furst (1994) provides a critical overview of humanistic issues and universal themes addressed by current scholarship. Relevant topics range from the shaman's ecological wisdom to ecstatic experience and healing etiology. Furst (*ibid.*:2) regards the shamanic worldview as "the common property of humankind," which he feels helps to account for widespread public interest in the subject.

American psychologist Roger Walsh (1990:3-7) contends that shamanism is currently "in" among

Douglas Sharon, ed., *Mesas & Cosmologies in Mesoamerica*. San Diego Museum Papers 42, 2003.

Western professionals and laymen alike. He attributes this to a growing interest in non-Western cultures, the short-term effectiveness of shamanic techniques, the enormous impact of the books of Carlos Castaneda dealing with his alleged apprenticeship to a Yaqui shaman, the emergence of scientific research on the topic, and firsthand experience with shamanism by scholars and the public.

In this symposium, the ethnographic depictions of shamanic paraphernalia and associated cosmological concepts provide graphic examples of Furst's theses regarding New World shamanism. They also illustrate how shamans are instrumental in meeting the needs of the people they serve in rural areas and—to an increasing degree—in urban and international environments as well (Press 1971, 1978; Campos 1997).

In effect, the "take-away message" of this symposium is that—despite its great antiquity and the disruption wrought by European contact—New World shamanism in general and Middle American shamanism in particular is extremely viable in meeting the needs of the communities where it is found today. Furthermore, it is proving to be particularly relevant in addressing issues and concerns of the postmodern world. In this regard, the February 1997 issue of *Natural History* contains a series of articles on contemporary shamanism.

In the article "Shamanisms Today," published in the *Annual Review of Anthropology*, Jane Atkinson (1992) comments on "neo-shamanism" which she traces to environmental activism, the human potential movement, interest in non-Western religions, and popular anthropology. Although anthropologists have reason to be dismayed by the "veritable cottage industry" that encourages the romanticizing and commercialization of shamanism, she contends that the widespread interest in the topic is a significant phenomenon that anthropologists should be studying. Given the present role of shamans in spiritual movements and cultural discourse, she asserts that it is incumbent upon anthropologists to "attend to the wider conversations, both popular and academic, not only to devise new ways of being heard but also to engage reflexively these contemporary inventions" (ibid.:321).

Themes and Interpretation

The principal challenge in this symposium is to de-mystify an important subject which is currently very topical, even trendy, with a broad general audience. However, at the same time, we need to strive to avoid a scholarly reductionism that is insensitive to the religious values of the ethnic groups who have shared their beliefs and practices with the members of the academic panel participating in this project. In seeking to achieve a balance between engagement and education, we are motivated by a conviction that the anthropological perspective can be extremely relevant in bridging the gap between indigenous and Euro-American spiritual traditions.

The questions addressed by the symposium include:

1. What cosmology is expressed by *mesas* and what is the nature of the sacred world they map?

2. What transformations has this shamanic tradition undergone and why is it still with us?

3. What needs does it serve in native cultures and among urban populations?

Mesa rituals are used by shamans to invoke a stratified, geocentric cosmos in which the earth's plane is midway between an upper sky world and a lower underworld. A central navel or world axis (a tree or mountain) oriented to the four cardinal directions links these realms. The seasonal cycle is delineated by the passage of the sun through both the sky world and the lower realm. Everything is animated, often with spirit beings situated at the zenith, nadir, and intervening strata as well as the cardinal and/or intercardinal quadrants. It is a world in which all things are connected and interdependent through the web of life and the cycles of nature. The Central Mexican term *teotl* conveys the indigenous notion of the sacred essence in all things, animate and inanimate, seen or unseen, fixed and mobile; the equivalent Mayan term is *itz*.

The interpretation of contemporary Middle American *mesas* utilizes the comparative method. Ethnographic reports describe shamanic power objects in symbolic configurations laid out on the ground or arranged in shrines or temples. Ethnohistoric and archaeological information is used to demonstrate how these artifacts are patterned to form microcosmic models of indigenous cosmologies.

The single most powerful transformation that this indigenous cosmology has undergone came with the advent of Christianity. Throughout Spanish America during the colonial period, a major campaign was waged to "extirpate idolatry" and win souls for the Church. In the process, native beliefs and practices were demonized in an effort to break their hold on the hearts and minds of the native population. However, Church fathers consistently failed to recognize the eclectic nature of native religion and its capacity to assimilate new concepts while maintaining the old as attested by the archaeological record, colonial ethnohistory, and modern ethnography. Colonial period examples record the frustration of Catholic priests who discovered that their Indian parishoners would hide idols under the altars of local churches. A contemporary example is provided by the Ch'orti' Maya where sacred stones form a quincunx under the altar cloth (Girard 1966:33).

Regarding native needs served by shamanic *mesas*, a review of the ethnographic literature reveals that they are used in order to cure, divine, locate lost property, punish thieves, harm enemies, retrieve runaway spouses, perform love magic, assure a safe journey, consecrate a new house, overcome bad luck, guarantee good fortune, influence the weather, avoid or overcome punishment by ancestors and deities, pay tribute to the spirits inhabiting the supernatural, and promote health and fertility of crops, herds, and humans.

Neo-shamanism contrasts markedly with the indigenous model (see Furst's and Schaefer's 1996b:504-512 critique of "Don Juan seekers"). Relatively free from the pressures of daily subsistence, middle-class urbanites can afford the indulgence of an idealized New Age shamanism in search of an escape from the alienation of the postmodern world. And there is no shortage of "plastic medicine men" waiting to meet these needs (Kehoe 1990). The irony in this situation is that the indigenous shaman has proven to be very effective in helping migrants adapt to an urban environment.

In spite of the differences between "neo" and "native" shamanism, the one thing that they have in common and the central theme of this symposium is the perennial human need to find meaning in existence. In the final analysis, shamans are the repositories of the spiritual wisdom of their respective societies, the intermediaries between the natural and the supernatural, the known and the unknown. By placing a range of Middle American shamanic complexes in cultural and historical context, this symposium seeks to help the public develop an appreciation and respect for the richness and complexity of this subject as well as the ability to distinguish between authentic traditions and deceptive imitations. Ultimately, we hope to assist our audience in achieving a better understanding of culture and its role in shaping our perceptions of the world.

Work to Date

In the late 1970s, Sharon (1976) surveyed the anthropological literature on the use of *mesas* in Latin American indicating how they often were projections of indigenous cosmologies (Sharon 1978:183-196). The review of Middle America included information on the Tepehua of Veracruz and the Mazatec of Oaxaca, as well as a variety of Maya communities, e.g., the Tzotzil of Chiapas and the Mam, Tz'utujil, and Ch'orti' of Guatemala. However for Central Mexico, Sharon overlooked the principal monograph on the Tepehua by Williams García (1963) and the photographs of Johnson in Madsens (1969:43-52) as well as Dow's (1974, 1975) work on paper cult-figures among the Otomí of Puebla. Sharon also missed the work by Ichon (1973) among the Totonac of Puebla and the Mazatec field notes of Ichaústegui cited by Benítez (1970:3:35-62).

In the Maya area, Sharon did not include Vogt's 1976 classic *Tortillas for the Gods* on the Tzotzil of Zinacantán in which the elders' *mexa* is a "small-scale model of the universe" (ibid. 132) and rising sun symbolism is employed in altar rituals (ibid.:128, 1992). He also omitted the pioneer ethnographic work from the lowlands of the Yucatán Peninsula where, "The center of ceremonial activity is the table-altar...often referred to as *mesa*..." which is "the world itself with heaven above" (Redfield and Villa Rojas 1934:131, 115; see Villa Rojas 1945:107 for "*zuhuy-mesa*" or "holy table" as well as Gann 1917, 1918 for the *ch'a chàak* rain ceremony and Tozzer 1907 for Yukatekan cosmology and Lacandon censer rituals—at times performed on a table, ibid.:113).

In spite of the lacunae noted above, the survey established that the *mesa* complex was widely distributed among the indigenous peoples of Middle America, especially the Maya where it graphically portrayed native cosmology. This *imago mundi* was best described by Holland (1964:14-15) based upon his work among the Tzotzil. Here the earth:

> ...is conceived as the center of the universe, the flat and rectangular surface of which is sustained on the shoulders of a bearer at each of the corners. The heavens, formed by thir-

teen levels, are conceived as a cupola or cup over the earth: six layers in the east, six in the west, and the thirteenth one in the zenith, heart of the heavens...

[T]he ceiba...ascending from the center of the earth, penetrates and connects the thirteen levels...Beneath the earth there exist nine...layers that form the underworld...

[T]his sphere looks like a huge mountain or pyramid. The concept of "the mountain of the earth" is...in the pre-Hispanic codices...

The sun ascends the thirteen layers of the heavens, which form a path ornamented with flowers...Ascending a layer every hour, it reaches noon at the thirteenth...In the afternoon, it descends the western layers...During the night it passes by under the layers of the...[underworld].

Work in Middle America since Sharon's survey has shown that *mesas* are even more pervasive than originally anticipated. They have been documented among the Huichol of Nayarit and Jalisco (Schaefer 1996a, 1996b), the Teenek Maya of San Luis Potosi (Alcorn 1984), the Nahua of Veracruz (Sandstrom 1991), the Otomí of Puebla (Dow 1986), the Mixtec (Monaghan 1995) and Mixe (Lipp 1991) of Oaxaca, the Yukatek Maya (Bartolomé 1978, Love and Peraza 1984, Ku Ché 1985, Sosa 1989, Hanks 1990, Freidel et al. 1993:252), and the Maya of Guatemala, i.e., the Mam (Watanabe 1992), Ixil (Colbys 1981, i.e., the *meeša* or divining bundle), K'iche' (Tedlock 1982), Kaqchikel (Betts and Libbey 1993), and the Tz'utujil (Carlsen and Prechtel 1991, 1994, Carlsen 1997). Also, the ethnological analysis of *mesa*-related paper cult figures among the Nahua, Otomí, and Tepehua by the Sandstroms (1986) demonstrated contemporary persistence of pre-Hispanic pantheism as delineated earlier by Hunt (1977).

More in-depth studies of indigenous cosmologies—past and present—have demonstrated the manner in which shamanic paraphernalia and sacred architecture express cosmological principles in ritual contexts (see Hanks 1984, Sosa 1986, Carrasco 1990, Schele and Freidel 1990, Freidel et al. 1993, Broda 1996, López Austin 1996, and Aveni 2001:148-152). Among the Maya, Sosa (1986), working with Gossen's (1974:18-36) data on Tzotzil (Chamula) cosmology, compares pre-Hispanic evidence with the ethnographic present to delineate four conceptual continuities, i.e., celestial domed layers, anthropomorphic celestial deities, an organizing solar deity, and cosmic directional values. In Larráinzar, Ochiai (1991) documents the microcosmic ritual platform (*moch*) as the ancient abode of *Chak*. Carrasco (1990:xvii) characterizes Mesoamerican religion as "world making (cosmovision and sacred space), world centering (cosmovision and the human body), and world renewing (ritual rejuvenation of time, human life, agriculture, and the gods)." This worldview encompasses "a strong sense of parallelism between the celestial supernatural forces of the cosmos (macrocosmos) and the biological human patterns of life on earth (microcosmos);" time and space are inseparable.

Specifically, tables have been archaeologically documented in dry caves in the Central Depression (Hayden 1987:176), at Chich'en Itza (Schele and Matthews 1998:241-243) and Copán (Altar Q?) while a *ch'a chàak* ceremony has been identified in a pre-Hispanic Maya vase from the Pacific slope of Guatamala (Kerrs 1995:844). In Central Mexico, the priest-chronicler Durán describes "a platform" used for rituals in the Aztec home (Durán in López Austin 1997:31).

Among the highland Tzotzil Maya, Vogt (1976:58) has shown how the cosmology of "four corners and the center" manifests in every aspect of daily life:

Houses and fields are small-scale models of the quincuncial cosmogony. The universe was created by the ... gods who support it at its corners and who designated its center, the "navel of the world"... Houses have corresponding corner posts; fields emphasize the same critical places, with cross shrines at their corners and centers. These points are of primary ritual importance.

Among the lowland Yukatek Maya, "Altars, yards, cornfields, the earth, the sky and the highest atmospheres are described in terms of the five-point cardinal frame" (Hanks 1990:349). The altar's surface is "a model of the quadrilateral earth" with arched tree branches lashed at the four corners forming "four domes...to represent the sky" and supporting a platform suspended over a central candle, constituting a "hole in the sky," or "cosmological conduit" to the zenith or "middle of the sky" (Sosa 1989:139-140). Underworld symbolism is expressed in a canoe and jars (containing sacred spring water and ritually captured "winds") placed under Ch'orti' Maya *me*-

sas (Girard 1966:24-28) and by a red dwarf under Kaqchikel (Betts and Libbey 1993:56-57).

As Freidel (in Freidel, Schele, and Parker 1993:127-129) points out, scholars now know that the first act of the Creation according to the Ancient Maya consisted of centering the world by placing the three stones of the cosmic hearth. The second act was to raise the sky by establishing the sides and corners of the cosmic house. The Maya at pre-Columbian ceremonial centers and in contemporary peasant communities have been centering the world and creating the four sides ever since. Like the gods before them, shamans ritually create a five-part image to sanctify space and open a portal to the Otherworld: "Centering the world is thus a way of re-creating a spatial order that focuses the spiritual forces of the supernatural within the material forms of the human world, rendering these forces accessible to human need" (ibid.:131).

A drawing from the Aztec Codex Borbonicus may provide a clue to possible pre-Hispanic *mesa* antecedents (Oakes 1951:180). The drawing depicts the primeval human couple: old Cipactonal, the first man and his wife Oxomoco, who are similar in some ways to the Maya primordial couple Xpiacoc and Xmucane, parents of the twin brothers of the Popul Vuh. They were seers, doctors, and inventors of the calendar. Their four sons were identified with the four cosmic directions. They are shown seated on benches with tobacco gourds on their backs. Cipactonal holds a pointed bone for sacrificial bloodletting, a copal incense pouch, and a ladle censer, the paraphernalia used by Aztec priests. Oxomoco divines with corn grains—a ritual that is still practiced in Middle America (*pito* seeds from the Mayan tree of life are used in Guatemala). Guardians of "the place of duality" at the zenith, they are seated within a rectangular enclosure, from which water flows. It is described by scholars as a cave or mat (for the mat symbol in Maya art see Robicsek 1975). Deer-headed staffs mark the entrance. This sacred space may be the mythical prototype for rectangular *mesas* used by shamans today for divination, curing, and fertility rituals.

Costumbre Religion:
Mountains, Water, and Pilgrimages

The foregoing leads to the question regarding the specific nature of the Middle American cosmos as manifest in popular religion. A recurring term found throughout the ethnographic literature in describing indigenous religious beliefs and practices is the Spanish word *costumbre* (custom). Perhaps the best characterization of this worldview is provided by Sandstrom (1991:319) who describes the Huastecan Nahua universe as

> composed of forces in equilibrium, of a balanced exchange between people and spirits, polluted by disruptions that shamans endeavor to smooth out through elaborate and deeply symbolic ritual offerings.

In concrete terms a layered and quartered cosmos traversed by the sun manifests as a landscape of sacred mountains (including caves, Heyden 1991) and water sources encompassing the local community often delineated by temples, oratories, shrines, and crosses. It is a participatory, animated universe sustained by ritual sacrifice and pilgrimage. Townsend (1992:171-185, 2000:136-162) describes the Aztec version of this sacred geography and its ritual sustenance through two pilgrimage and fertility ceremonies held at the end of the dry season. The first ritual took place in a microcosmic rectangular temple and symbolic womb on top of Mt. Tlaloc (Tlalocan) where earth and sky meet. Here the image of the rain god *Tlaloc* and idols symbolizing hills (*Tlaloque*) were dressed and sprinkled with the blood of sacrificed children. The second ceremony began on the Tlaloc side of the twin-towered Great Pyramid of Tenochtitlan from which a central tree of five was transported and "planted" near a sumphole at the middle of Lake Tezcoco[1]. (See Albores 1997 for "planting" and "dressing" of crosses today.) Founded as an "earth altar," the Great Pyramid was the sacred center of the Aztec world at the juncture of four roads. It was conceptualized as a "water mountain" fed by four springs and as a cosmic model ritually reinforced at the beginning of each year by pilgrimages to seven sacred sites (6 hills/sump) (Aveni 1991, Broda 1991, 1993).

Remnants of this ritual landscape are found all over indigenous Middle America. Sandstrom (1991:6.1) has located the major sacred hills recognized by the Nahuas of northern Veracruz and their neighbors. These are "living entities that are the dwelling places of the seed and rain spirits associated with crop growth" (ibid.:24). Shamans make pilgrimages to the tops of certain hills and to lakes to make special offerings on behalf of their communities. Regarding the lakes, in the early twentieth century, Starr (1908:258, 261) was told that two to three hundred Indians would make offerings to *la Sirena* of seeds, fowl, money, and *muñecos* in times of drought, excessive rains, or crop damage. Modern presidents of Mexico have been known to perform lake pilgrimages (Roberto Campos, personal communication 1997). (For the mountain cult in Mesoamerica see Broda 1987:224-237; for the ecology of water mountain see Townsend 1987:385-390, especially Figure 12; for *graniceros*, mountain rituals, and *mesas* see Glockner 1996, Albores and Broda 1997).

López Austin (1997) in his study of Tamoanchan and Tlalocan, the Central Mexican realms of creation and death has developed an ethnographic model for interpreting these mythical places, which he sees as complementary components of the cosmic tree of life. In summarizing the literature from the highland Nahua, Otomi, Tepehua, and Totonac, he provides information that is particularly relevant:

> The...principal source of "seeds" is the great mythical mountain which contemporaneous Nahua call Tolokan (Aramoni Burgete 1990: 62). The hills and natural water reservoirs are secondary sources from which "seeds" can be obtained, which they place and keep in images made of cut paper (Williams García 1963:200, 209) [López Austin 1997:152].

The projection of this *imago mundi* in space and its relation to the built environment and nature is explained as follows:

> A settlement is a microcosm (Ichon 1973:319). Domestic space is the image of the universe (Galinier 1990:154). A domestic altar represents and summarizes the four corners of the terrestrial place (Ichon 1973:39). All the cavities, caverns, and springs can generate clouds and rain because they are replications of the Wind Gods' and the Rain Gods' houses (Galinier 1990:555). The Tepehua temple, the *lacachinchin*, with its boxes where the "spirits of the seeds" are kept, can also be a secondary image of the great mountain where the world's riches are stored. The powers of the cosmos are reproduced in a pyramid ruled by the hierarchy [ibid.:152].

The archetypal nature of tables and their relation to mountains of abundance is clearly indicated in the ethnographic record:

> According to the Totonac, a Golden Table or a Table of Offerings where the great gods live, a place covered with flowers and food, is in the East (Ichon 1973:130, 157)...The Tepehua believe that the "ancients" live in the east on the Golden Mountain...(Williams García 1963:144-145). The "ancients" gather at the Hill of Gold around a table with an iridescent tablecloth (Williams García 1963:198)...It is the image of a place from which all riches flow, as in the Otomi chant "I am the Table, I am the Mother, and I am in your midst/Because of that I am called the Table..." (Galinier 1990:292). That is similar to the Silver Table of the Mazatec that lies on the other side of the Sacred Sea, where the four posts, upon which the archetypes, or "samples," of living things dance, or stand (Incháustegui n.d.:fol. 3 [4], [5], 7, 77) (ibid.:155).

The highland Tzotzil Maya have similar beliefs about the sacred nature of mountains and water:

> Almost all mountains...located near Zinacanteco settlements are the homes of ancestral gods (*Totil-mé iletik*,..."Fathers-Mothers"). These ancestral gods are the most important Zinacanteco deities...and they were ordered to take up residence inside the mountains by the Four-Corner Gods in the mythological past...
>
> Next to the ancestral gods, the most important deity is the "Earth Owner" (*Yahval Balamil*)...[A] cave, a limestone sink, or a waterhole...serves as a means of communication with him. He...controls the lighting and the clouds that are believed to emerge from caves, rise up into the sky, and produce the needed rain for crops [Vogt 1970:6].

Rectangular tables play pivotal roles in shamanic initiation (inside sacred mountains), civil-religious hierarchical processions, ritual meals, curing pilgrimages (to five or more mountains), and as models of the cuadrilateral cosmos delineated by the sun's seasonal journey. Mountains, cross shrines, and seven waterholes where ancestors bathe play prominent roles in much of their ritual life (Vogt 1976:11, 27-30, 38-50, 61-83). The *me' santo* is the traditional ritualist par excellence (Holland 1963:199-206).

López Austin (1997:143) offers the following interpretation of the cosmic forces at work in the seasonal cycles portrayed in Tzotzil beliefs and rituals:

> The basic division of the annual cycle into two halves is marked by the feasts of the Holy Cross and the Days of the Dead. It is

the alternation of the rule of the two opposed and complementary forces. It is the struggle between the aquatic, feminine, and terrestrial force, manifested in the rainy season, and the fiery, masculine, and celestial force of the dry season. Each one of the periods ends with a deifying, culminating moment: the rainy season with the reunion of the cold forces, assembled at the Feast of the Dead; the dry season with the celebration of the Holy Cross, where the Mesoamerican fire symbol is united to the colonial image of Christ-Sun.

In highland Guatemala, Christenson (2001) relates how Maya traditionalists consider mountain caves as "mouths of the world" leading to the realms of sacred beings who control the formation of rain clouds and the winds that bear them. In order to guarantee fertility and new life, ritual specialists conduct ceremonies within actual caves or at effigy caves such as clefts in stones, holes in the ground, altars with cave-like recesses made of stones or pottery shards, and church altarpieces conceptualized as mountains with cave-like recesses for patron saints. In Santiago Atitlán, the Tz'utujil Maya view their *cofradía* houses as sacred mountains with doorways serving as cave-portals into the otherworld realm of the deified ancestors. The interiors of sacred mountains and *cofradía* houses are believed to be the birthplaces of life-giving power. "Maize, incense/rain clouds, water, fertility, earth, all combine to give birth to life itself" (ibid.:8). Pre-Columbian antecendents are sacred temple-mountains with open-jawed earth-deity entrances found at Chicanná and Copán.

Freidel (in Freidel, Schele, and Parker 1993:143) shows how among the Ancient Maya and their ancestors the ritual mountain-water circuit, e.g., the mountain-path-pool design of Chich'en Itza, was incorporated in the layout of their settlements:

> So we find that the Olmec and the early Maya defined sacred space in fundamentally similar ways: plazas shimmered with the hidden currents of the Primordial Sea, stairways descending from the summits of Creation mountains shaped paths between worlds. Threshold buildings and ballcourt alleyways marked out the liminal space for dance, ritual sport and...for sacrifice. In each case, we find evidence for centering the world and anchoring it in the original moments of its birth.

Tedlock (1982) provides an insightful view into the world of the K'iche' Maya priest-shamans (*chuchkahawib*, "mother-fathers") of Momostenango in the central Guatemalan highlands. Following initiation, they are trained concerning the "six-place" (*wakibal*) shrine located on Paclon Hill in the town center (for six in Zinacantán see Vogt 1976:189). This hill is "the 'heart' (*c'ux*) or center of the Momostecan world...spiritually connected to four inner hills of the four directions or corners" (Tedlock 1982:71). After being presented to Paclon, the ritual specialists' duties are expanded to include offerings at Paclon and the altars of the inner four corners (ibid.).

Originally initiated as calendar diviners, dream interpreters, curers, and prayer-makers, Momosteco priest-shamans are hierarchically ranked at the lineage, canton, and town levels. Candidates for these positions are determined by divination after the death of their predecessors, followed by a series of permissions and trainings at a variety of shrines, including paired water sources and mountaintops. Lineage shrines are known as "sowing places, planting places" (ibid.:76-77).

One town priest-shaman's duties include a four-part pilgrimage, stretching over a 40-day period, that takes him to each of the mountains of the four directions, located at or near the boundaries of the municipality where he petitions the gods and ancestors for health, rain, and protection from natural disasters. The southern mountain, is called the "four corners of the sky" while the northern mountain is referred to as the "four corners of the earth."

> This sacred circuit is called both the "sowing and planting" (*awexibal ticbal*) of the town and the "stabilization" (*chac' alic*) of the town. The K'iche' term *chac' alic*, which in everyday usage refers to the firm placement of a table on its four legs, here refers to the firm placement of the town within its four mountains, so that it will not wobble or tip over during a revolution, earthquake, landslide, or other catastrophe [ibid.:82].

Tedlock (ibid.:53, 54, 139, 155, 157) describes an interesting feature of Momosteco cosmology, i.e., four sacred lakes which correlate with the four directions. Shaman-priests are distinguished from ordinary mortals by the fact that they are born on a special day in the sacred calendar which confers on them a kind of soul called "lightning" (*cayopa*) originally bestowed upon humans by the prototypical mountain spirit *(Tzitzimit)*, the axe-bearing red dwarf-shepard who is annually portrayed all over Guatemala in the Dance of the Conquest (ibid.:147-150; see him using his divining table in Freidel, Schele, and Parker 1993:Photos 7, 24, 25). The medium by which messages are received from the natural and supernatural worlds, this soul manifests in shamans' bodies like sheet lightning moving over the lakes at night which indicates good or bad weather. Lakes figure prominently in the "divine election" of shaman-priests, e.g., to dream of a lake below a mountian indicates that the supernatural is calling one to make a pilgrimage to the lake and the mountaintop, symbolizing the paired low (water)-high (mountain) public shrines. Whenever diviners visit the lakes, they return with a container of water to deposit at the low-water shrines in their community. This purifies the springs and adds curing power from the sacred directions.

In addition to calendrical divination and cyclical visits to shrines, ritual specialists may seek training in one of five specialties. For our purposes, that of spiritualist (*ajnawal mesa*, "worker with the spiritual essence of the table") is especially relevant (ibid.:74). Rectangular *mesas* are the focal point of divination with sacred *pito* seeds.

The Uto-Aztecan Huichol peoples of Jalisco and Nayarit (and Zacatecas and Durango) ritually reinforce their sacred geography by regular pilgrimages apparently integrated into a ritual itinerary of visits to sacred sites associated with the four world directions (Lemaistre 1996:317). Mountains and water sources are integral parts of these journeys as summarized by López Austin (1997:173-174):

> The caves are essentially replications of the aquatic goddesses' world. Moreover, there is a grand replication, a sacred place par excellence. It is Wirikúta, where the Huichol go each year to collect peyote. The journey is made amid ecstatic experiences, and the entire journey is marked by power places. Everything is filled with reproductive force: water from the sacred springs cures sterility (Furst 1972b). Before reaching Wirikúta, their final destination, they pass by the sacred springs of Tatéi Matiniéri ("Where Our Mother Lives"), the house of the eastern rain goddess. They cross steppes. The first one is the Cloud Gate; the second, Where the Clouds Open. From there, they go to the Vagina. Wirikúta is the ancestral deities' home, where the peyote seekers are received by the Great Mother, who gives to children, before their births, the vital animistic force (*kupúri*) (Furst 1972b). The largest area for the ritual collection of peyote is the "Grandparent's Patio," located between two mountain ranges. The peaks of those ranges are said to be the homes of Kakauyarixí, a generic name given by the Huichol to the "ancestors," the "ancients," or to the ancestral gods (Furst 1972b). [*Kauyumari*—culture hero and spirit helper of the old fire god and his human counterpart the shaman—inhabits the Central Hill in Wirikúta where the blessing and eating of peyote commences, Schaefer 1996a:149.]

The realm of the vegetation and rain goddesses is in the sea and at the four corners of the earth. *Nakawé*, the old earth goddess, wife of the fire god, *Tatewarí*, is under the earth. Caves, springs, and clouds belong to the goddesses. The Stars are shared by *Nakawé* and Father Sun (ibid.:173). In the beginning *Tatewarí* set up four trees to support the sky at the corners, and a fifth at the center. He also provided a god chair for the sun's western journey (Schaefer and Furst 1996a:14).

The essence of the gods inhabits sacred places and microcosmic temples. The latter have a hierarchical order including buildings, altars, and baskets of ceremonial objects and crystals (the souls of ancestors). God-disks placed in cornfields convert them into sanctuaries (ibid.:172-173). The circular temple interior consists of a cane-and-pole altar (*mesa*) or a rock-and-mortar pyramid-like "stairway to the Sun" symbolizing the sun's sky journey, located on the west side; three emergence holes in the floor (one under the fire pit) for Our Mother, Venus, and Grandfather Fire; and a twin *axis mundi* of two posts (Thunder/Lightning and a Rain Goddess) uniting the Middle World with the Upper World and the Underworld. God stones and offerings are placed in wall niches or crypts and decorated with deer antlers. Five sacred plants tied beneath the roof's interior delineate the four directions and sacred center. The east-west axis divides the temple into rainy season (left) and dry season (right). Openings in the wall (on either side of the eastern entrance) and roof are used to track the daily and annual paths of the Male Sun and Female Moon, "owners" of complementary halves of the temple. The temple at San Andrés, Jalisco is the ceremonial center for a system of five sacred compounds arranged in the shape of a quincunx (Schaefer 1996b:335-361).

The ceremonial precinct of the Uto-Aztecan Cora of Nayarit is a veritable *imago mundi*. It consists of a dance circle focused on a central fire pit with an altar of four poles and planks located on the east side. Between the fire and the west side of the circle are the seats of the twin gods, Morning Star and culture hero *Hátzikan* and his sister Evening Star *Tatei*. To the west is the house of *Tatei Wáwata*, God of Water, Evil, and Night, to the north that of *Tatei Sáreme*, Godess of the Left, and in the south the home of *Tatei Kuámeche*, Goddess of Pinole. Crowned with two arches decorated with cotton cloth and flowers, the altar is the ritual focus representing the East, direction of the sunrise and mythical Wirikúta, land of peyote and the ancestors. Point of departure and culmination of fertility rituals, the altar is the sacred space par excellence. Above it is the zenith abode of *Kuajrave*, Lord of the Eagles; below it the subterranean domain of *Teheté Tétewas*, Goddess of the Earth. Behind the altar is the mysterious space inhabited by the *Shuká Tujaninei*, "those who are beyond the East," including deities related to birth, life, planting, corn, clouds, light, and rain (Benitez 1970:3:443-453).

Returning to López Austin's ethnographic model, he contends that, in spite of differences in world view between the contemporary peoples discussed, "one can see a conceptual basis that they all had in common at one time" (ibid.:189). He proceeds by drawing up a list of basic principles for interpreting the beliefs of other Mesoamerican groups. The central role of mountain imagery in his model is indicated by the following:

> The gods' dwelling in this complex is a great hill. Inside the hill enormous agricultural wealth, animals, and currents of water are kept. Caves are the chief communication points with this world and the places from which the winds and clouds emerge…
>
> The great hill is at the same time, the "heart" of the Earth. It is the great source from which the "seeds" come, and to which they return when they have completed the terrestrial part of their cycle. One of the great hill's representations is a tub, an image that is also used for the hill's goddesses.
>
> A tree which produces flowers of different colors stands at the center of the hill, and it also holds the children who will come to the world.
>
> The great hill is located in the east, and it contains both the creator gods and the humans who shared in a special way in the essences of those gods.
>
> All other hills are replications of the great hill. It is also reproduced in different sacred places to which the faithful go on pilgrimages, in unusual geographical places, and in the temples. The temples are used to keep the images containing "seeds."

Carrasco (1990:147-153) delineates the dynamics of a contemporary Maya pilgrimage based upon Robert Carlsen's description of the twelve-hour ritual procession around the symbolic quarters of Santiago Atitlán, Guatemala, the home of the Tz'utujil Maya. Beginning and ending at a hole in the middle of the church considered to be the umbilicus or center of their microcosmos, the town's religious leaders understand their journey as "walking the sky." (Ch'orti' Maya pilgrimages imitate the sun's movement to inaugurate the native year, Girard 1966:11-14.) The sacred circuit is undertaken "to renew the cosmos…by symbolically retracing the cosmic image of the center and the four quarters." Landa described the same process in 16th-century Yukatek New Year's processions (Freidel et al. 1993:164). Carrasco compares the *atiteco* microcosm to the cosmology of the great pre-Hispanic cities of Teotihuacan, Tollan, and Tenochtitlan.

In Zinacantán Vogt (1976:43) shows that ritual processions "set out from the direction of the rising sun and flow along its path," as well as "symbolically mark out time in a manner that can be related directly to the ancient concept of *Kinh* (León-Portilla 1968)." He suggests that the ritualists are "symbolically re-enacting the ascent and descent of the sun through the layers or steps of the sky."

Freidel (in Schele and Freidel 1990:114) identifies a pre-Hispanic Maya precedent for this cosmological sun-circuit performed by kings at the late pre-Classic sacred temple-mountain with its four world trees located at Cerros on the eastern coast of the Yucatán Peninsula.

> Since this building faces to the south, a person gazing at its colorful facade would see the sun in its jaguar aspect "emerging" from

the sea on the eastern side of the building and "setting" into the sea on the western side. Thus, these terrace panels symbolize the sun at the two most spectacular moments of the tropical day: dawn and dusk. Together, these sun masks display both linear time...through the day and year and cyclical time in the return of the cycle to its beginning point over and over again; and it is significant that this path encircles the stairway along which the king must travel on his ritual journeys.

Ashmore (1989) demonstrates that cosmology provided the template for settlement patterning during the Late Classic at the Maya sites of Tikal, Palenque, Copán, and Quiriguá. There were four cosmological bases for site planning: 1) the concept of a multilayered universe with the sky above and the underworld below; 2) temporal unification of the cosmos by the cyclical movement of the sun, moon, and Venus through the upper and lower worlds; 3) vertical links between the earth and other realms such as four corner gods, mountains (up), and caves (down); and 4) a horizontal division of the world into four quarters and a center. Directional references (horizontal and vertical) also manifest in hieroglyphs painted on the walls of the tomb of Six Sky excavated at Rio Azul in northeast Guatemala (Adams 1986, Tedlock 1992).

For Oaxaca, Lipp (1991) and Monaghan (1995) have greatly enhanced our knowledge of indigenous cosmology in the southern highlands of Mexico. Mixe divinities are partial manifestations of a transcendental, formless being. Dual in nature, they derive their titles from the natural world, i.e., *Poh 'Ene* or "wind thunder" (also rain god), *Na Swi ñ* or "earth surface," *Yu:k* or "mountain," *Higi ny* or "life" (also known as Four Rivers or "queen where the water springs forth"), *co'k* or "guardian spirit," and *Mihkú*, lord of the underworld who is master of illness and wealth. *Poh* or Wind is a diffuse concept, part of *Ene* (Thunder) as expressed in the term for the rain god (*Poh'Ene*), but also encompassing the spirits of the dead and mischievous dwarfs. In Atlixco there are four winds: the hot south wind of March, the green north wind of June, the gray or purple southeast wind of December, and the cold northeast wind of November. All are beneficial except for the green north wind. The directions of the four winds reflect Mixe spatial orientation which includes two intercardinal solstitial points linked to the corners of the earth and intersected by the fixed cardinal points defined by sunrise (east) and sunset (west) as well as the hot (south) and green (north) winds. The spiritual nature of ritual numerology—an essential element in Mixe ceremonies—is derived from the winds (Lipp 1991:26-33, 86, 88).

Lipp (ibid.:61-62) provides important information on the native calendar, which is:

> ...visualized as a series of stairs or a ladder leading up and down a mountain from a celestial table where the divine elders, forefathers, and chiefs, who have received the "burdens" of kings, overseers of nature, hold their reunions...The day signs are used as seats by the deities for their councils and as steps where they "place their feet," or journey, ascending and descending from the celestial table at the apex. When offering a sacrifice, the shaman sees herself or himself as standing before these stairs and the offering as rising to the deities, who descend the stairs to receive it. When no offerings are given, the deities descend, resulting in illness for the negligent.

Table symbolism is also associated in curing rituals with a person's alter ego, specifically the placing of one's table in the abode of the guardian spirits (ibid.:89, 90, 172, 174). Actual tables are used in astronomical rituals performed by shaman curers for good results in their work or as a general protection rite for villagers. Performed at night on a mountain, these rituals take place at two tables made of poles and pine boughs with five holes forming a quincunx in the ground underneath. The first table is oriented to the midnight appearance of Venus, while the second is oriented to the appearance of the Southern Cross. The quincunx pattern also occurs in village protection rites, maize divination, and marriage ceremonies (ibid.:105-112).

The ritual paraphernalia for Mixe rituals consists of bundles of pine splints, a brazier, five holes in a quincunx pattern, mescal, and sacrificial fowl to provide blood for sprinkling over the splints and in the holes. A complex numerical system derived from the native calendar governs pine-bundle enumeration prior to burning. The system may have its origins among the Mixe-Zoque-speaking peoples of the Olmec core area. Similar ritual bundles are used by the Totonac, Tlapanec, and Chontal. They are commonly depicted in native codices, and early chroniclers described the ritual burning of stick bundles. Aztec "new fire," and "binding of the years" rituals, including sculptural stone bundles representing the conclusion of time periods are also related. Finally Lipp interprets page five of the Fejervary-Mayer Codex as related to sorcery (ibid.:72-116).

Monaghan's (1995:97-166, 193-232) study of Mixtec sociality in Santiago Nuyoo, Oaxaca documents the covenants of Nuyootecos with Earth *(Nu'un)* and Sky *(Sukun)* mediated by rain *(Savi)* and the people's emergence from *Soko Usha* ("Seven Womb" or 'Seven Well") in the mythic first times, which he compares with the birth of the Aztecs from the womb of Mount Chicomoztoc ("Seven Caves"). He shows how their partitioning of the cosmos into two halves is consistent with the ancient scheme of the Mixteca Alta as manifest at the mountaintop shrine near Apoala where Earth and Sky were believed to meet.

Earth refers to the physical presence of the earth as specifically manifest in a mountain, rock, or soil. Corporal images are used when speaking about Earth, which manifests through the *Nu Nu'un* ("the face of the earth"), bearded old men (sometimes with the face of a puma) or as a seven-headed snake living in underground houses. Like everything in existence, they are endowed with a life principle *(yii,* or *fuerza* in Spanish). The sphere of mortal life is described metaphorically as "seven mountains, seven valleys, seven lakes, seven swamps," encompassing all of the world's geographical features. Earth shrines are located in fields, caves, and on mountaintops.

Rain is part of everything related to the Sky and moisture. Like Earth, it is a fecund and sacred substance, which stimulates growth. It has several "faces" or manifestations such as "Rain People" who appear as lightning bolts, spotted "Rain Serpents" who travel in the center of a rainstorm, "Rain Lizards" found in mist and dew, and multicolored "Rain Saints" who manifest as rain clouds with dark bellies. The "Rain People" live in "Rain Houses," mountaintop caves containing pools of water regarded as shrines. Four mountains are particularly significant. It is believed that mountains contain large amounts of water and that "Rain Houses" or shrines act as conduits for these storehouses.

The interaction between the male Sky (specifically its semen, the Rain) and the womb of the female Earth engenders their daughter, the Corn. *Tachi* (Wind) is seen as a destructive force with many faces (including the "Grandparents"). The creative movements and acts of Jesus, the Sun define a mediating process operative at all levels of society, i.e., between Earth and Sky, night and day, the living and the dead as expressed in baptismal and marriage rites, the growth of corn, ecological exchanges, the pooling of tortillas at *fiestas,* and the ritual circulation of saints' images.

As in most indigenous highland communities, Nuyooteco altars and shrines are found in the home, the fields, and the mountains. The household altar consists of a table holding saints' images, stones, flowers, candles, and incense, often with an arch of canes over the top (ibid.:Figure 3). During All Saints' Day, food is placed on the altar for the deceased and an additional table may be placed in front (ibid.:Figure 14). Mountain shrines are discussed above. In the fields, a harvest ritual involves piling the ears of corn on a mat. A flowery cross or cornstalk resembling a cross is placed in the middle and candles are placed at the corners. Then the sponsor circles the pile with an incense burner thanking *San Marcos* (the earth deity or "face" associated with the Covenant) and the "Rain People" for the harvest while pouring pulque over the four corners. Pozole is offered on a table to passers-by after it has rested for a day on the corn. Monaghan draws parallels between Aztec and Nuyooteco sacrifice.

Of particular interest to this review is the *tenuvi* or "transforming man," who can diagnose illness with a glance, predict the weather, and cause rain clouds to form. His guardian spirits include powerful animals, lighting bolts, and rainfall in general. These rain-makers, who are sometimes called "people of the mountain," are baptized in a special ceremony at mountain ponds inhabited by their patron, the "Rain Serpent," who emerges from the water to bless *(sicuchi,* "to bathe") the initiate by licking. The *tenuvi* make it rain by climbing four special mountains and smoking seven cigars (cognate with rain clouds) at cave-shrines or "Rain Houses."

In Northwestern Mexico the Uto-Aztecan Tarahumara of Inápuchi, Chihuahua have a broad definition of "curing," which in addition to medical practices, encompasses the annual ceremony to assure rain and good crops as well as rituals to protect animals and people from lightning, disease, and sorcery. Fertilization of the fields is also referred to as curing. The principal religious leader is the *owerúame* or "great curer" who is a combination of priest and doctor. His or her most important power is the ability to "see" what is happening with people's souls and to intervene by projecting his or her own soul (Kennedy 1978:139).

The focal point of a curing ritual is the wooden "ceremonial table" placed to the east of the dance patio. Three wooden crosses draped with white muslin and decorated with strings of beads are placed on the east side of this altar and one or two smaller crosses are placed beneath it along with a broken pottery shard, bits of refuse, and "medicines." (For the "dressing" of crosses see Vogt 1976:49 and Freidel et al. 1993:252: "The Cross-Tree stands, blessed, dressed, and adorned, as the symbol of ancient understanding in contemporary homes and shrines…the Foliated Cross at Palenque wears a necklace and jewelry like the living being it was.") The refuse is buried as an offering to *Diablo* or Devil after the ritual. Jars of corn beer (*tesgüiño*), the primary ritual substance, are placed on the east behind the table, which is covered with native foods offered to *Onorúame* or Great Father. All ceremonies are dedicated by tossing ladles of *tesgüiño* to the four directions. *Tesgüiño* jars and blood are dedicated the same way. Other ritual gestures include marking crosses in the air with cedar smoke, *tesgüiño*, or "medicines." Ceremonies involve dancing, eating, drinking, animal sacrifice, and speeches (Kennedy 1978:139-149). Lumholtz (1902:172-174) claimed that the altar crosses represented the three major aboriginal deities, Father Sun, Mother, and Morning Star.

Merrill (1988:71) describes Tarahumara (Rarámuri) cosmology as manifest in public speeches and daily life at Rejogochi:

> The speeches divide the universe into three levels: the domain of the Rarámuri's heavenly parents is above, that of the Devil below, with the Rarámuni in the middle. In their everyday cosmology, the Rarámuri often organize the universe into a hierarchy of seven levels, although the relations among the levels remain the same in the sermons. We live on the fourth or middle level, with the three levels above associated with God and God's wife, the three below with the Devil. They call the levels above the earth *riwigáchi* (sky or heaven), which they preface with *sine* (first), *osá* (second), and *bisá* (third) to distinguish each successively higher plane from the others. God and his wife reside in the highest heaven, called *bisa riwigáchi*. The Rarámuri tend not to name the levels below the earth separately, referring to them collectively as *riré* (below) or *riré pachá* (below underneath). There is nothing above the highest plane or below the lowest.

Except for mountains, each level is flat, with the underside of each level serving as domed sky of the level below. Beginning at the bottom, columns rise along the edge of each level to support the sky and level above. Earthquakes occur when the Devil shakes the supporting columns. The speeches treat time as linear and link the Rarámuri to events at the beginning of the world while everyday cosmology sees time as manifest in the annual agricultural and ceremonial cycles and the idea that this world is the fourth in an ongoing cycle of creation, destruction, and renewal (ibid.:72-74).

In his study of the "living saints" revivalism of the Uto-Aztecan Mayo of Banari in the lower Mayo River Valley of Sonora, Crumrine (1979: 121-129) documents the altars and "dressed" crosses of sacred ramadas. Planted in the ground, the cross represents the *santo*. (For the classification of crosses with saints' images see Vogt 1976:49; as "doorways" to the abodes of the ancestral gods, ibid.:6, 11). At the foot of the cross, boxes of earth from a hole near the mesquite tree where Our Father appeared to a Mayo prophet in 1957 express the connection between sacred earth (symbol of Our Mother) and the ancestors. Red flowers adorning crosses represent Hell; blue is peace and white, hope. Palm arches may symbolize heaven or the sky.

The Uto-Aztecan Papago of Sonora and Arizona hold a curing and fertility ceremony (*wi'igita*) each year at Laguna Quitovac and a sacred cave on Cerro Petaca where dance costumes are protected by a local female saint. All-night dances and a ritual hunt celebrate Montezuma's defeat of the lake monster as well as protecting Quitovac from the waters of the sea and the possibility of excessive summer rains. Prior to the *fiesta* five ramadas oriented to the sun are built behind the sacred cemetery and offerings are deposited at four earth shrines marking the cardinal directions. Dancers commit to four successive years of service. For the Arizona Papago this consists of four annual pilgrimages. The ceremony is seen as maintaining a state of harmony between the Papago and the desert.

Spicer (1969:789) summarizes pre-contact beliefs shared by Uto-Aztecans of Northwestern Mexico:

> The cosmology included conceptions of stages in creation and a universal flood, a view of life as involved in an opposition between supernaturals controlling wet and dry seasons, a belief in serpents associated with springs and other sources of water which were the source of supernatural power, a dominant male and a dominant female supernatural probably connected with heavenly bodies, and the attachment of high value to the deer and to flowers.

Conclusion

Ethnoarchaeologist Ed Krupp (1997:4) describes beliefs regarding the association between mountains and rainwater:

> [I]n Mesoamerica, storm clouds were thought to form and simmer inside the mountains. This association was inspired by the fact that clouds do condense over the mountains, as if they emerged from them. The peaks themselves seem to make contact with the sky where the clouds appear, and springs sprout from the mountain slopes. Rainwater is shed by the mountains and funneled down their flanks to the cultivated valleys below. The mountain's interior is a hall of the underworld, to which caves provide entry.

He also indicates how mountain imagery expressed pre-Hispanic cosmological notions:

> Most Mesoamerican pyramids were artificial cosmic mountains, and they were also said to symbolize the realms of heaven and the levels of the underworld in the stack of platforms they pushed into the sky. They were, in fact, pictures of the cosmos organized around a world axis. Sometimes this axis was defined by the zenith and the nadir, and in other circumstances it was the polar axis, centered on the sky's rotation. These pyramids could also represent the place of Creation, permit communication with the gods, and mark the center of the world [ibid.:299].

In many parts of Middle America one finds the concept of a four-cornered cosmos supported by posts or deities and a central axis as demarcated by the diurnal (zenith/nadir) and seasonal (intercardinal) movements of the sun. Working with Ichaústegui, Benítez (1970:40-41) describes a version of the indigenous *imago mundi*:

> [T]he Mazatecs conceive the world as a flat quadrilateral extension sustained by four posts submerged in water. It is a giant table, the eastern border of which is fixed by the rising sun; the western border by the setting sun. The hours and days are born in the east. Daylight represents all that is positive, the domain of the beneficial powers, while darkness implies all that is negative and dangerous...
>
> Beyond the water that supports the table extends the "Sacred Sea," abode of the Eternal Father seated at a silver table, destination of the souls of dead shamans on which all the animals of the world are forged in silver.
>
> At night, the sun makes a subterranean journey beneath the cosmic table to the realm of the "Grau," little men..., naked, with straight hair and bodies blackened by the strong rays of the sun, which travels very close at hand compensating for burning them by bathing them in gold. The table is surrounded by seven celestial layers contained in a crystalline sphere on which the stars are fixed.

When this *imago mundi* is portrayed in ritual, the microcosmic table-altar becomes a symbolic prop with profound and powerful cultural connotations.

End Note

1. Regarding the five trees planted and roped together in honor of Tlaloc in the temple's courtyard, according to López Austin (1997:116), the central one symbolized the mythical Tamoanchan tree which was "the synthesis of the four trees, and was itself the axis of the universe." Its pivotal role was "expressed by an image of a tree covered with alternating stripes of four colors that gyrated in spirals...just as the cosmic currents moved in each of the four trees of different colors" (ibid.:100). The spiral or helix known as *malinalli* in Aztec iconography was formed by two intertwined currents, fire from the heavens and water form the underworld (ibid.:99).

The helicoidal maypole-like circulation of energy associated with these trees persists today in the Dance of the Ribbons conducted as part of fertility-promoting pilgrimages to the volcanoes

Popocatépetl and Iztaccíhuatl as performed by shamanic weather magicians or *graniceros*. The colored ribbons symbolize the rainbow. Their intertwining is an allegory for the cosmic forces driving the interaction between the wet and dry seasons and the harmonizing of sun and rain (Glockner 1996:215-216, 221-222).

Douglas Sharon
P.A. Hearst Museum of Anthropology
103 Kroeber Hall #3712
University of California, Berkeley
Berkeley, CA 94720
(510) 642-3682

References Cited

Adams, R.
1986 Rio Azul, Lost City of the Maya. *National Geographic* 169(4):545-563.

Aguilar, A.
1992 *Flora Medicinal Indígena de México.* 3 vols. México, D.F.: INI.

Albores, B.
1997 Los Quicazles y el Árbol Cósmico del Olotepec, Estado de México. In: B. Albores and J. Broda, eds., *Graniceros: Cosmovisión y meteorología indígenas de Mesoamérica.* México, D.F.: El Colegio Mexiquense, A.C. UNAM.

Albores, B., and J. Broda, eds.
1997 *Graniceros: Cosmovisión y meteorología indígenas de Mesoamérica.* México, D.F.: El Colegio Mexiquense, A.C. UNAM.

Alcina Franch, J.
1997 Cosmovisión andina y mesoamericana: una comparación. In: R. Varon and J. Flores, eds., *Arqueología, Antropología e Historia en los Andes: Homenaje a María Rostworowski,* pp. 653-675. Lima: IEP.

Alcorn, J.
1984 *Huastec Mayan Ethnobotany.* Austin: University of Texas Press.

Armon Burgete, M.
1990 *Talokan Tata, Talokan Nana: Hierofanías y testimonios de un mundo indígena.* México: Consejo Nacional para la Cultura y las Artes.

Ashmore, W.
1989 Construction and Cosmology: Politics and Ideology in Lowland Maya Settlement Patterns. In: W. Hanks and D. Rico, eds., *Word and Image in Maya Culture: Explorations in Language, Writing and Representation,* pp. 272-286. Salt Lake City: University of Utah Press.

Atkinson, J.
1992 Shamanisms Today. *Annual Review of Anthropology* 21:307-330.

Aveni, A.
1991 Mapping the Ritual Landscapes: Debt Payment to Tlaloc During the Month of Atlcahualo. In: D. Carrasco, ed., *To Change Place: Aztec Ceremonial Landscapes,* pp. 58-73. Niwot: University Press of Colorado.

2001 *Skywatchers.* Austin: University of Texas Press.

Bade, B,
1994 Contemporary Miztec Medicine: Emotional and Spiritual Approaches to Healing. In: G. Johnson and D. Sharon, eds., *Cloth and Curing: Continuity and Change in Oaxaca,* pp. 61-69. San Diego Museum Papers No. 32.

Bartolomé, M.
1978 *Dinámica social de los mayas de Yucatán.* México, D.F.: INI.

Benítez, F.
1970 *Los Indios de México.* 5 volumes. México, D.F.: Ediciones Era S.A.

Betts, R., and D. Libbey
1993 Speaking with Dios: A Costumbre in Highland Guatemala. *Shaman's Drum* 33:50-57.

Broda, J.
1982 Astronomy, Cosmovisión, and Ideology in Pre-Hispanic Mesoamerica. In: A. Aveni and G. Urton, eds., *Ethnoastronomy and Archaeoastronomy in the American Tropics,* pp. 81-110. New York: The New York Academy of Sciences.

1987 The Provenience of the Offerings. In: E. Hill Boone, ed., *The Aztec Templo Mayor,* pp. 211-256. Washington, D.C.: Dumbarton Oaks Trustees for Harvard University.

1991 The Sacred Landscapes of Aztec Calendar Festivals: Myth, Nature, and Society. In: D. Carrasco, ed., *To Change Place: Aztec Ceremonial Landscapes,* pp. 74-120. Niwot: University Press of Colorado.

1993 Astronomical Knowledge, Calendrics, and Sacred Geography in Ancient Mesoamerica. In: C. Ruggles and N. Saunders, eds., *Astronomies and Cultures,* pp. 253-295. Niwot: University of Colorado Press.

1996 Calendarios, cosmovisión y observación de la naturaleza. In: S. Lombardo and E. Nalda, eds., *Temas mesoamericanas,* pp. 427-469. México, D.F.: INAH.

Campos, R.
1997 *Nosotros los curanderos.* México, D.F.: Nueva Imagen.

Carlsen, R.
1997 Ceremony and Ritual in the Maya World. In: M. Schevill, ed., *The Maya Textile Tradition,* pp. 177-216. New York: Harry N. Abrams, Inc.

Carlsen, R., and M. Prechtel
1991 The Flowering of the Dead: An Interpretation of Highland Maya Culture. *Man* (n.s.) 26:23-42.

1994 Walking on Two Legs: Shamanism in Santiago Atitlán, Guatemala. In: G. Seaman and S. Day, eds., *Ancient Traditions: Shamanism in Central Asia and the Americas,* pp. 77-111. Niwot: University Press of Colorado.

Carrasco, D.
1990 *Religions of Mesoamerica: Cosmovision and Ceremonial Centers.* Prospect Heights, IL: Waveland Press, Inc.

1991 *To Change Place: Aztec Ceremonial Landscapes.* Niwot: University Press of Colorado.

Christenson, A.
2001 In the Mouth of the Jaguar: Caves and Maya Cofradía Worship in Highland Guatemala. *The PARI Journal* 11(2). Spring.

Colbys, B. and L.
1981 *The Daykeeper: The life and Discourse of an Ixil Diviner.* Cambridge, Mass.: Harvard University Press.

Crumrine, N.
1977 *The Mayo Indians of Sonora: A People Who Refuse to Die.* Tucson: University of Arizona Press.

Dow, J.
1974 *Santos y supervivencias: Funciones de la religión en una comunidad Otomí, México.* Colección SEP-INI, No. 33. México, D.F.: INI y SEP.

1975 *The Otomí of the Northern Sierra de Puebla, Mexico: An Ethnographic Outline.* LASC Monograph Series, No. 12. East Lansing: Michigan State University

1986 *The Shaman's Touch. Otomí Indian Symbolic Healing.* Salt Lake City: University of Utah Press.

Friedel, D., L. Schele, and J. Parker
1993 *Maya Cosmos: Three Thousand Years on the Shaman's Path.* New York: William Morrow and Company, Inc.

Furst, P.
1972a *Flesh of the Gods: The Ritual Use of Hallucinogens.* New York: Praeger Publishers.

1972b Para encontrar nuestra vida: El peyote entre los huicholes. In: S. Nahmad, E. Klineberg, P. Furst and B. Myerhof, eds., *El peyote y los huicholes,* pp. 109-194. México: SEP (Sep Setentas 29).

1973-74 The Roots and Continuities of Shamanism. In: *Stones, bones and skin. Ritual and Shamanic Art,* pp. 33-60. Toronto: artscanada.

1994 Introduction: An Overview of Shamanism. In: G. Seaman and J. Day, eds., *Ancient Traditions: Shamanism in Central Asia and the Americas,* pp. 1-28. Niwot: University Press of Colorado.

Galinier, J.
1987 Los pápagos, la lluvia y la frontera. *México Indígena* #14, año III:22-23.

1990 *La mitad del mundo. Cuerpo y cosmos en los rituales otomíes.* México: UNAM/CEMCA/INI.

Gann, T.
1917 The Chachac, or Rain Ceremony, as Practiced by the Maya of Southern Yucatán and Northern British Honduras. *Proceedings 19th ICA,* pp. 409-418, Washington, D.C.

1918 *The Mayan Indians of Southern Yucatán and Northern British Honduras.* Smithsonaisn Institution, Bureau of American Ethnology, Bulletin 64, Washington, D.C.: Government Printing Office.

Girard, R.
1966 *Los Mayas.* México, D.F.: Libro Mex.

Glockner, J.
1996 *Los Volcanes Sagrados: Mitos y rituals en el Popocatépetl y la Iztaccíhuatl.* México, D.F.: Grijalbo.

González, H.
1989 Bi' kita: ceremonia pápago. *México Indígena* #26, año V:61-63.

Gossen, G.
1974 *Chamulas in the World of the Sun: Time and Space in Maya Oral Tradition.* Cambridge: Harvard University Press.

1986 The Chamula Festival of Games: Native Macroanalysis and Social Commentary in a Maya Carnival. In: G. Gossen, ed., *Symbol and Meaning beyond the Closed Community: Essays in Mesoamerican Ideas,* pp. 227-254. Albany: Institute for Mesoamerican Studies, SUNY Albany.

Green, J.
1968 *The Days of the Dead in Oaxaca, Mexico.* San Diego Museum of Man Popular Series No. 1.

1972 The Days of the Dead in Oaxaca, Mexico: An Historical Inquiry. *Omega* 3:3:245-261.

Greenberg, J.
1981 *Santiago's Sword: Chatino Peasant Religion and Economics.* Berkeley: University of California Press.

Hanks, W.
1984 Stratification, Structure, and Experience in a Yucatec Ritual Event. *Journal of American Folklore* 97(384):131-166.

1990 *Referential Practice: Language and Lived Space Among the Maya.* Chicago: University of Chicago Press.

Hayden, B.
1987 Past to Present: Uses of Stone Tools in the Maya Highlands. In: B. Hayden ed., *Lithic Studies Among the Contemporary Highland Maya,* pp. 160-234. Tucson: University of Arizona Press.

Heyden, D.
1991 La matriz de la tierra. In: J. Broda, S. Iwaniszewski, and L. Maupomé, eds,. *Arqueoastronomía y Etnoastronomía en Mesoamerica,* pp. 501-515. México, D.F.: UNAM.

Holland, W.
1963 *Medicina maya en los altos de Chiapas.* México, D.F.: INI.

1964 Conceptos Cosmológicos Tzotziles como una Base para Interpretar la Civilización Maya Prehispánica. *America Indígena* 24(1):11-28

Huber, B., and A Sandstrom, eds.
2001 *Mesoamerican Healers.* Austin: University of Texas Press.

Hunt, E.
1973 *The Transformation of the Hummingbird: Cultural Roots of a Zinacantecan Mythical Poem.* Ithica: Cornell University Press.

Incháustegui, C.
n.d. La Mesa de Plata. Cosmogonía y curanderismo entre los mazatecos de Oaxaca. Typescript.

Ichon, A.
1973 La Religión de los Totonacas de la Sierra. *Colección SEP-INI,* No.16. INI y SEP

Kehoe, A.
1988 Primal Gaia: Primitivists and Plastic Medicine Men. In: J. Clifton, ed., *The Invented Indian: Cultural Fictions and Government Policies,* pp. 193-209. New Brunswick, N.J.: Transaction Publications.

Kennedy, J.
1978 *Tarahumara of the Sierra Madre: Beer, Ecology, and Social Organization.* Arlington Heights, Illinois: AHM Publishing Corporation.

Kerr, J., and B. Kerr, eds.
1995 *The Maya Vase Book, Vol. 5.* The Hudson Museum. Orono: University of Maine.

Krupp, E.
1997 *Skywatchers, Shamans & Kings: Astronomy and the Archaeology of Power.* New York: John Wiley & Sons, Inc.

Ku Ché, F.
1985 Ch'a cháak: La Lluvia entre los mayas. *México Indígena* 6:38-40.

Lemaistre, D.
1996 The Deer That Is Peyote and the Deer That Is Maize. In: S. Schaefer and P. Furst, eds., *People of the Peyote: Huchol Indian History, Religion, & Survival,* pp. 308-329. Albuquerque: University of New Mexico Press.

León-Portilla, M.
1968 *Tiempo y Realidad en el Pensamiento Maya.* México, D.F.: UNAM.

Lipp, F.
1991 *The Mixe of Oaxaca: Religion, Ritual, and Healing.* Austin: University of Texas Press.

López Austin, A.
1996 La cosmovisión mesoamericana. In: S. Lombardo and E. Nalda, eds., *Temas mesoamericanas,* pp. 471-507. México, D.F.: INAH.

1997 *Tamoanchan, Tlalocan: Places of Mist.* Niwot: University Press of Colorado.

Love, B., and E. Peraza
1984 Wahil Kol: A Yucatec Maya Agricultural Ceremony. *Estudios de Cultura Maya* 15. México, D.F.: Universidad Nacional Autónomo de México.

Lumholtz, C.
1902 *Unknown Mexico.* Vol. 1. New York: Scribner's Sons.

Madsen, W., and C. Madsen
1969 *A Guide to Mexican Witchcraft.* Mexico, D. F.: Editorial Minutiae Mexicana.

McKeever Furst, J.
1995 *The Natural History of the Soul in Ancient Mexico.* New Haven: Yale University Press.

Merrill, W.
1988 *Rarámuri Souls: Knowledge and Social Process in Northern Mexico.* Washington, D.C.: Smithsonian Institution Press.

Monaghan, J.
1995 *The Covenants with Earth and Rain: Exchange, Sacrifice, and Revelation in Mixtec Sociality.* Norman: University of Oklahoma Press.

Natural History
1997 Worlds of the Shaman. *Natural History* 10(2): 32-53.

National Geographic
1989 America's Ancient Skywatchers. *National Geographic* 177(3):76-107.

Oakes, M.
1951 *The Two Crosses of Todos Santos: Survivals of Mayan Religious Ritual.* Bolligen Series XXVII. New York: Pantheon Books.

Ochiai, K.
1991 Bajo la mirada del sol portátil: representación social y material de la cosmología tzotzil. In: J. Broda, S. Iwaniszewski, and L. Maupomé, eds., *Arqueoastronomía y Etnoastronomía en Mesoamérica,* pp. 205-218. México, D.F.: UNAM.

Prechtel, M.
1998 *Secrets of the Talking Jaguar: A Mayan Shaman's Journey to the Heart of the Indigenous Soul.* New York: Jeremy P. Tarcher/Putnam.

Press, I.
1971 The Urban Curandero. *American Anthropolgist* 73(3):741-756.

1978 Urban Folk Medicine: A Functional Overview. *American Anthropologist* 80(1):71-84.

Redfield, R., and A. Villa Rojas
1934 *Chan Kom: A Maya Village.* Carnegie Institution of Washington, Publication No. 448. Washington, D.C: Judd & Detweiler, Inc.

Robicsek, F.
1975 *A Study in Maya Art and History: The Mat Symbol.* New York: The Museum of the American Indian Heye Foundation.

Sandstrom, A.
  1991 *Corn Is Our Blood: Culture and Ethnic Identity in a Contemporary Aztec Indian Village*. Norman: University of Oklahoma Press.

Sandstrom, A., and P. Sandstrom
  1986 *Traditional Papermaking and Paper Cult Figures of Mexico*. Norman: University of Oklahoma Press.

Schaefer, S.
  1996a The Crossing of the Souls: Peyote, Perception, and Meaning Among the Huichol Indians. In: S. Schaefer and P. Furst, eds., *People of the Peyote: Huichol Indian History, Religion, & Survival*, pp. 138-168. Albuquerque: University of New Mexico Press.

  1996b The Cosmos Contained: The Temple Where Sun and Moon Meet. In: S. Schaefer and P. Furst, eds., *People of the Peyote: Huichol Indian History, Religion, & Survival*, pp. 332-378. Albuquerque: University of New Mexico Press.

Schaefer, S., and P. Furst
  1996a Introduction. In: S. Schaefer and P. Furst, eds., *People of the Peyote: Huichol Indian History, Religion, & Survival*, pp. 1-25. Albuquerque: University of New Mexico Press.

  1996b Conclusion. In: S. Schaefer and P. Furst, eds., *People of the Peyote: Huichol Indian History, Religion, & Survival*, pp. 503-521. Albuquerque: University of New Mexico Press.

Schele, L., and D. Freidel
  1990 *A Forest of Kings: The Untold Story of the Ancient Maya*. New York: William Morrow and Company, Inc.

Schele, L., and P. Matthews
  1998 *The Code of Kings: The Language of Seven Sacred Temples and Tombs*. New York: Touchstone.

Sharon, D.
  1976 Distribution of the Mesa in Latin America. *Journal of Latin American Lore* 2(1):71-95.

  1978 *Wizard of the Four Winds: A Shaman's Story*. New York: Free Press.

Sosa, J.
  1986 Maya Concepts of Astronomical Order. In: G. Gossen, ed., *Symbol and Meaning Beyond the Closed Community: Essays in Mesoamerican Ideas*, pp. 185-196. Albany, New York: Institute for Mesoamerican Studies, SUNY Albany.

  1989 Cosmological, symbolic and cultural complexity among the contemporary Maya of Yucatán. In: A. Aveni, ed., *World Archaeoastronomy*, pp. 130-142. Cambridge University Press.

Spicer, E.
  1969 Northwest Mexico: Introduction. In: E. Vogt, ed., *Handbook of Middle American Indians, Volume 8*, pp. 777-791. Austin: University of Texas Press.

Starr, F.
  1908 *In Indian Mexico: A Narrative of Travel and Labor*. Chicago: Forbes & Company.

Tedlock, B.
  1982 *Time and the Highland Maya*. Albuquerque: University of New Mexico Press

  1992 The Road of Light: Theory and Practice. In: A Aveni, ed., *The Sky in Mayan Literature*, pp. 8-42. New York: Oxford University Press.

Townsend, R.
  1987 Coronation at Tenochtitlan. In: E. Hill Boone, ed., *The Aztec Templo Mayor*, pp. 371-409. Washington, D.C.: Dumbarton Oaks Trustees for Harvard University.

  1992 *The Ancient Americas: Art from Sacred Landscapes*. Chicago.: The Art Institute of Chicago.

  2000 *The Aztecs*. London: Thames & Hudson, Ltd.

Tozzer, A.
  1907 *A Comparative Study of the Mayas and the Lacandones*. Archaeological Institute of America. New York: The MacMillian Company.

Villa Rojas., A.
  1945 *The Maya of East Central Quintana Roo*. Carnegie Institution of Washington, Publication No. 559. Baltimore: The Lord Baltimore Press.

Vogt, E.
  1970 *The Zinacantecos of Mexico: A Modern Maya Way of Life*. New York: Holt, Rinehart and Winston.

  1976 *Tortillas for the Gods: A Symbolic Analysis of Zinacanteco Rituals*. Cambridge: Harvard University Press.

  1992 The Persistence of Maya Tradition in Zinacantán. In: R. Townsend, ed., *The Ancient Americas: Art from Sacred Landscapes*, pp. 61-69. Chicago: The Art Institute of Chicago.

Wagley, C.
  1969 The Maya of Northwestern Guatemala. In: E. Vogt, ed., *Handbook of Middle American Indians, Volume 7*, pp. 46-68. Austin: University of Texas Press.

Walsh, R.
  1992 *The Spirit of Shamanism*. New York: J.P. Tarcher.

Watanabe, J.
  1983 In the World of the Sun: A Cognitive Model of Mayan Cosmology. *Man* (n.s.) 18:710-728.

  1992 *Maya Saints and Souls in a Changing World*. Austin: University of Texas Press.

Williams García, R.
  1963 *Los Tepehuas*. Xalapa, Veracruz: Universidad Veracruzana, Instituto de Antropología.

Central and Northern Mexico

Curanderos' Altar-*Mesas* in Mexico City

Roberto Campos-Navarro

It is a known fact that the majority of Mexicans are Catholics. And their customs include the development of altar-*mesas* dedicated to the saints and virgins of their particular choice. These altars always include offerings and decorations, flowers, and candles that are almost always lit since "light for the saints should never be lacking" (Scheffer 1986:94).

The use of altar-*mesas* is a fundamental element among the resources utilized by the rural and urban *curanderos* of Mexico—the majority of whom are Catholics. It is a focal point for multiple symbolic and ritual activities related to therapy. It is not a simple scenographic element, but the most important space of the *curandero* in relation to the other social actors involved in the curing act.

In contemporary urban curing the altar synthesizes the ideology and cosmovision of the specialist. In it are amalgamated his or her thoughts, prayers, and practices. It is the very expression of the known heterogeneity of form and cultural content characteristic of urban *curanderos* as described by Irvin Press (1971).

Also in contemporary urban curing we find that continuous change is another characteristic structural element (Campos 1997). As a result, in the altars we witness successive modifications in form and content as much in space as in time. The transformations in altar-*mesas* maintain tradition, but also incorporate modernizing modalities of the cultural globalization of which we are all a part.

Mexican culture is a living combination of Mesoamerican and European cultural currents in which the Amerindian elements have not disappeared, nor will they disappear given the 10 to 15 million Indians residing in indigenous regions as well as important migrants to the large cities and megalopolis of Mexico (León-Portilla 2001: 26). And, at the same time, there is constant and incomplete penetration of Western elements, first Spanish Catholic and then American Protestant as well as other ethnic minorities, such as Chinese, Lebanese, Jews, etc. settled throughout the length and breadth of the country. Given this diversity, our multi-ethnic and pluri-cultural composition is undeniable.

In this sense of racial and ethnic admixture, contemporary urban curing is reflected in the intimate and specific development of curing altars. In them are expressed with clear transparency this multiple and hybrid cultural composition.

Doña Marina

In this paper I will describe the altar-*mesa* of a *curandera* who lives in eastern Mexico City, comparing it with altars of *curanderos* who live on the outskirts of the city.

Doña Marina is a *mestiza curandera* born in the northern part of the country, who migrated to Mexico City in the 1950s, and who has been a practicing *curandera* for 40 years. In Figure 1, we see Gómez Palacio, Durango, her birthplace where she spent her childhood (foreground), and, in the background, the city of Torreón, Coahuila.

Douglas Sharon, ed., *Mesas & Cosmologies in Mesoamerica*. San Diego Museum Papers 42, 2003.

Figure 1. Gómez Palacio, Durango (foreground)—Doña Marina's birthplace—and Torreón, Coahuila (background).

At the present time, she resides in Iztapalapa, to the east of Mexico City. Her house is no different from those in the rest of the colony, however, near the entrance she maintains a small garden of medicinal plants such as *zábila (Aloe barbadensis* Will.), *muicle (Justicia spicigera* Schlechtend), *epazote (Chenopodium ambrosioides* L./*Teloxys ambrosioides* L. Weber), and other vegetable species (Figure 2).

Figure 2. Doña Marina's house in Iztapalapa, to the east of Mexico City.

In her small waiting room, one can observe several contradictory symbols: on one side a cross of wood and *pericón (Tagetes lucida* cav.) tied together with red ribbons surrounded by *zábila*, which is used in Mexico to prevent "bad airs" and to keep out "negative energies" (Figure 3). On the other side, on a small table, there is statue of Buddha as a guardian of the home. On the wall is a propitiatory floral arrangement.

Figure 3. Cross surrounded by zábila.

In a close-up, we observe the protective cross with a plastic toy representing a little sorceress beside it. Mexican ambivalence is worth mentioning here, where *curanderos* are considered to be good and sorcerers represent evil, in spite of the fact that there are sorcerers who carry out curing activities and *curanderos* practicing activities related to sorcery.

Once we enter the room, our attention is drawn to a niche used as a small altar which expresses the hybridization inherent in *curanderismo* as revealed by Catholic images of Saint Martin, the Christian cross, Child Jesus richly adorned in blue and gold as well as the presence of an enigmatic naked woman with oriental features.

Completing the setting is a poster of Ernesto "Ché" Guevara, which has its origin in a direct personal experience of Doña Marina, who says that she met Ché at the General Hospital of Mexico where he worked as an allergy specialist. She also claims that she administered herbal treatment for his asthma from which he, in effect, suffered from childhood (Figure 4).

Figure 4. Poster of Ernesto "Ché" Guevara.

Figure 5. Doña Marina's grandmother.

Regarding the curandera´s family, it should be noted that Doña Marina inherited her knowledge and curing practice from her grandparents (above all her grandmother, Figure 5), uncles, and parents and that she transmits this legacy to her extensive family, sons, daughter-in-laws, and grandchildren.

The principal demands for her services involve fright sickness *(susto)*, sorcery *(mal puesto* or *daño)*, muscular ailments treated with massage and "cupping," digestive problems such as indigestion *(empacho)*, among others. In her therapy, she uses herbal remedies and ritual procedures.

Returning to the description of Doña Marina´s home, the garage is used as her consulting room. There we find the principal altar occupying a fundamental space surrounded by stored herbs and a long couch where the majority of her consultations and curing take place. On the altar the color red dominates in the textil covering the table which in turn is covered by an apparently chaotic aggregate of crosses, images, pictures and printed prayers, small Catholic and Asiatic sculptures, triangles, and pyramids (Figure 6). Concentrated in several metal trays, we find coins, scissors opened in the form of a cross, photo i.d.'s of patients, and shapeless fragments of iron and iron pyrites (Figure 7). Other items include candles and candle holders of all sizes and colors, images of saints consecrated by the Church or rejected by it (as in the case of Holy Death), rosaries in the form of the cross, tree branches for cleansings, empty glasses to be used in "cupping," and others containing water and eggs used in patient "cleansings."

It is evident that this is an active, working table holding all kinds of sacred objects sacralized by the *curandera*. In the following scenario we observe the treatment of a family suffering from fright sickness, a clinical syndrome involving soul loss, the therapy for which is choreographed in the consultation room with the altar-*mesa* in the background.

The case involved a 9-year-old boy who nearly drowned in a swimming pool, but ended up with the symptoms of fright sickness, i.e., no appetite, weakness, weight loss, nightmares. The popular

Figure 6. Objects on Doña Marina's altar.

Figure 7. Objects concentrated in metal trays include photo i.d.'s and fragments of iron and iron pyrites.

treatment consists of retrieving the lost soul. This involves "cleansing," i.e., rubbing the naked body of the patient with his own clothing. Note that on the altar a metal cross from a cemetery has been added. Also note the array of cups for "cupping" on the edge of the couch (Figure 8).

Catching the patient by surprise, Doña Marina throws holy water on the child and calls out his name. He is wrapped in a sheet, and the procedure makes him cry. The curing continues with the child sitting down. Behind him, note the re- cipients with liquids, tree branches for cleansings, a star of David, and a plastic pre-Hispanic Atlantean figure (Figure 9).

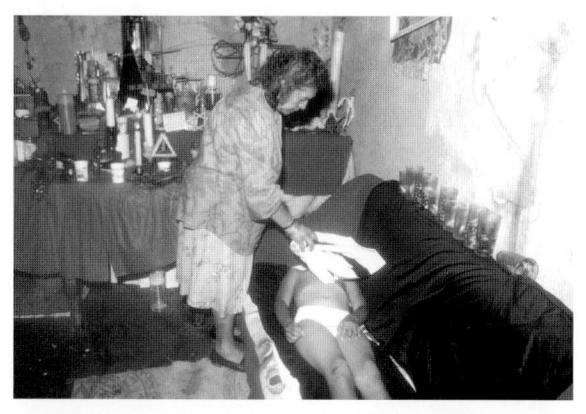

Figure 8. Curing ritual for a 9-year-old boy with symptoms of fright sickness. Note cups for "cupping" (right).

Figure 9. Objects on Doña Marina's altar during ritual procedures for curing the boy.

After the child, the parents—equally frightened by the possible loss of their son and his subsequent ailment—are treated. Here we can place the participating social actors within the scenographic context: Doña Marina and her patients, her son and assistant—the principal actors in the therapeutic drama—not to mention the spectators, i.e., the photographer and the meddling anthropologist. All are framed by the altar-*mesa* as theatrical backdrop.

Other *curanderos* in the Valley of Mexico show similarities and differences. In Xochimilco, D.F., Don Miguel, a merchant herbalist, has a simple *mesa* with a white tablecloth, candleholders, fruits, flowers, and a central sculpture of a red

Holy Death. The *mesa* of another *curandero*-merchant, Don Humberto holds flowers, Christ images, saints, and virgins, once again with Holy Death in the forefront.

Considering that Doña Marina also works with medallions and prayers alluding to Holy Death, it is apparent that its presence in urban curing is quite extensive (Figure 10). We know very little about this personage. It is not mentioned in the colonial chronicles (Quesada 1989) and does not appear in the Encyclopedic Dictionary of Traditional Mexican Medicine (Zolla 1994).

Figure 10. La Santa Muerte—Holy Death.

From the ethnographic point of view, a variety of sources confirm the generalized presence of Holy Death in the last century (Sepúlveda 1983: 174). It is known that there are three manifestations recognizable by the color of their clothing. According to Don Humberto, the white Holy Death serves "to solicit peace and harmony in the home," the red "to bring back a loved one," and the black is "for removing those who cause harm, drive off undesirable persons or impair them" (Aguilar et al. 1999). For Don Miguel, the white is "for work, business and to remove and cut the evil vibration," the red "to produce the energy to attract a person or things that have been lost," and the black "to reject everything negative" (ibid.). In recent years, the latter has been converted into the protective figure of Mexican narco-trafficking gangs (Suaverza 2002:26-27).

Final Comments

As we have seen, the majority of urban *curanderos* have a special, sacred space for exercising their public and private activities related to curing. The elaboration of altar-*mesas* corresponds to a social and ideological construction of the *curandero* in which cosmovision plays a fundamental role.

This cosmovision as expressed in altars is the product of a long process of cultural blending in which Catholic, Oriental, and unconventional elements are mixed.

To date, in the collective construction of urban altars we do not find a structural pattern of antagonistic divisions as is the case for shamanic *mesas* from the Andean region as described by Douglas Sharon. However, there could actually exist some contradictory elements, for example, the growing cult of the Holy Death, which is not accepted by the Catholic Church.

From the foregoing, we believe that the altar-*mesa* in urban contexts is essential to the creation of a therapeutic atmosphere. Its heterogeneity with regard to form and content, meaning and significance will probably continue to be a characteristic trait of urban curing.

Roberto Navarro-Campos
Facultad de Medicina
Universidad Nacional Autónoma de México
Brasil #33 Centro Historico
Mexico, D.F. 06220, MEXICO
(5) 55 49 78 42
rcampos@servidor.unam.mx

References Cited

Aguilar, Eberth, Boris Calderón, Mary Díaz, and Rosario González
  2001 Altares de curanderos de Xochimilco. Unpublished manuscript. Facultad de Medicina. UNAM.

Buenrostro, Marco
  2002 Altar de Dolores. *La Jornada*, March 20, 2002, p. 28a. México, D.F.

Campos-Navarro, Roberto
  1997 *Nosotros los curanderos. Experiencias de una curandera tradicional en el México de hoy.* México: Nueva Imagen.

León-Portilla, Miguel
  2001 La conquista de México. *Arqueología Mexicana* IX (51):20-27.

Press, Irvin
  1971 The Urban Curandero. *American Anthropologist* 73:741-76.

Quesada, Noemí
  1989 *Enfermedad y maleficio. El curandero en el México colonial.* México: Universidad Nacional Autónoma de México.

Ruiz Méndez, Teresita de Jesús
  2002 *Ser curandero en Uruapan, Zamora*. Michoacán: El Colegio de Michoacán/Instituto Michoacano de Cultura.

Scheffler, Lilian
  1986 *Magia y brujería en México*. México: Editorial Panorama.

Sepúlveda, María Teresa
  1983 *Magia, brujería y supersticiones en México*. México: Everest Mexicana.

Sharon, Douglas
  1980 *El chamán de los cuatro vientos*. México: Siglo XXI Editores.

Suverza, Alejandro
  2002 La santita. *Rev. Cambio* I (37):26-27.

Zolla, Carlos (coord.)
  1994 *Diccionario Enciclopédico de la medicina tradicional mexicana*. México: Instituto Nacional Indigenista.

Central and Northern Mexico

Sierra Otomí Religious Symbolism: Mankind Responding to the Natural World

James W. Dow

My goal is to view the symbolic world of the Sierra Otomí. I will look at the most public symbols in their religion and then examine the native concepts that lie behind them. These interpretations were developed during more than 30 years studying and writing about their culture.

The Sierra Otomí are a cultural group of Mesoamerican Indians who live in the mountains to the northeast of Mexico City. Although not often stated, the difficulty that Euro-Mexicans have with the Otomí language has inhibited the understanding of the group. This situation is now being corrected by a more intense effort to study the language and culture (e.g., Bernard and Salinas Pedraza 1989, Lastra 2001). As an illustration of the problems created by the language one can cite the issue of pronouncing the correct name of the linguistic group. The proper name is "Ñähñu." In the International Phonetic Alphabet Ñähñu is written as *nanu* and is derived from "*na*" meaning "word" or "speech" and *nu* meaning "nose." Thus Ñähñu means "nasal word" or "the nasal language." European language speakers have difficulty recognizing and pronouncing the voiceless palatal nasal *n* in this word. It is pronounced by putting the tongue to the roof of the mouth and expelling air without sounding the vocal chords.

The Ñähñu people have a very old culture that predates the Aztecs. Most of the speakers of Ñähñu live in the highlands. The culture there was changed most radically by the Spanish because it was a region of haciendas during the colonial period. The haciendas lasted through the 19th century. However, the hacienda system did not reach into the mountains to the east where the sierra branch of this group lives. Figure 1 shows the location of the Sierra Ñähñu in 1990.[1] There were approximately 49,300 speakers of Ñähñu there in 2001.

The Sierra Ñähñu population is located in the states of Hidalgo (28,300) and in adjacent regions of the states of Puebla (5,900) and Veracruz (15,100).[2] Although the Indians are the largest ethnic group in some *municipios*, the *municipio* governments are usually controlled by smaller Spanish-speaking elites.[3] Profits to be made from trade, cattle ranching, and coffee production have attracted such elites into the sierra. The Indians are the poorest segment of this multi-ethnic society. *Municipio* government usually represents the interests of a town-dwelling *mestizo* elite.

In the 16th century, Augustinian monks brought the Holy Catholic Church to the area and attempted to evangelize the Indians. The Augustinian chronicler Esteban García (1918) reported that the Sierra Ñähñu were still worshiping their own idols in the 17th century after considerable effort by the Augustinians to convert them. When I first went to study the area in 1967, the Catholic Church in Tutotepec was still unable to attract the Indian population. The Catholics had offended the Ñähñu by deprecating some of their most sacred idols. Even today Catholic ideas and customs are only part of the native religion. Although the Augustinian monks left in the 18th century, leaving behind many buildings, only a

Douglas Sharon, ed., *Mesas & Cosmologies in Middle America*. San Diego Museum Papers 42, 2003.

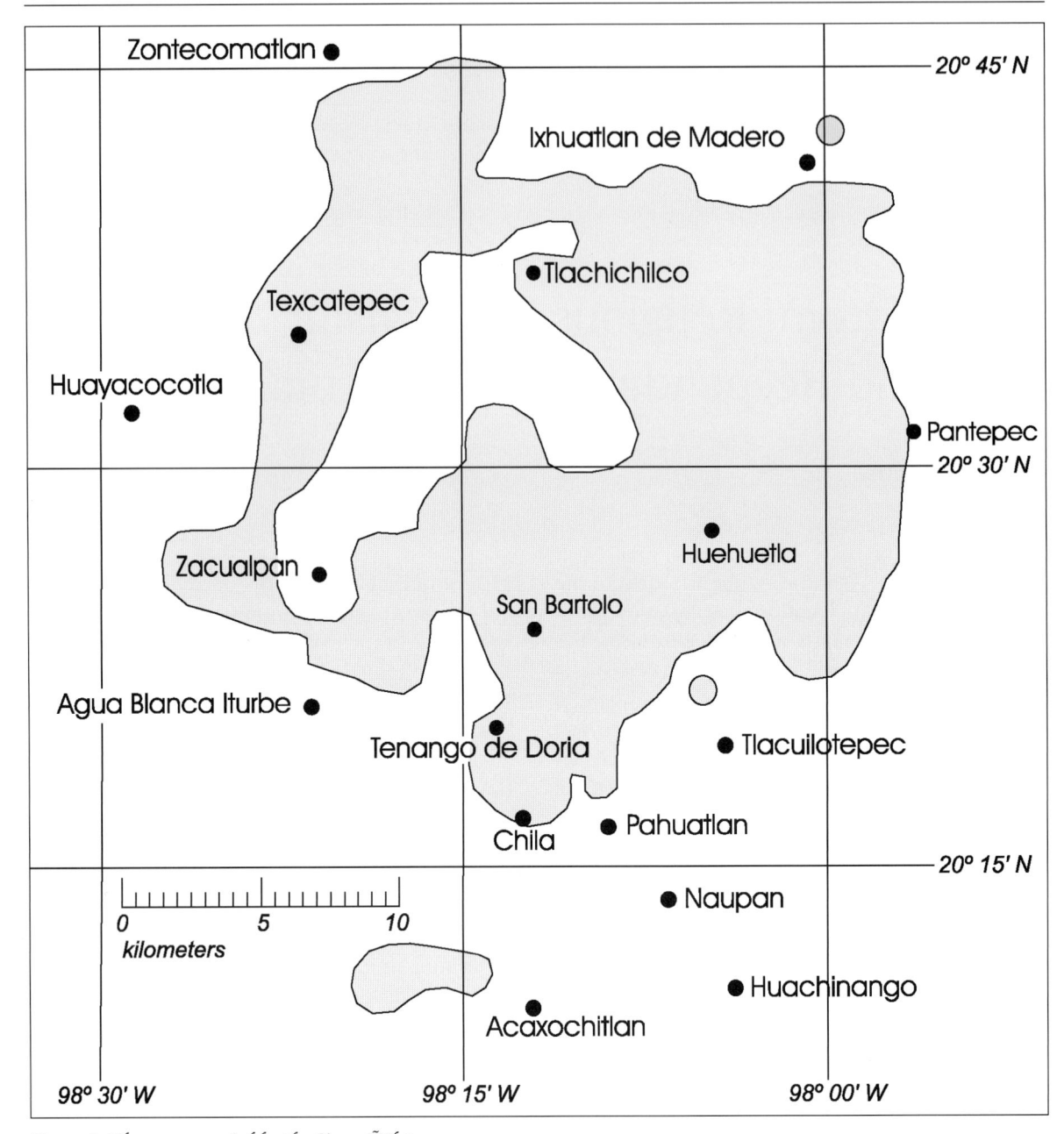

Figure 1. *The area occupied by the Sierra Ñähñu*

partial impression of Roman Catholicism remained. Today, because it is the religion of the powerful classes and, hence, the most politically correct religion, Catholicism in the region is more visible to outsiders. This makes it an excellent entry point for our view of Sierra Ñähñu religion.

Each *municipio* has a parish church with a resident priest. The church is located in the capital town *(cabecera)* of the *municipio*. Sometimes the Bishop will visit the parish church to baptize infants and in general show support by the priestly hierarchy. People, especially the townsfolk, appreciate his presence because it lends status to their *municipio*. But the Bishop never—and the priest seldom—visits the other communities in the *municipio*, the *pueblos* and *rancherías*. However, the *pueblos* do have churches left over from the evangelizing work of the Augustinians. For example, the *pueblo* of San Pablo El Grande in the *municipio* of Tenango de Doria, Hidalgo, has an old church, the origins of which seem to be in the 17th century. During the annual *fiesta* of Saint Paul *(San Pablo)* the doorway of the church is festooned with leaves and flower images. An image of Saint Paul is kept inside and is paraded around the village with other images in the evenings of the *fiesta* days. There is a cross associated with this church, but it is not inside. It is outside the church and is decorated with a large flower design made of palm leaves (see Figure 2) during *fiestas*. Crosses are important symbols for the Sierra Ñähñu, but they always are covered with flowers and foliage during rituals, so much so, that they look more like the pre-Columbian foliated cross than the Christian cross. The cross with its flower decorations actually symbolizes Jesus and God Sun together. Every holy building, church and oratory *(oratorio)*, has a cross associated with it. A small private *oratorio* may have its cross inside on the wall opposite the altar, but a larger *oratorio* or church will display its cross more prominently, outside and in front, on its own altar. So stands the cross of the San Pablo church.

Figure 2. The Cross and Sun-Flower in front of the San Pablo church.

Appointed officials, *mayordomos*, care for the images that belong to the *pueblo* as a whole. Every image also has a *padrino* (godfather), but if the image is owned by a family, no *mayordomo* is necessary, because the owners and the *padrino* share the leadership of the *fiesta*. I have been told that the *padrino* is the most important steward of an image. However, the prestige created by the conspicuous public spending of *mayordomos* sometimes overshadows that of the *padrinos* in larger communities. The San Pablo church has three images on the main altar: the Virgin of Guadalupe, Saint Paul *(San Pablo)*, and Saint Peter *(San Pedro)*. Two Christ *(Cristo)* images in niches on opposite walls flank the main altar.

In 1990, the village elders appointed only three *mayordomos*, one each for the images on the main altar. They promised to make the offerings and to hold feasts to honor their saints. The rituals for the *Cristos* were supported by public contributions, not by a single *mayordomo*. This situation illustrates a change in religion that is taking place throughout the Sierra Ñähñu area. Men are no longer willing to bear all the expenses of sponsoring a *pueblo* image as a *mayordomo*. In the past, each image had several ranked *mayordomos*, and men vied to be allowed to accept this honor of sponsorship. But the economy has changed and along with it the religion. Wages are coming into the communities from migrants who go as far away as the United States to earn money. At home, this largess can be well invested in houses or land, so the urge to capture prestige by sponsoring a public image has diminished. San Pablo has solved this problem by opening up *mayordomo* sponsorship to ambitious young men who have earned enough excess wealth that they can afford to spend some of it on public displays. In previous years, mayordomoships only went to the older and respected conservative members of the community. In the background, however, today the older men watch over the *fiesta* to make sure that the village saints are well treated, hence, the community support for rituals for the two *Cristos* who would otherwise be neglected. In other Sierra Ñähñu *pueblos*, the changing economy and the pressure to spend all one's wealth on religious *fiestas* has encouraged the growth of Protestant sects that have reduced expenditures on *fiestas* (Dow 2001).

Mobile altars on which the three saints are carried stand at the back of the church. They are decorated with flower fans and stalks of corn. The *fiesta* takes place each year when the corn is just beginning to ripen and when the fresh ears *(elotes)* can be eaten. It is a festive time. In the evening, the images are taken from the church on their mobile altars to enjoy the fireworks outside with the people. They are lit by candlelight on the hill next to the plaza and wait with their supporters to see the fireworks ordered by the *mayordomos*. A tower of fireworks *(castillo)* bursts with an ascending fumarole of sparks, smoke, and noise to reach a crowning pinwheel that sails off into the night sky.

This public view of religion appears somewhat Catholic; however, when one looks at what people believe and practice in their homes, something different emerges. One sees an animistic view of the world that is closely attuned to nature. For example, away from the church in San Pablo another scene takes place. Men sit in front of a oratory all day, drinking, chatting, and meticulously making flower offerings to be laid in front of the images in the church. It is a particularly auspicious place for men to gather, for inside the oratory are other images belonging to an old family in the *pueblo*.

Oratories are small buildings built very carefully to be the homes of religious images. Of all cultural features beyond language, this is the one that most closely links the Sierra Ñähñu to their Ñähñu brethren in the rest of the highlands. Otherwise, the current religion of the Sierra Ñähñu bears a closer resemblance to the religions of the Tepehua and Nahua than it does to the religion of the highland Ñähñu, who have assimilated more of the post-colonial Spanish-speaking culture.

A well-off Sierra Ñähñu family will build an oratory to house its most precious images. They may be of Catholic saints, but they may also be images of non-Catholic beings. These other precious images are called *antiguas* or ancients, an appropriate name because some of them are pre-Columbian in origin. These *antiguas* have their own myths of power. Shamans are able to identify them and pass on their names. The Catholic priest in Tutotepec in the 1960s failed to recognize people's belief in these images thus causing many people to become angry with him and the Catholic Church in general. In the Indian language, all the beings whose images are kept in oratories and churches are known as zidähmu, "respected great lords." The images are the points in space to which the life force of the beings are called by ritual.

The concept of life force *(zaki)* is probably the most important idea in Sierra Ñähñu religion. *Zaki* is an animating force that brings all living things to life. Without *zaki* the world would be a dead place. Nothing would change. The sun would not move in the sky. Plants would not grow. Animals would not move. Sierra Ñähñu shamans are experts who study and understand this other dimension, the dimension of *zaki*.

Shamans study the hidden nature of *zaki* and are respected for their work, which may involve visionary contact with unseen beings. Not all that happens in the world of *zaki* is good. Sorcerers are the incompetent fools who try to manipulate these forces for selfish ends. Shamans say that sorcerers outnumber good folk. I have not met any sorcerers, but they are not likely to reveal themselves. One must seek out sorcerers secretly, because if other members of the community found one doing this there would be serious repercussions. They are not an easy group to study. I know that sorcery exists because I have found sorcery figures by the Tenango graveyard. Figure 3 shows one of these figures. It has been burned and the eye and feet have been mutilated. The intent here was to destroy the *zaki* of the person by attracting it and mutilating it near the graveyard where the souls of those who have died a bad death would attack it.

Shamans have to fight these evil forces. Don Antonio is a shaman who works in the *municipio* of Tenango de Doria (Dow 1986). The following items for the fight can be found on his altar.

(1) Paper figures representing the *zaki* of a patient (see Figure 4). Around the edges of the human figure are the figures of the patient's animal companions, his *rogi*.

(2) Plant and flower offerings.

(3) Long candles to illuminate the evening offering to the gods.

(4) Votive candles for the altar.

(5) The shaman's wands covered with ribbons and paper figures. These attract the *zaki* of tutelary beings that help the shaman in his visions.

(6) A chest containing *antiguas,* two of which are the special teachers of the shaman.

(7) A censer used to activate the figures and offerings and to divine solutions for problems.

A shaman, too has his or her oratory. Here, he or she conducts healing rituals on a daily basis and, from time to time, rituals for the adoration of the traditional deities, the non-Catholic ones. Before a ritual of adoration, called a *costumbre,* the shaman will divine how many offerings are required. Many unseen beings participate as well. Don Antonio puts it this way:

When you make a *costumbre* there in your land, and as you remember your friends, call

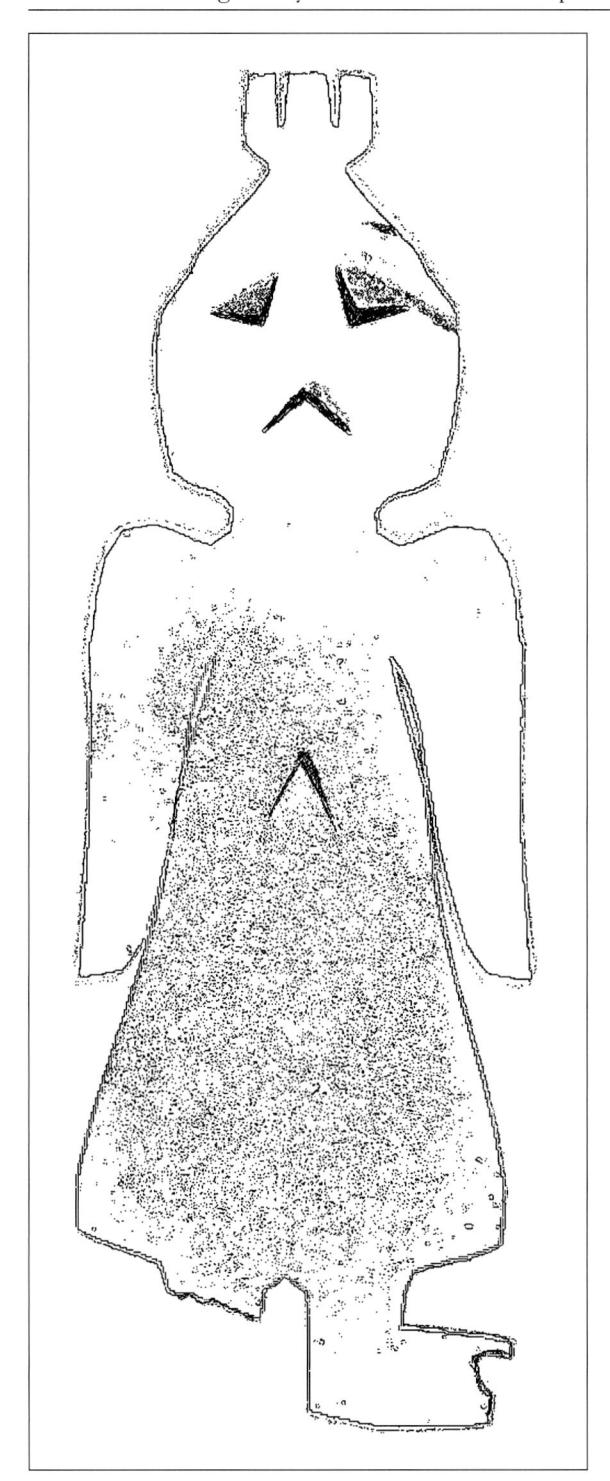

Figure 3. A Sorcery Figure.

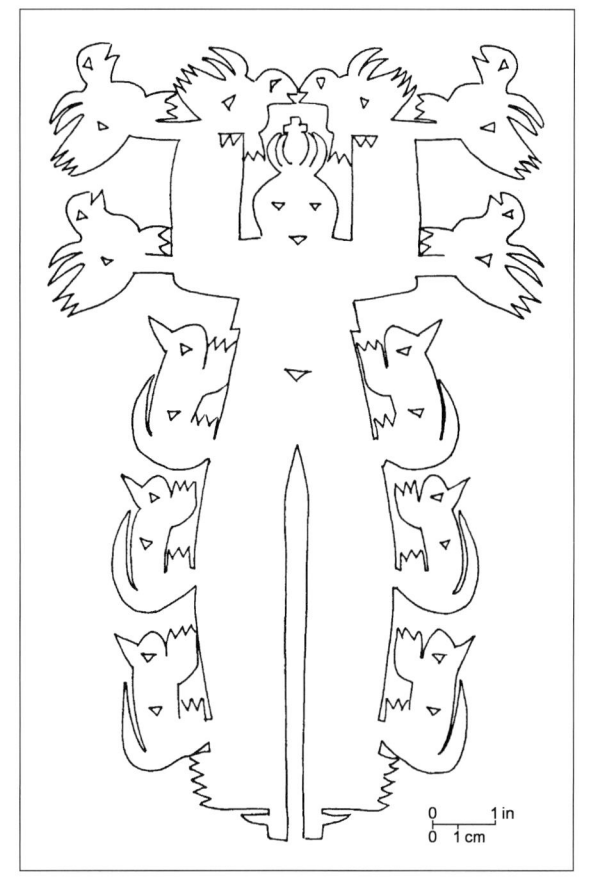

Figure 4. A Figure of the zaki of a Patient with Animal Protectors.

them to the meal with the censer. Put incense in the embers four times, and the spirits of your friends will arrive. Even though they're sleeping and far away, they'll come. The spirit of someone does not sleep. They'll not delay in arriving. Just think of them and they'll come. My friends number 60. I've selected those who are good. I call only upon them and not on bad friends. So, all will come to the *costumbre*, and all will share with me [Dow 1986:73].

The ritual of adoration is just one of the many traditional rituals. The Sierra Ñähñu are noted for their use of paper figures in these rituals (Sandstrom and Sandstrom 1986). The paper figures represent the *zaki* of the beings that are addressed. The shaman gains some power over the beings by manipulating the figures. Let us take a particular case, the healing of a sick patient. The patient can be healed magically at a distance, but usually he or she comes to the oratory of the shaman. He or she sits in the oratory for a while to personally pray to the shaman's *zidähmu*, whose images are on the altar. Then, the shaman comes in for a consultation not just with the patient but with other unseen beings. Don Antonio puts it this way:

A shaman never has to ask someone else about a illness. The little virgin (an *antigua* called Delfina) I have here tells me everything about an illness. No matter what time of day it is, she informs me that patients will be coming. She gives me the information as if it were a dream. When I look like I'm resting or catnapping, she's telling me how to do one thing or another. So everything is detailed. So always remember there is nothing to worry about. There in your consciousness everything will be left [Dow 1986:55].

Inside a chest on the altar, Don Antonio has an image of Delfina, one of his two most important *antiguas*. The image has a tiny porcelain female face, which seems to have come from an antique doll. A patient may be allowed to hold this image with the hope of receiving some of the healing power of this miraculous tutelary being.

After the consultation, a paper figure representing the *zaki* of the patient may be left on the altar to receive the protection of the beings that arrive there. If the patient has been attacked by evil winds *(dahi)*, a cleaning *(hokwi)* is required. The shaman cuts figures of the evil winds from tissue paper and lays them out on a bed of tissue paper and newspaper. If the sickness is particularly bad, the shaman may see that the evil winds have been commanded by a higher evil being who was bribed by a sorcerer. In this case, an appeal also needs to be made to this being. A *hokwi* that makes an additional appeal to higher evil beings is called the "large" *hokwi*. Otherwise it is just the "regular" *hokwi*.

Santa Catarina is one of these beings. I was never able to determine where its name came from. It is a male monster that is aided by evil companion animals. In a large *hokwi* involving *Santa Catarina*, the figures of the evil animal companions are then tied to the figure of *Santa Catarina*. The "altar" on which these figures are placed is the dirt floor of the house. They would never be placed on the raised altar, for that is for good beings. They are surrounded by candles and threads with magical powers that prevent the *zaki* from escaping the encirclement. They are offered money, rum, and cigarettes to attract the *zaki* into the circle. After the offerings have been made, the bundle is wrapped and passed over the patient, other persons present, the house, and its furnishings. Because the *zaki* of these beings are dangerous, the bundle is thrown away after the patients and house have been swept clean with it. I was able to photograph the figures before the ceremony began, because they had not started to attract *zaki* at that time. They have to be bathed in the smoke of the censer and sprinkled with the blood of a sacrificial chicken before they begin their work.

There are many other evil beings that can command the evil winds such as Lightning Bolt and The Devil. Traditional bark paper is used for the worst beings. The tradition of making bark paper has continued among the Sierra Ñähñu in order to supply shamans with the material they need to cut figures of evil beings. Plain writing paper and tinseled paper are used for the *zaki* of the good beings. The Sierra Ñähñu of San Pablito have also started a business selling the paper to outsiders through handicraft markets. Outsiders evaluate the paper in a reverse fashion. They believe the handmade bark paper, closely resembling pre-Columbian paper, to be the most valuable. Yet these beliefs in evil beings provide a rationale and a means for psychologically escaping some of the hardships of life, a very valuable cultural trait in itself. If shamans did not have the bark paper, they would not be able to do their good work.

An animistic view of the world underlies all the rituals and symbolism of the Sierra Ñähñu religion. Everything that has *zaki* is a being, and beings are ranked by the power of their *zaki*. The most powerful being of all is *Maka Hyādi* (God Sun) who transmits his powerful *zaki* to all living beings below him. On the top of a nearby sacred mountain, *Maka Hyādi* is worshiped at a shrine of crosses. *Maka Hyādi* and Jesus are regarded as the same, and the foliated cross is his symbol. Thus Christianity has entered the religion at the top. However it is the historical *Maka Hyādi* who governs the cosmology not the historical Jesus. This religion is very ecological, for according to modern science, the sun is the primary source of energy for all life on earth. Another life-giving god is *Maka Sumpe Dehe* (Goddess Lady Water). Again, Sierra Ñähñu cosmology recognizes the fundamental sources of life in the biosphere.

Animals have a lesser *zaki* than humans with one exception, the animal companions called *rogi*. These are thought to be real animals with supernatural protective power to help other beings, especially humans, to whom they belong. They are born at the same time as their human companions and they protect them throughout their lives.

Thus, the religion relates people to nature. It evolved from centuries of living close to nature in a subsistence-based agricultural economy. Although it is a profound expression of the relationship between humans and the natural world, it would be a mistake to equate it with modernistic Euro-American environmental concepts. It does not contain an ethic of technological conservation or sustainability. It is a religious rather than technical solution. It sees humans as part of a web of life with moral imperatives that are different from those being generated by scientific biological ecology. It tries to solve ecological problems through ritual rather than through technological change.

The Sierra Ñähñu rituals do have some material consequences that help to regulate the human environmental ecosystem such as those discovered by Rappaport in New Guinea (Rappaport 1967). For example, only the best seeds are selected to present to *Maka Hyãdi* in the spring fertility ritual.[4] Thus ritual supports good plant breeding. However, it has failed to control human population. The area is now overpopulated relative to the agricultural resources and consequently suffers from high rates of poverty. So although we as humans build these spiritual links to nature and to ourselves, modern science still has something to tell us about our actions and our fate.

End Notes

1. This map was produced by the author with the help of the bilingual school teachers who live and work in the region.

2. Note that the speakers do not include children less than five years of age, so the actual Ñähñu population is larger.

3. In these states, the executive power of the state is divided into *municipios*, each of which is governed by a president *(presidente)*. The territory of most sierra *municipios* is smaller than an American county.

4. Seeds contain the *zaki* of plants. The paper figures representing the *zaki* of plants are called "seeds."

James Dow
Oakland University
Rochester, Michigan
dow@oakland.edu

References Cited

Bernard, H. Russell, and Jesús Salinas Pedraza
 1989 *Native Ethnography: A Mexican Indian Describes His Culture.* Newbury Park, California: Sage Publications.

Dow, James W.
 1986 *The Shaman's Touch: Otomí Indian Symbolic Healing.* Salt Lake City: University of Utah Press.

 2001 Demographic Factors Affecting Protestant Conversions in Three Mexican Villages. In: James W. Dow and Alan R. Sandstrom, eds., *Holy Saints and Fiery Preachers: The Anthropology of Protestantism in Mexico and Central America,* pp. 73-86. Westport, Connecticut: Praeger.

García, Esteban
 1918 *Crónica de la Provincia Agustineana del Santísimo Nombre de Jesús de México.* Libro Quinto. Madrid: G. Lopez de Horno.

Lastra, Yolanda
 2001 *Unidad y diversidad de la lengua: Relatos otomíes.* Mexico City: Instituto de Investigaciones Antropológicas, UNAM.

Rappaport, Roy A.
 1967 *Pigs for the Ancestors: Ritual in the Ecology of a New Guinea People.* New Haven: Yale University Press.

Sandstrom, Alan R., and Pamela E. Sandstrom
 1986 *Traditional Papermaking and Paper Cult Figures of Mexico.* Norman: University of Oklahoma Press.

Central and Northern Mexico

The Annual "Royal Ceremony" on Mt. Tlaloc: Mountain Fertility Ritualism in the Late Pre-Hispanic Basin of Mexico

H. B. Nicholson

The promotion of fertility through ritual programs designed to propitiate the supernaturals believed to control this aspect of nature clearly constituted the core of the religious/ritual systems that played such pervasive roles in indigenous Mesoamerican civilizations. As Fray Diego Durán (1971:265), reporting on the peoples of Central Mexico at the time of the Conquest, expressed it:

> ...on all the feasts of the calendar (which were eighteen) the entire aim in celebrating them—with so many men's deaths, with so many fasts and shedding of blood of their own bodies—everything was directed toward the procuring of food, of prosperous seasons, of the prolonging of human life.

Owing to the extensive investigations of some of the earliest Spanish missionaries, much more information concerning these fertility-promoting rituals is available for the late pre-Hispanic Basin of Mexico and adjoining territory than for any other Mesoamerican region. The massive compilations of Fray Bernardino de Sahagún— the *Primeros Memoriales* (1993, 1997) and the *Historia General (Universal) de las Cosas de (la) Nueva España* (1950-1982, 1982)—are especially valuable. They provide two of the most comprehensive accounts, in Mesoamerica's Conquest Period *lingua franca*, Nahuatl, of a non-Western ritual system ever recorded until modern times—and Sahagún's accounts are usefully supplemented by a variety of other missionary chronicles and native language sources.

Many years ago (Nicholson 1971:Table 4), I very concisely summarized the most important of the major pre-Hispanic Central Mexican rituals, the eighteen *veintena* ceremonies that were performed, as a highly structured system, throughout the seasons of the solar year. The majority were clearly devoted, to a greater or lesser degree, to the promotion of agricultural fertility. They involved the propitiation of a host of deities, both male and female, who expressed significant aspects of the second of the three major themes that I discerned in the crowded pantheon of this rich, complex religious/ritual system: Rain-Moisture-Agricultural Fertility. Five deity complexes were assigned to this theme, each designated by its most prominent member: A) Tlaloc; B) Centeotl-Xochipilli; C) Ometochtli; D) Teteoinnan; E) Xipe Totec. The first and preeminent one, the Tlaloc Complex, bore the name (probably = "He Who Is The Embodiment of the Earth" or something quite similar; Sullivan 1974:213-219) of the major rain god of the Nahua-speakers (Figure 1). I (Nicholson 1971:414-416) very briefly summarized his cult at Contact thus:

> No deity enjoyed a more active or widespread cult than the ancient supernatural believed to control the indispensable crop-fertilizing rain. Tlaloc was the deity most clearly conceived in quadruple and quintuple form, each Tlaloque assigned, with his distinctive color, to one of the four cardinal directions (plus, in some cases, the Center). Various of the Tlaloque, who were conceived as dwarf-

Douglas Sharon, ed., *Mesas & Cosmologies in Mesoamerica*. San Diego Museum Papers 42, 2003.

Figure 1. Tlaloc, fronting Mt. Popocatepetl. Codex Vaticanus A fol.: 20r. From Codex Vaticanus 1996.

ish assistants to a preeminent Tlaloc, were individualized and known by proper names (Opochtli, Nappatecuhtli, Yauhqueme, Tomiauhtecuhtli, etc.). The clouds and rain were believed to be brewed in caves on prominent peaks; each of the latter were apparently conceived as one of the Tlaloque, bearing the name of the eminence in question. In this role, the Tlaloque were also the Tepictoton, the mountain deities, to whom a very active cult was rendered in Central Mexico, especially in and around the Valley of Mexico, centered on Mt. Tlaloc, between Tetzcoco and Huexotzinco.

To this complex I also assigned the goddess Chalchihuitlicue. She was regarded, in some sense, as the conceptual counterpart of Tlaloc but seems to have exercised more explicit jurisdiction over water and its sources. She was also intimately blended with the numerous maize/earth goddesses of the Teteoinnan Complex. In addition, I assigned the wind god, Ehecatl, an aspect of Quetzalcoatl, to this complex. Since gusty winds characteristically preceded the onset of rain, Ehecatl was regarded as the *in tlachpancauh in tlaloque*, "the road-sweeper of the rain gods"

(Sahagún 1950-1982, Number 14, Part II:3). He also constituted, as Quetzalcoatl, one of the Tepictoton, an eminence known by this name in the Mt. Tlaloc range, near Coatepec in the southeast Basin of Mexico.

In heavily populated Central Mexico at the time of the Conquest, with a subsistence pattern based primarily on intensive agriculture, the timing of the onset of the rainy season, usually in May/June, its duration, normally until some time in October, and the overall amount of rain that fell during this period were all of critical importance to the survival and well-being of the inhabitants of the Basin. Drought years could be catastrophic. The most devastating that had occurred in late pre-Hispanic times, 1453-1457, was abundantly recorded in the native historical annals. It was obviously all too well remembered and its possible recurrence greatly feared. It is hardly surprising, therefore, that an intensive ritual program designed to induce the relevant deities to provide the necessary quantity of rain each year played a leading role in the galaxy of elaborate ceremonies that occupied so much of the time and effort of the Basin populace. And the locational foci of these ceremonies—as would be expected owing to the belief that it was there that the clouds, mist, rain, lightning, hail, and snow were brewed—were precisely the hills and mountains that constituted such a striking feature of the landscape of Highland Central Mexico.

As is well known, these eminences were conceptualized as giant *ollas* filled with water, or, as Sahagún's informants (Sahagún 1950-1982, Number 14, Part XII:247) eloquently put it:

> The people here in New Spain, the people of old, said ... that the mountains were only magic places, with earth, with rock on the surface; that they were only like *ollas* or like houses; that they were filled with the water which was there. If sometime it were necessary, the mountain would dissolve; the whole world would flood. And hence the people called their settlements *altepetl*. They said, "This mountain of water, this river, springs from there, the womb of the mountain. For from there Chalchihuitlicue sends it—offers it.

Highlighting the importance of the Tlaloc cult was the sharing of the principal shrine of this deity with that of Huitzilopochtli, the tutelary deity of the most powerful member of the Triple Alliance that ruled most of western Mesoamerica

Figure 2. Veintena ceremony Tepeilhuitl. Fray Bernardino de Sahagún, Primeros Memoriales, Códice Matritense del Palacio Real de Madrid: fol. 252r. From Sahagún 1993.

at the time of the Conquest, the Mexica (Tenochca/Tlatelolca), atop the Templos Mayores of Tenochtitlan, Tlatelolco, and Tetzcoco—and probably those of other communities in the Basin as well. Also, four of the preeminent ceremonies of the annual ritual cycle, those geared to the twenty-day periods, the *veintenas*, into which the year, *xihuitl*, was divided, were primarily devoted to the propitiation of the Tlaloc Complex deities: Cuahuitlehua/Atlcahualo (II:14-III:3 [Caso (1967) correlation for 1519]), Etzalcualiztli (V:25-VI:13), Tepeilhuitl (X:12-X:31; Figure 2), and Atemoztli (XII:11-XII:30). The deities of this complex were also prominently involved in the related rituals of Tozoztontli (III:26-IV:14) and Hueytozoztli (IV:15-V:4). The sacrifice of children—simulacres of the dwarfish Tlaloque—of both sexes on hill and mountaintops was featured in these *veintenas*, particularly those that were celebrated in late winter and spring, the height of the dry season when maximum ritual effort was directed toward initiating a successful rainy season. The offerings of the Tepictoton, "the Little Molded Ones," the amaranth dough images that personified the Tlaloque (Figure 3), were particularly featured in the dry season *veintenas* of Tepeilhuitl and Atemoztli, highlighting the fertility promotion emphasis of the overall ritual system.

The importance of these hill/mountain rainmaking rituals has long been recognized and much studied, especially by Johanna Broda (e.g., 1971, 1982, 1983, 1989, 1991a, 1991b, 1993, 1997, 2001). Most of the relevant primary ethnohistorical accounts that describe them have been

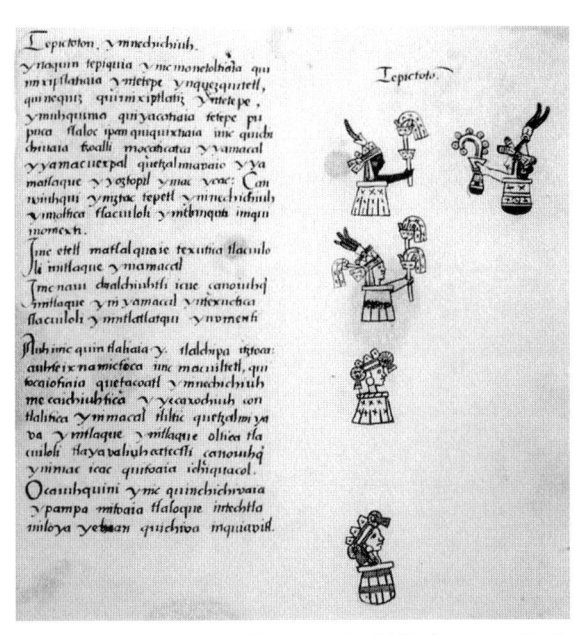

Figure 3. Tepictoton (images of deified mountains): Popocatepetl, Iztactepetl (Iztaccihuatl), Matlalcueye, Chalchiuhtlicue, Quetzalcoatl. Fray Bernardino de Sahagún, Primeros Memoriales, Códice Matritense del Palacio Real de Madrid: fol. 267r. From Sahagún 1993.

analyzed and discussed. Considerable archaeological investigation has also been undertaken on hill and mountaintop sites in and around the Basin of Mexico that were clearly devoted primarily to rainmaking rituals (e.g., Charnay 1887, Lorenzo 1967, Iwaniszewski 1991a, 1991b, 1994). This brief article, utilizing both ethnohistorical and archaeological data, will focus on the one that appears to have been the most important of all. Unmentioned by Sahagún, it was described in considerable detail by his Dominican counterpart, Fray Diego Durán., in his 1580/1581 *Historia de las Indias de Nueva España e islas de Tierra Firme*.

This was the pilgrimage and sacrificial ceremony celebrated annually in the spring at the most important Basin of Mexico shrine of the paramount deity of rain, which was located on the summit of the high mountain, southeast of Tetzcoco, that bore, and still does, the name Tlaloc (Tlalocatepetl, Tlalocan). To emphasize its crucial role within the superactive, incessant ritual universe of Conquest Period Central Mexico, Durán's detailed account is worth quoting virtually in full.

First, however, it is pertinent to note that the profound sanctity of the Mt. Tlaloc shrine had obviously been enhanced from the point of view of the Contact Period peoples of the Basin by its antiquity. In his 1582 *relación geográfica* of Tetzcoco, the *mestizo* chronicler connected with the royal dynasty of that important pre-Hispanic polity, Juan Bautista de Pomar (1986:60-61; cf. Torquemada 1975-1983, III:77-78, essentially a copy of Pomar's account), described in detail the image of Tlaloc that occupied the north shrine of the Tetzcoco Templo Mayor (a virtual replication of the Templo Mayor of Tenochtitlan). He then goes on to say that the idol *"más antiguo en esta tierra"* was the Tlaloc discovered by the Colhuaque—who, migrating from the Northwest, settled in Tetzcoco, alongside the Acolhuaque Chichimeca, during the reign of Quinatzin (ca. 1398-1457?). Soon after their arrival, they encountered it on the summit of the most prominent eminence east of Tetzcoco. They did not know who had deposited it there, but *"hay sospechas [que] lo hicieron un género de gentes q[ue se] llamaron tulteca[s] q[ue] hubo antiguamente en esta tierra, [que] se despoblaron deella muchos a[ñ]os antes q[ue] los chichimecas la tornasen a poblar."* A human figure seated on a quadrangular base, facing east, it was carved from a white, hard stone, similar to pumice. On its head was a *"vaso como lebrillo"* in which *"aquel licor llamado olli"* was deposited,

> Y, en él había de todas las semillas de las q[ue] usan y se mantienen las naturales, como maíz blanco, negro, colorado y amarillo, y frijoles de muchos géneros y colores, chia, huauhtli y michhuauhtli y ají de todas las suertes q[ue] podían haber los que lo tenían a su cargo, renovándole cada año a cierto tiempo.

Pomar goes on to say that Nezahualcoyotl, who ruled Tetzcoco, 1431-1472, *"por reverencia a este ídolo,"* ordered the installation of the Tlaloc image, earlier mentioned, that was enshrined in the Templo Mayor of Tetzcoco, *"en compañía de Huitzilopochtli."* His son and successor, Nezahualpilli, who ruled 1472-1516, wanting to enhance the Mt. Tlaloc shrine, replaced the ancient idol with a larger one, the size of a man, carved from a more durable black stone. But, after a time, *"fue hecho pedazos por un rayo que dio en él, y atribúyenlo a milagro."* Accordingly, they dug up the venerable old image, which had been buried nearby, and set it up again. It was discovered after the Conquest—one arm attached with three thick nails of gold and one of copper—and the first Bishop of Mexico, Fray Juan de Zumárraga, ordered it destroyed.

Fernando de Alva Ixtlilxochitl, another *mestizo* descendant of Acolhuaque royalty, who wrote somewhat more extensively on the history and culture of his ancestors, also referred to this idol, similarly dating it to the Toltec period. In his (Alva Ixtlilxochitl 1975-1977, I:272-273) description of some of the principal Toltec deities, he mentioned

> otro ídolo a quien han adorado hasta cuando vinieron los españoles, que es Tlaloc, que tenía su templo en las más alta sierra de Tezcuco, y allí estan todavía sus pedazos. Y dicen que este ídolo era dios de las lluvias temporales, y que fue un rey de los quinametin que son los filisteos, y hizo grandes cosas, y por eso lo colocaron por dios.

The *Anales de Cuauhtitlan* (Bierhorst 1992:86), of unknown authorship, recorded a somewhat recondite tradition concerning a miracle of Nezahualcoyotl's youth. He was magically transported by supernatural powers to the summit of Mt. Tlaloc (here called Poyauhtecatl), where he was seemingly anointed in a ritual that presaged his future greatness.

We now turn to Fray Diego Durán's account of the great annual spring ceremony at this mountaintop shrine. In Fernando Horcasitas' and Doris Heyden's excellent translation (Durán 1971:156-165), it reads as follows:

> On the summit of the mountain stood a great square courtyard surrounded by a finely built wall about eight feet high, crowned with a series of merlons and plastered with stucco.... On one side of this courtyard was a wooden chamber neither large nor small, with a flat roof. It was stuccoed both within and without and possessed a beautifully

worked and handsome [castellated] crown. In the middle of this room, upon a small platform, stood the stone idol Tlaloc, in the same manner in which Huitzilopochtli was kept in the temple [of Mexico]. Around [Tlaloc] were a number of small idols, but he stood in the center as their supreme lord. These little idols represented the other hills and cliffs which surrounded this great mountain. Each one of them was named according to the hill he stood for. These names still exist, for there is no hill lacking its proper designation. Thus the small idols which stood around the great god Tlaloc had their own names, just like the hills which encircle the great mountain.

The feast of this god fell on the twenty-ninth of April, and it was celebrated in such a solemn way that men came from all parts of the land to commemorate it, to the point that no king or lord great or small failed to bring his offerings. This god was honored on one of the principal feasts of the calendar. It was called Huey Tozoztli [Great Vigil], which indicated that the feast was most solemn and elaborate with double ceremonies and rites.... The purpose of this feast was that of asking for a good year, since all the maize which had been sown had now sprouted.

As I have mentioned, the mighty King Moteczoma, together with all the great men of Mexico—knights, lords, and nobles—came to the celebration on the great mountain. Nezahualpiltzintli, King of Acolhuacan, [arrived] with all the nobility of his land and kingdom. At the same time came the rulers of Xochimilco and of Tlacopan with their leading chieftains. So everyone came to the Mountain of Tlalocan: the entire nobility of the land, princes and kings, and great lords, both from this side of the snowy mountain [Iztaccihuatl] and from the other, Tlaxcala and Huexotzinco. For these lords large, fine shelters of boughs were made, according to their rank, for these were mighty kings and lords, greatly feared and venerated. For each sovereign and his followers were built, on different parts of the mountain, houses of straw with their rooms and apartments, as if they had been meant to be permanent. All of them were constructed around the great courtyard which, as I have mentioned, was at the summit.

Just after dawn these kings and lords with their followers left [their shelters]. They took a child of six or seven years and placed him within an enclosed litter so that he could not be seen. This was placed on the shoulders of the leaders. All in order, they went in the form of a procession to the courtyard, which was called Tetzacualco. When they arrived before the image of the god Tlaloc, the men slew the child within the litter, hidden [from those present]. He was slain by the god's own priests, to the sound of many trumpets, conch shells, and flutes. The child dead, King Moteczoma, together with all his great men and chieftains, approached [the idol] and presented finery and a rich garment for the god. They entered the place where the image stood and [Moteczoma] with his own hands placed a headdress of fine feathers on its head. He then covered it with the most costly, splendid mantle to be had, exquisitely worked in feathers and done in design of snakes. The idol was also girded with a great and ample breechcloth, splendid as the mantle. They threw about its neck valuable stones and golden jewels. Rich earrings of gold and stones were placed upon him, and on his ankles also. [The king] adorned all the small idols who stood next [to Tlaloc] in a similar fashion. After Moteczoma had dressed the idol and had offered it many splendid things, Nezahualpilli, king of Tetzcoco, entered. He was also surrounded and accompanied by great men and lords, and he carried a similar garment [for the idol]; and if it was superior [to that offered by Moctezuma], so much the better. He dressed it and the smaller images with much splendor, except that he did not place the headdress upon the head but hung it from the neck and down its back. Then he departed. The king of Tlacopan then came in with another garment and offering. Finally the [sovereign of] Xochimilco, accompanied by all the rest, entered with more fine adornments: textiles, bracelets, necklaces, wristbands, and earplugs, just as the others had done. The headdress was placed at the feet [of the idol]. Thus everyone came in to make his offerings: one of them a mantle, another a jewel, another a precious stone or feathers, exactly as [people] enter [the church] on Good Friday for the Adoration of the Cross. After the offerings had been made, all went outside, leaving the chamber so rich in gold, jewels, stones, cloths, and feathers that [this wealth] might have enriched many paupers.

The idol and the smaller images had now been dressed in the manner described. Then was brought forth the sumptuous food which had been prepared for each king [to offer the god]: turkeys and their hens and game with a number of different kinds of bread. Moteczoma himself, acting as steward, entered the chamber where the idol stood, and his great men aided him in the serving of the food. The rest of the chamber was filled to bursting with stews of fowl and game, many small baskets of various breads, and gourds of chocolate. Everything was beautifully prepared and cooked, and there was such abundance in the room that some of it had to be left outside. At that time the king of Tetzcoco entered with his viands, which were no less rich and superb. And he fed the god in the same way as Moteczoma, he himself as steward. Then came [the ruler] of Tlacopan, who did likewise. And after him that of Xochimilco. They offered so much food that those who tell this story (they are men who actually saw these things) affirm that the food was so plentiful—stews, breads, and chocolate in the native style—that most of the courtyard was crowded, and it was a sight to see. It was especially notable that all the pottery was new, and so were the baskets and the vessels—never used before. When the food had been put in its place, the priests who had slit the throat of the child came in with his blood in a small basin. The high priest wet the hyssop which he held in his hand in that innocent blood and sprinkled the idol [and] all the offerings and food. And if any blood was left, he went to the idol Tlaloc and bathed its face and body with it, together with all the companion idols, and the floor. And it is said that if the blood of that child was not sufficient one or two other children were killed to complete the ceremony and compensate for what had been lacking.

When all these rites had terminated, everyone descended to the living quarters to dine, since they could not eat in that place because of their pagan superstition. Meanwhile, in the neighboring towns down below an abundant and sumptuous repast, for kings, princes, and great lords, had been prepared. So it was that each returned to his city.

When one of the sovereigns found himself unable to go in person (because of some urgent matter), he sent his envoy or delegate with all the pomp and offerings described, so that these might be offered in his name and all the ceremonies of which we have spoken might be performed.

When all these things had been done, a company of one hundred soldiers was formed—the most courageous and valorous to be found, [led by] a commander. They were left to guard the rich offerings and abundant victuals which had been presented. This was done to prevent the foe (from Huexotzinco and Tlaxcala) from robbing and sacking. If by chance [the Mexicas] were neglectful of placing that guard or the sentinels of their watch, the enemy came at night and, having stripped the idol, stole all the wealth that had been offered. Should this happen, the Mexicas and all the other provinces of the Mexica country were greatly offended and outraged. Thus the soldier who was careless paid for his neglect with his own life. Nevertheless, since the cunning and trickery of the Mexicas was always great, it is said that more often than not, while pretending to be asleep, they allowed the enemies to enter with their riches as bait, and after they had been thus baited and were at the mercy [of the Mexicas], the latter appeared suddenly in an assault which left no man alive. This guard lasted until all the food baskets and gourds rotted and the feathers disintegrated from the moisture. Everything else was buried there, and the chamber was walled in until the next year, for in that place there were no priests or ministers in attendance, only the guard we have mentioned, which was changed every six days. [To maintain this guard], certain nearby towns had been chosen to provide soldiers to keep watch as long as there was any fear that the foe might sack the idol and the offerings. After the oblations on the mountain [of Tlaloc] and everything had ended, the lords hastened to descend to the celebration and sanctification of the waters, which were performed on that same day in the lake, streams, springs, and cultivated fields. Here sacrifices and oblations were offered...

At dawn the lords celebrated the Feast of Tlaloc on the mountain (this Mountain of Tlalocan) with the solemnity and lavishness I have mentioned, in great haste, since they wished to be present at the sacrifice of the waters. [While these rites were being performed], those who had remained in the city [of Mexico], where the image of the god, sumptuously and richly adorned, was kept in the temple of Huitzilopochtli, prepared for the same feast of the waters. This was especially true of the priests and dignitaries of the temples and of all the youths and boys who lived in seclusion and in the schools. [All of them] donned new ornaments and performed many different dances, farces, and games. They wore various disguises as if it were their principal feast day, very much the way [our] students celebrate the feast of San Nicholas. All these games and festivities were carried out in an artificial forest set up in the courtyard of the temple in front of the image of the god Tlaloc. In the middle of this forest was placed a very large tree. It was the tallest that could be found in the woods, and it was called Tota, which means Our Father. This indicated that the idol was the god of the woods, forests, and waters. When the news arrived [that the lords who had been on Mount Tlaloc] were descending from the mountains and drawing close to the waters to embark in the canoes which awaited them, this solemnity and feast ended in the lagoon. These [canoes] were as numerous as the lords, chieftains, and men who had made the journey, and they covered the shores of the lake. All were richly adorned and covered with awnings, especially those of the sovereigns, each one possessing his own boat with a great number of rowers who propelled it swiftly.

Durán then proceeds to recount how they obtained from the "Cerro de Colhuacan" (= Huixachtepetl [modern Cerro de la Estrella]), south of Tenochtitlan, the tall tree trunk that served as the Tota, which was set up, surrounded by four smaller ones, in an artificial forest fronting the north stairway of the Tenochtitlan Templo Mayor.

A little girl of seven or eight, dressed in blue—the equivalent of the boy who had been sacrificed on the mountaintop—was placed on a covered litter. All chanted before her until they were notified that the lords had descended from the mountain and were ready to board their canoes. The child was then sent off in a canoe, escorted by the priests and all the worshippers, along with the Tota on a raft. Meeting out in the lake with those who had descended the mountain at a "drain"/whirlpool called Pantitlan, "Place of Banners," the great tree trunk was erected in the water by thrusting it into the mud. Then the girl was sacrificed by slitting her throat with a small spear for hunting ducks. While her blood stained the waters, she was cast into the whirlpool, never to be seen again, following which the sovereigns and their retinues threw in after her as offerings "as many rich things (such as jewels, stones, necklaces and bracelets) as had been given on the mountain."

This effectively concluded Durán's vivid account of this theatrical and complex mountain/lake rainmaking ceremony. He went on, however, at some length to discuss the different explanations for the mysterious aquatic phenomena that characterized Pantitlan, as well as the reputed "great treasure of Moteczoma" that had been cast into it. He cited his own experiences while crossing the lake by canoe, seeing there the "great hoary tree trunks rising out of the water."

Clearly, Durán is describing a particularly important ceremony within the cycle of the basically standardized eighteen annual *veintena* rituals—one devoted to the successful initiation of the late spring/early summer rainy season upon which the survival of the massive population of the Basin of Mexico literally depended. Its most remarkable feature was the active participation of the highest levels of leadership of the Tenochtitlan/Tetzcoco/Tlacopan Triple Alliance. In effect, it constituted a virtually unique annual "royal ceremony."

Undeniably, it is somewhat puzzling that, considering the importance of the Mt. Tlaloc shrine and the spectacular annual rainmaking ritual in which the paramount rulers personally participated, it receives no mention anywhere in Sahagún—who otherwise provides the fullest accounts of the *veintena* ceremonies—or any other chronicler. There may be an understandable reason, however, for this omission. Sahagún's versions of these ceremonies in Book I, Chapter 2, of his *Primeros Memoriales* were obtained in Tepepolco, a community that, while of undoubted Acolhuaque affiliation, was politically just a dependency of the Acolhuaque capital, Tetzcoco. And, as is well known, the community where the Franciscan obtained his even fuller account of the *veintena* rituals was Tlatelolco, politically subservient after 1473 to Tenochtitlan. Although Hueytozoztli (Figure 4), generally described as a

Figure 4. Veintena ceremony Hueytozoztli. Codex Borbonicus 25. In a group of four suppliants, a child, arrayed with sacrificial ritual papers, is being borne toward a Tlaloc temple on a mountain—possibly Mt. Tlaloc, but more likely (?) Huixachtepetl (Cerro de la Estrella), near Itztapallapan, from which this screenfold possibly derives. From Codex Borbonicus 1991.

fertility promoting ritual that included the propitiation of the Tlaloque, was undoubtedly celebrated throughout the Basin and adjacent areas of Central Mexico, clearly here Durán was describing the particular Mt. Tlaloc version of the ceremony, the only one that involved the supreme lords of the Triple Alliance and their retinues. I think it probable, therefore, that Durán's account of the ceremony, although typically quite Europeanized in its style of presentation, can be generally accepted as reliable—particularly since he avers that it was told to him by persons who had actually participated in it. His April 29 date for it, however, should probably be corrected to May 4, at least for 1519, following the widely accepted Caso (1967) correlation.

The inclusion, as a fourth royal participant, of the ruler of Xochimilco is interesting. This major *chinampaneca* polity had been one of the earliest conquests of the Triple Alliance and thereafter had served as one of the principal bulwarks of the specifically Tenochca domain (Carrasco 1999:101). There may have been some special reason that the Xochimilca ruler was included, of which we are simply unaware.

Aftermath

Tenochtitlan/Tlatelolco surrendered to the besieging Cortesian army on August 13, 1521, effectively terminating any further "official" celebrations of what seems to have constituted the greatest of all the annual Central Mexican rain-making ceremonies. As indicated, Juan Bautista de Pomar stated that Bishop (later Archbishop) Fray Juan de Zumárraga, who had arrived in New Spain in 1528 and had pursued a vigorous campaign to extirpate all traces of idolatry, ordered the destruction of the ancient, putatively Toltec image on Mt. Tlaloc. This is generally confirmed by a 1539 *proceso inquisitorial* in the Archivo General de la Nación, Mexico City (*Proceso inquisitorial del cacique de Tetzcoco* 1910), which provides additional information concerning the image and its fate.

On Sunday, June 22, 1539, an inquisitorial proceeding (for which Fray Bernardino de Sahagún and two other Franciscan friars served as translators) was initiated in the Iglesia de Santiago in Tlatelolco. It was conducted in person by Bishop Zumárraga, who was also serving as the *"Inquisidor Apostólico contra la herética pravedad y apostasía."* Francisco Maldonaldo, a native of Chiconauhtlan, near Tetzcoco, was bringing formal charges of heresy and apostasy against his uncle, Don Carlos Ometochtzin Chichimecatecuhtli, natural son of Nezahualpilli. The latter had been raised in the household of Cortés and was a leading *principal* of Tetzcoco, where he resided. During the next few days Francisco's testimony was expanded upon by other witnesses.

These included the native *gobernador* of Tetzcoco, Don Lorenzo de Luna, another nephew of the accused, and seven other Tetzcocanos, including various functionaries of the community government. After further allegations involving Don Carlos, it came out, from the testimony of Don Lorenzo de Luna and others, that smoke had been observed rising from *"la sierra que se dice Tlalocatepetl"* that indicated possible continued ceremonial activity in the shrine on its summit. Consequently, the governor and his advisors sent various teams to investigate. Although they failed—after repeated attempts, even including watchdog observers posted in shifts—to catch the ritual celebrants in the act, they concluded, from the sacrificial paraphernalia that had been left behind and the direction of the cleared access trails, that they were natives of Huexotzinco, east of the *sierra*. Regarding the ancient, supersacred stone image of Tlaloc, their testimony is somewhat discrepant, but it was almost certainly discovered and broken up—for which they were reproached by members of other leading communities of the area who, after learning of its destruction, clearly dreaded the possibility of consequent droughts.

No very clear description of the image itself was provided in their varying testimonies—and more than one *ídolo* was reportedly discovered. The most circumstantial, those accounts that described it as having been repaired with gold and copper wires and smeared with unguents composed of liquid rubber, tobacco, and various seeds of comestible plants, are generally congruent with Pomar's description of it. However, although this was testimony provided by Tetzcocanos, including descendants of Nezahualpilli himself, the refurbishing of the celebrated idol was attributed not to him but to Ahuitzotl, eighth official ruler of Mexico Tenochtitlan, after the Huexotzinca, *"por hacer enojo a los de Mexico,"* had broken it up. An intriguing element of their testimony is the mention of *"una piedra verde chalchuy con una figura por la una parte, que dicen es cuenta de seis dias, que el dicho ídolo tenía en el frente."*

Interestingly, the shrine itself, with its extensive double stone walls, was never mentioned or described. As a follow-up to what can be called his Mt. Tlaloc project, on July 7, 1539, Zumárraga ordered the mutilation and defacement of the extensive sculptured gardens and shrines of Tetzcotzinco, in the northern part of the *sierra*, that had been constructed during the reigns of Nezahualcoyotl and Nezahualpilli. As for Don Carlos, after his conviction by the Santo Oficio as a *"hereje domatizador,"* he was publicly executed in Mexico City's Zócalo on November 30, 1539.

What happened subsequently can only be conjectured. Possibly a certain amount of surreptitious rainmaking ritual continued at or near the shrine. Certainly, with their exposed position on the mountaintop and the propensity of the darkest, most moisture-laden storm clouds to gather on this prominent peak, the stone walls of the processional pathway and the great quadrangular enclosure, under the bombardment of wind and rain, partly disintegrated. In any case, however often through the years the shrine might have been visited and even ritually utilized, it seems to have been largely forgotten until Constantine G. Rickards, the British Vice Consul in Mexico City—who had developed a strong interest in Mexico's pre-Hispanic past—explored and recorded the site, publishing a brief article on it in 1929 in the *Journal de la Société des Américanistes* (Paris).

He begins by stating:

Of the many ruins found near the City of Mexico none are so rarely visited by people interested in archaeological research as those which are known as the Ruins of Tlaloc, named after the mountain which bears the same name. [For exact location, see Figure 5.]

He gives the height of the ruins as "1890 meters above the Lake of Texcoco." He names "Tequisquenahuac" as the nearest village, about 14 miles to the southeast, pointing out that from this community there is a mountain trail for about eight miles and from there barely a beaten path to the site "through a wild region on which only grass can grow." He then describes the long narrow entrance to the large squarish enclosure that was bounded by a partially disintegrated double wall, approximately 50 meters on a side, composed of roughly cut stones set without mortar. He includes a simplified plan of the site, to scale, which reveals its essential features (Figure 6). He points out that from the summit both Mexico City and Puebla, in opposite directions, can be seen. He describes, in the center of the enclosure, "the remains of a monolith of dark volcanic rock," regarding its top fragment as a representation of Tlaloc "with the eyes with a large ring around them."

Rickards mentions a pit that was dug within the enclosure and that bits of pottery and flakes of obsidian could be surface-collected. He also

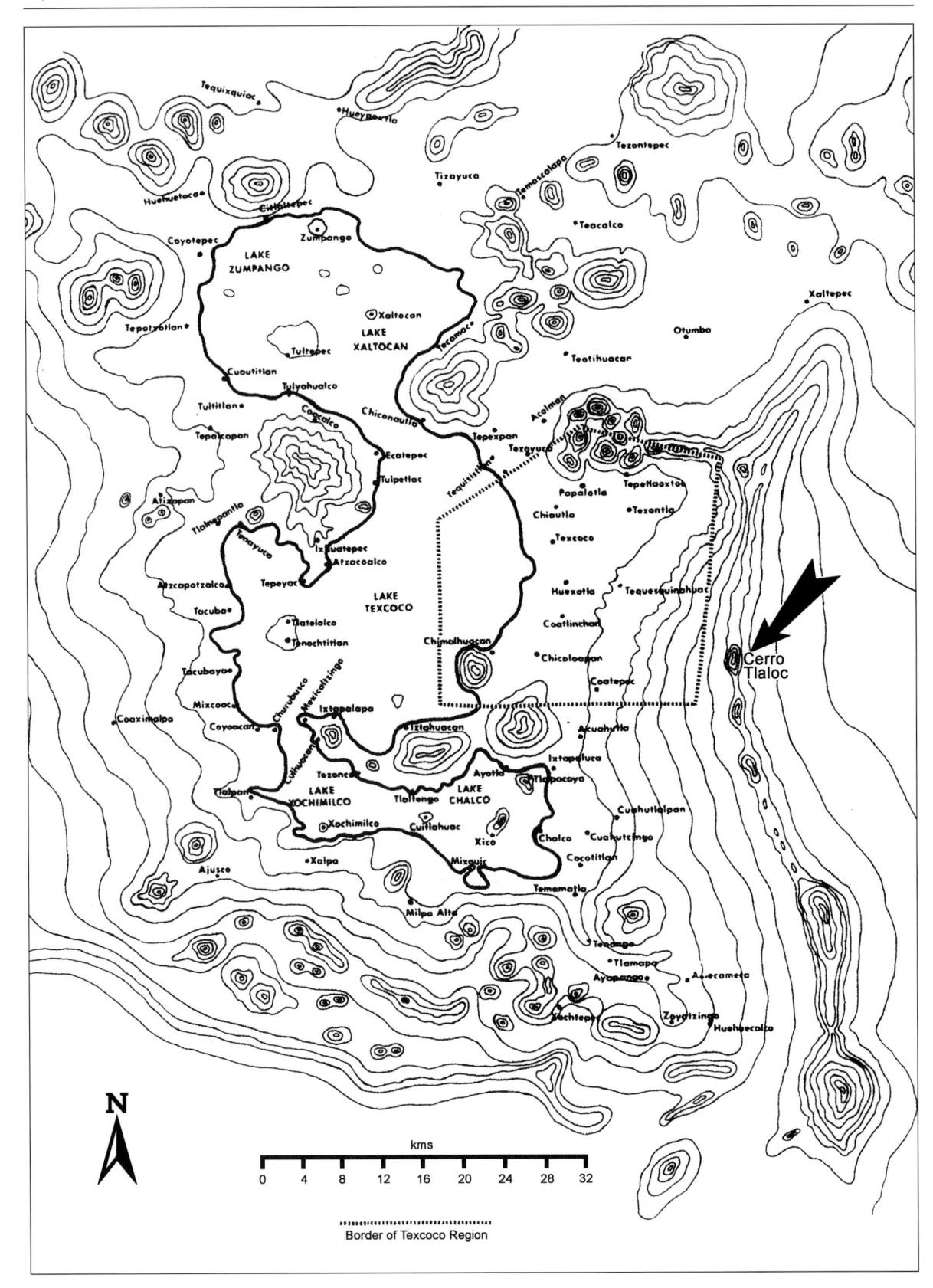

Figure 5. Map of the Basin of Mexico, showing the approximate extent of Lake Texcoco at the time of the Conquest and the location of the most prominent peaks, including Mt. (Cerro) Tlaloc (indicated by arrow). From Parsons 1971:Map 2.

photographs of the ruined walls and one of the fragments of the "monolith" in the center of the enclosure.

A more extensive investigation of the site was conducted some years later, in 1953, by Charles Wicke and Fernando Horcasitas, and reported on in an article in *Mesoamerican Notes*, published in 1957. They gave the altitude of Mt. Tlaloc as 13,270 feet above sea level and suggested that the ruins of the shrine on the summit constituted "the highest archaeological site in the Mexican Republic" (now known not to be the case). They visited it twice, reaching it from the east, from Río Frío.

Wicke and Horcasitas began by citing various colonial references to the pre-Hispanic shrine, including Pomar and Durán, concisely summarizing the latter's account of the annual Hueytozoztli ceremony there. They did not cite Rickards' article or refer to his investigation of the site. They described its physical features in more detail than their British predecessor and included a somewhat similar plan of it. They identified a nearby quarry southeast of the site as the source of the rough cut stones composing the walls of the entrance passageway and the double enclosure walls. They suggested that masses of fallen stones at three corners of the enclosure might have originally constituted walls of structures at these locations. They also described a 1 x 2.5-meter pit cut into the living rock in one of these foundations and speculated that, with no source of this element at the site, it might have served as a cistern for storing water—or possibly as a pit into which the bodies of sacrificial victims were cast.

They illustrated with a photograph the upper fragment of what appears to be a very stylized image of Tlaloc—apparently the one referred to by Rickards—noting that it bore no resemblance to those described by Pomar and Durán. They characterized it as stylistically Aztec. Contradicting Rickards' assertion that many stones had been removed from the site for construction purposes by the inhabitants of nearby villages, they state that, due to its isolated position: "Indeed it is difficult to imagine that a single stone has been carried away during the last four hundred years." While recognizing that "the sixteenth century sources describe the structures on Mt. Tlaloc as being covered with stucco," like Rickards they found no trace of it. They speculate that the constant bombardment of the wind and rain might have denuded the rock of this original coating.

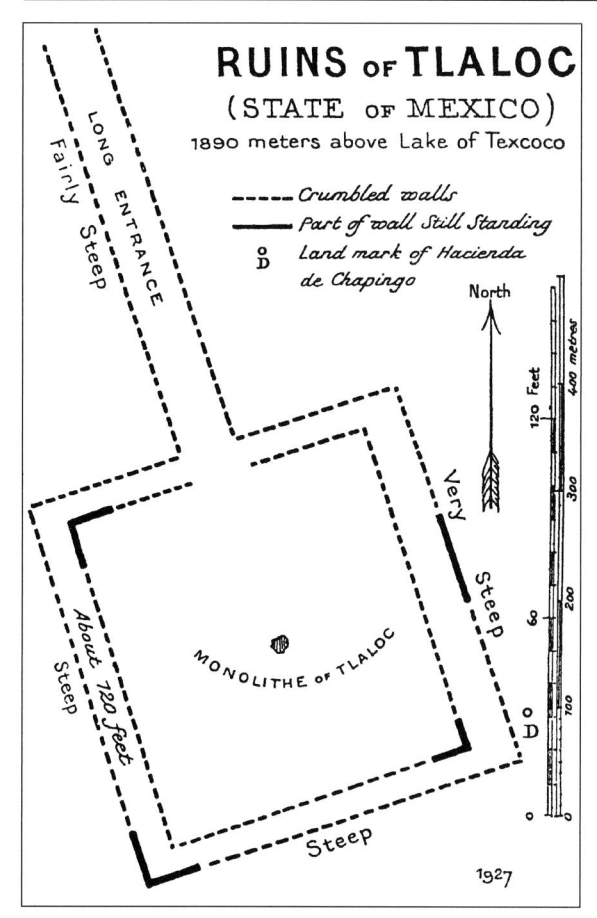

Figure 6. Constantine G. Rickards' plan of the ruins of the Mt. Tlaloc shrine to Tlaloc. From Rickards 1929:Fig. 13.

states that: "Many stones have been carried away by the Indians to build houses in their villages." He speaks vaguely of "many legends told by the old Indians regarding this place" but adds that "no facts appear to be known regarding the history of this romantic spot." He was apparently unaware of references to it in what would be called today the published ethnohistorical literature, especially the accounts of it in Pomar and Durán. However, somewhat surprisingly, he does state that: "The old legends claim that this was one of the places where the eagle settled on the cactus plant to indicate to the Mexicans where to settle."

Finally, he opines that, in addition to its use as a shrine, "It must also have been used as a fortress on account of its position and thick walls," concluding with the observation that "The ruins, although very simple, are most interesting and if restored, would make a very imposing sight especially on account of its surroundings." The article includes, in addition to the site plan, five

A 1 x 1-meter stratipit, with 3-inch levels, was dug within the enclosure. No trace of a stucco floor was encountered, but sherds were found to a depth of 15 inches. A black-on-red type and "Aztec complex" sherds were relatively common, but the latter lacked the characteristic fine-line decoration, possibly due to weathering. Many sherds belonged to incense burners. All of the ceramics found, including those of the "Tula-Mazapan complex," appeared to date to the Postclassic. A fragment of the handle of a Tlaloc effigy vessel, almost identical to one found by Acosta at Tula, was illustrated. A number of minute bits of turquoise, cut in quadrilaterals, were recovered, possibly originally forming parts of mosaics. No arrow or spearheads were found.

Their illustrations included—in addition to drawings of the Tlaloc jug, a plan of the site, and a photograph of the fragmentary putative Tlaloc sculpture—an aerial photo of the site (Figure 7), a photo of the southeast corner of the enclosure, a sketch map pinpointing the location of Mt. Tlaloc, and drawings of two "gingerbread" figurines, two animal heads, and what they identified as a Mazapan figurine head.

They also reported that, according to the noted ethnohistorian, Robert H. Barlow, "the natives of the Tetzcoco region still remember comparatively recent times in which babies were sacrificed to Tlaloc on the peak of the mountain," the old men recounting tales of the villagers sacrificing unbaptized children to ensure good harvests. The authors themselves cited the testimony of a native of the village of Purificación, near Tetzcoco, who informed them that her mother had often told her that the sacrifice of the last child on Mt. Tlaloc had taken place in 1887. They were, however, unable to obtain any more details concerning this alleged survival of a lethal pre-Hispanic ritual within eyeshot of Porfirian Mexico City.

More recently, beginning in the 1980s, investigators from Mexico, Europe, and the United States have visited, photographed, mapped, and surface-collected the site, publishing a number of articles concerning it. Also, reflecting the recent rise of widespread interest in archaeoastronomy, various studies have been pursued focusing on the location of the site in relation to other sites within and without the Basin of Mexico—especially those on other peaks where similar archaeological remains have been found—with the possibility that the Mt. Tlaloc shrine constituted an important horizon observation point with astronomical and calendric implications.

A group headed by Johanna Broda, Anthony Aveni, and Stanislaw Iwaniszewski visited the site in 1984, photographing and recording it. Broda, in addition to her long term interest in and many publications (cited above) concerning the mountain-oriented rainmaking ritualism of the Basin peoples, was particularly interested in the possible links, archaeoastronomical and otherwise, between this great mountaintop shrine and the Tenochtitlan Templo Mayor, whose offerings—as she had emphasized in her publications (Broda 1987a, 1987b) concerning them—had displayed throughout a strongly aquatic orientation. Aveni (Aveni, Calnek, and Hartung 1988) and his associates also focused their research on a possible archaeoastronomical relationship between Tenochtitlan's paramount temple pyramid, which appears to have constituted the *axis mundi* of the

Figure 7. Aerial photograph of the ruins of the Mt. Tlaloc shrine to Tlaloc. From Wicke and Horcasitas 1957:Fig. 37.

Mexica cosmos, and the Mt. Tlaloc shrine. They noted that its orientation, Az 273°30', conformed with that of the former, raising the possibility that it may have played a role in its planning and orientation. Also, noting that the alignment (Az 281°30') of the 125-meter-long walled entrance to the enclosure was skewed by 8° relative to the enclosure itself, they speculated that it might have been deliberately misaligned to accommodate an orientation to the setting sun on a date close to that of the Hueytozoztli ceremony described by Durán. Other students, such as Arturo Ponce de León (1983, 1991) and Franz Tichy (1991), have also explored the possibilities of significant archaeoastronomical aspects of the site.

Stanislaw Iwaniszewski has beeen particularly active in promoting and carrying out various archaeological investigations at high altitude Basin of Mexico sites, including Mt. Tlaloc, within the framework of what has been denominated *"la arqueología de alta montaña en México"* (Iwaniszewski 1991a, 1991b). In 1994, he published a key article reporting on his own researches at the site and those of others. It constituted the most comprehensive summary and discussion up to that time of the archaeology, ethnohistory, and archaeoastronomy of the Mt. Tlaloc shrine. He included two plans of the sanctuary, based on his own measurements, plus photographs of details of the enclosure's interior and exterior walls, describing its architectural features in considerable detail. He suggested that it had been constructed in two stages, both of which could be dated to the Late Postclassic. For the site as a whole, he cited the artifactual, mainly ceramic, evidence— including that collected by Townsend and Solís—that indicated some occupation as early as the Late Preclassic.

Iwaniszewski (1994) particularly focused on the archaeoastronomy, citing and discussing the work of Aveni and associates and Broda, who had suggested that Mt. Tlaloc had constituted an important sunrise horizon marker as viewed from the Tenochtitlan Templo Mayor, serving to regulate calendric rituals. While accepting the general proposition that "Mesoamericans utilized a horizon-orientation calendar," he opined that "sunrise sightings from the Templo Mayor over Mount Tlaloc or vice versa seem to be of minor calendric importance." Rather, he regarded sunrise observations to the east as much more likely to have played a significant role in this regard, above all, the Mt. Tlaloc–La Malinche (Tlaxcala)–Pico de Orizaba (Veracruz) and Mt. Tlaloc–Xochitecatl (Puebla) alignments. Specifically, he hypothesized that the orientations of the walls of the Mt. Tlaloc sacred enclosure aligned with positions of sun-at-horizon events at calendrically significant 20-day intervals and, possibly, the 5-day Nemontemi period at the termination of the 365-day solar year. He also suggested that this strategically located peak might have served as a significant observation post for weather forecasting, noting that: "A keen observer…looking in the direction of La Malinche–Pico de Orizaba could notice the southern shifts of the confluence belt clouds during the period of weather transition (April–June) and thus anticipate the arrival of the rainy season."

The most ambitious project yet to investigate the Mt. Tlaloc site was launched in 1989 by Richard Townsend and Felipe Solís (Townsend 1991). They approached it from Tequexquinahuac on a dirt road that is paralleled by what Townsend, in his 1991 article describing the project, characterized as "a fifteenth-century Aztec aqueduct which still brings springwater from the high sources to the villages of the Texcocan plain." His description of the site essentially conforms with those of earlier investigators, while he advances new interpretational hypotheses concerning it. He suggests that the "critical clue" to the "subtle iconography" of the site is the intercardinal locations of the large protruding boulders within the walled enclosure—which reminded him of the scene on *Codex Borgia* 27 depicting the five varicolored Tlaloque standing at the intercardinal points and the center. He suggests the possibility that "the top of the mountain was modified in antiquity to remove other rock formations that might have interrupted the cosmological symmetry," and he further speculates that the remaining natural boulders "are the 'idols' of which Durán spoke." He believes that the interior of the temple was conceived as "an animistic microcosm of the Mt. Tlaloc range" and that the rectangular pit cut into the living rock must correspond to an *omphalos*, an "earth-navel leading down into Mt. Tlaloc's interior."

Townsend and Solís surface-collected the site, estimating that about 80% of the pottery was from Texcoco or Tenochtitlan and dated to the fifteenth and early sixteenth centuries. A few pieces, however, including fragments of mold-made figurines, were earlier, including some that were possibly of Toltec, Teotihuacan, or even of Preclassic date. As did Wicke and Horcasitas before them, they found tiny turquoise mosaic fragments, as well as jadeite and serpentine beads and obsidian blade fragments—which they sourced to the Cerro de las Navajas mines in Hidalgo. On the basis of their preliminary surface collection they believe that the temple enclosure is of fifteenth century origin but that "the site itself may have seen ritual use for some fifteen hundred years."

> They encountered a crude stone shelter piled around and over a natural boulder toward the center of the quadrangle. This is a small shrine where evidence of candles, copal incense, and bottles with seed grains testify to the use of the site by villagers today. A cross surmounts this feature, and other crosses are placed on the rubble of the western precinct wall.

Townsend's final interpretative hypothesis was derived partly from relevant pictorial images in the *Codex Borbonicus* and the *Historia Tolteca-Chichimeca*. He proposes that the Mt. Tlaloc temple enclosure was

> a diagrammatic womb of the earth, containing the source of water and regenerative forces.... The imagery of the rites, the architectural setting, and the natural landscape forcibly conveyed ideas of regeneration and expressed a concept of kingship embedded in the natural cycle. Indeed, the long pilgrimage of the kings to the mountaintop and its source of life, and their return with a boon to the cities of the Valley suggest the enactment of an ancient cosmogonic myth.

Most of these interpretational hypotheses were reiterated at greater length in a longer, well-illustrated article published by Townsend the following year (1992b). It included an aerial photograph, taken by the author, of the Mt. Tlaloc site, looking south toward the two great volcanoes, which strikingly captures its dramatic, high altitude setting. Townsend also covers much the same ground in his description of the Mt. Tlaloc site in his general book on the Aztecs (Townsend 1992a:132-137). He includes (1992a:Fig. 77) a very similar aerial photo of the site, plus a new one (1992a:Fig. 78), a closer view, from the west.

In the early 1990s, Rubén Morante López also conducted archaeoastronomical and archaeological researches at the Mt. Tlaloc site. His 1997 article summarizing them included a new plan of

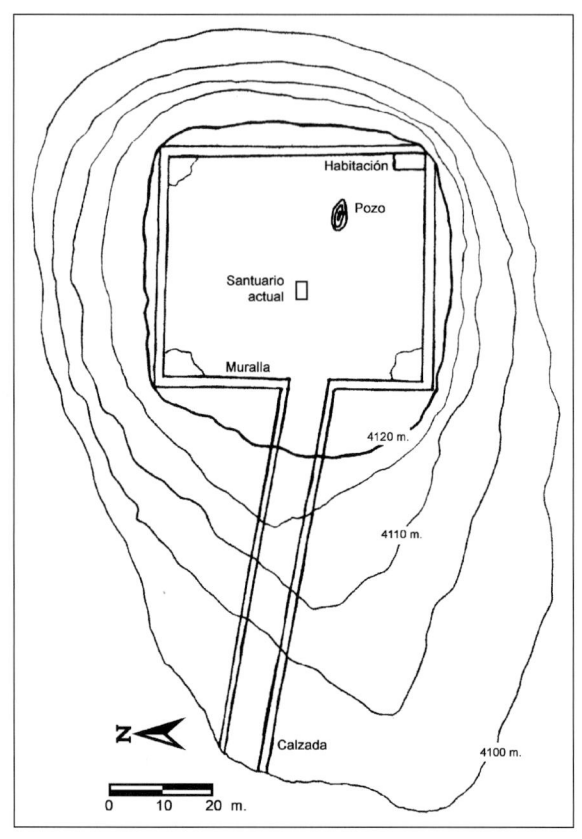

Figure 8. Morante López's plan of the ruins of the Mt. Tlaloc shrine to Tlaloc. From Morante López 1997:Fig. 1.

the walled enclosure (Figure 8), as well as a drawing (Figure 10), based on a photo taken in 1928, of the same fragmentary "Tlaloc" sculpture published by Wicke and Horcasitas, which he compared to a similar image (Figure 9) found on the Cerro de la Malinche in the western Basin of Mexico near San Bartolo Naucalpan (García Moll 1968). In basic agreement with the views of Stephan Iwaniszewski, he suggested that sunrise observations from Mt. Tlaloc southeastward along its alignment with the peaks of La Malinche and Pico de Orizaba might be connected with the February beginning of the pre-Hispanic solar year (cf. Morante López 2001). He also hypothesized a close connection between the temple pyramid of Tenayuca (Tenanyocan), a site traditionally founded by the semi-legendary Chichimec chieftain, Xolotl, and the Mt. Tlaloc shrine, based on both archaeoastronomical and ethnohistorical data.

In summary, clearly the Mt. Tlaloc shrine constituted one of the most important ritual loci at the time of the Conquest in all of Mesoamerica. In the final years before Cortés, it was the scene

Figure 9 (left). Tlalocoid stone image from Cerro la Malinche, near San Bartolo Naucalpan, western Basin of Mexico. Based on drawing published in García Moll 1968:Fig. 5.

Figure 10 (right). Fragment of similar image found in the ruins of the Mt. Tlaloc shrine to Tlaloc. From Morante López 1997:Fig. 6.

of one of the most elaborate and arduous ceremonies of the annual ritual cycle, in which members of the power elite of the Triple Alliance, including the supreme rulers themselves or their representatives, were actively involved. Their personal participation emphatically highlights the great importance they attached to this ceremony, featuring the propitiation of the deity who controlled and dispensed the annual rainfall upon whose timing and amount the lives of their people depended. In view of the crucial role that it played in the ceremonial life of the late pre-Hispanic inhabitants of the Basin of Mexico, its further archaeological, archaeoastronomical, and ethnohistorical investigation would appear to be a very desirable goal.

References Cited

Alva Ixtlilxochitl, Fernando
　1974-1977　*Obras históricas. Edición, estudio introductorio y un apéndice documental por Edmundo O'Gorman*. 2 vols. Mexico City: Universidad Nacional Autónoma de México, Instituto de Investigaciones Históricas, Serie de historiadores y cronistas de Indias 4.

Aveni, A. F., E. E. Calnek, and H. Hartung
　1988　Myth, Environment, and the Orientation of the Templo Mayor of Tenochtitlan. *American Antiquity* 53(2):287-309.

Bierhorst, John
　1992　*History and Mythology of the Aztecs: The Codex Chimalpopoca*. Translated from the Nahuatl by John Bierhorst. Tucson and London: The University of Arizona Press.

Broda, Johanna
　1971　Las fiestas aztecas de los dioses de la lluvia. *Revista Española de Antropología Americana* 6:245-327.

　1982　El culto mexica de los cerros y del agua. *Multidisciplina* 3(7):45-56. Escuela Nacional de Estudios Profesionales Acatlán, Universidad Nacional Autónoma de México.

　1983　Ciclos agrícolas en el culto: Un problema de la correlación del calendario mexica. In: Anthony F. Aveni and Gordon Brotherston, eds., *Calendars in Mesoamerica and Peru: Native American Computations of Time*, pp. 145-165. Oxford: British Archaeological Reports (BAR International Series 174).

　1987a　The Provenience of the Offerings: Tribute and Cosmovision. In: Elizabeth Boone, ed., *The Aztec Templo Mayor: A Symposium at Dumbarton Oaks, 8th and 9th October 1983*, pp. 211-256. Washington, D.C.: Dumbarton Oaks Research Library and Collection.

　1987b　Templo Mayor as Ritual Space. In: Johanna Broda, David Carrasco, and Eduardo Matos Moctezuma, eds., *The Great Temple of Tenochtitlan: Center and Periphery in the Aztec World*, pp. 61-123. Berkeley, Los Angeles, London: University of California Press.

　1989　Geography, Climate and the Observation of Nature in Prehispanic Mesoamerica. In: David Carrasco, ed., *The Imagination of Matter: Religion and Ecology in Mesoamerican Traditions*, pp. 139-153. Oxford: British Archaeologicl Reports (BAR International Series 515).

　1991a　Cosmovisión y observación de la naturaleza: El ejemplo del culto de los cerros. In: Johanna Broda, Stanislaw Iwaniszewski, and Lucrecia Maupomé, eds., *Arqueoastronomía y etnoastronomía en Mesoamérica*, pp. 461-500. Universidad Nacional Autónoma de México, Instituto de Investigaciones Históricas, Serie de Historia de la Ciencia y la Tecnología 4.

1991b The Sacred Landscape of Aztec Calendar Festivals: Myth, Nature, and Society. In: David Carrasco, ed., To *Change Place: Aztec Ceremonial Landscapes*, pp. 74-120. Niwot, Colorado: University Press of Colorado.

1993 Astronomical Knowledge, Calendrics, and Sacred Geography in Ancient Mesoamerica. In: *Clive L. N. Ruggles and Nicolas Saunders, eds., Astronomies and Cultures: Papers derived from the "Oxford" International Symposium on Archaeoastronomy, St. Andrews, UK, September 1990*, pp. 253-295. Niwot, Colorado: University Press of Colorado.

1997 El culto mexica de los cerros en la cuenca de México: apuntos para la discusión sobre graniceros. In: Beatriz Albores and Johanna Broda, coords., *Graniceros: Cosmovisión y meteorología indígenas de Mesoamérica*, pp. 49-90. Zinacantepec, Estado de México, El Colegio Mexiquense: Instituto de Investigaciones Históricas, Universidad Nacional Autónoma de México.

2001 Los mexicas en los cerros de la cuenca: Los sacrificios de niños. In: Johanna Broda, Stanislaw Iwaniszewski, and Arturo Montero, coords., *La Montaña en el paisaje ritual*, pp. 296-317. Mexico City: Conaculta—INAH, Universidad Nacional Autónoma de México.

Carrasco, Pedro
1999 *The Tenochca Empire of Ancient Mexico: The Triple Alliance of Tenochtitlan, Tetzcoco, and Tlacopan.* Norman: University of Oklahoma Press, The Civilization of the American Indian Series 234.

Caso, Alfonso
1967 *Los calendarios prehispánicos.* Mexico City: Universidad Nacional Autónoma de México, Instituto Nacional de Antropología e Historia, Serie de Cultura Náhuatl, Monografías 6.

Charnay, Desiré
1887 *The Ancient Cities of the New World: Being Voyages and Explorations in Mexico and Central America from 1857-1882.* Translated from the French by J. Gonino and Helen S. Conant. New York: Harper and Brothers.

Codex Borbonicus
1991 *El Libro del Cihuacoatl: Homenaje para el año del Fuego Nuevo. Libro explicativo del llamado Codice Borbónico. Codex du Corps Legislatif, Bibliothèque de l'Assemblée Nationale Francaise, Paris, Y 120.* Introducción y explicación: Ferdinand Anders/ Maarten Jansen/Luis Reyes García. Codices Mexicanos, III. Graz: Akademische Druck- und Verlagsanstalt; Mexico City: Fondo de Cultura Económica; and Madrid: Sociedad Estatal Centenario.

Codex Vaticanus A
1996 *Religión, costumbres e historia de los antiguos Mexicanos: Libro explicativo del llamado Códice Vaticano A, Codex Vatic. Lat. 3738 de la Biblioteca Apostólica Vaticana.* Introducción y explicación: Ferdinand Anders/Maarten Jansen. Codices Mexicanos, XII. Graz: Akademische Druck- und Verlagsanstalt, and Mexico City: Fondo de Cultura Económica.

García Moll, Roberto
1968 Un Adoratorio a Tlaloc en la Cuenca de México. *INAH Boletín*, Diciembre:24-27.

Iwaniszewski, Stanislaw
1991a De Nahualac al Cerro Ehécatl: una tradición prehispánica más en Petlacala. In: *Arqueología y etnohistoria del estado de Guerrero*, pp. 497-518. Mexico City: Instituto Nacional de Antropología e Historia-Gobierno del Estado de Guerrero.

1991b La arqueología de alta montaña en México y su estado actual. *Estudios de Cultura Náhuatl* 18: 249-273.

1994 Archaeology and Archaeoastronomy of Mount Tlaloc, Mexico: A Reconsideration. *Latin American Antiquity* 5(2):158-176.

Lorenzo, José Luis
1957 *Las zonas arqueológicas de los volcanes Iztaccihuatl y Popocatepetl.* Mexico City: Instituto Nacional de Antropología e Historia, Dirección de Prehistoria 3.

Morante López, Rubén B.
1997 El Monte Tlaloc y el calendario mexica. In: Beatriz Albores and Johanna Broda, coords., *Graniceros: cosmovisión y meteorología indígenas de Mesoamérica*, pp. 49-90. Zinacantepec, Estado de México, El Colegio Mexiquense: Instituto de Investigaciones Históricas, Universidad Nacional Autónoma de México.

2001 El Pico de Orizaba en la cosmovisión de México prehispánico. In: Johanna Broda, Stanislaw Iwaniszewski, and Arturo Montero, coords., *La Montaña en el paisaje ritual,* pp. 52-63. Mexico City: Conaculta–INAH, Universidad Nacional Autónoma de México.

Nicholson, H. B.
1971 Religion in Pre-Hispanic Central Mexico. In: Robert Wauchope, general editor, Gordon Ekholm and Ignacio Bernal, volume editors, *Handbook of Middle American Indians, Volume 10, Part 1*, pp. 395-445. Austin: University of Texas Press.

Parsons, Jeffrey R.
1971 *Prehistoric Settlement Patterns in the Texcoco Region, Mexico.* Contributions by Richard E. Blanton and Mary H. Parsons. Memoirs of the Museum of Anthropology, University of Michigan 3.

Pomar, Juan Bautista de
1986 Relación de la Ciudad y Provincia de Tezcoco. In: René Acuña, ed., *Relaciones geográficas del siglo XVI: México*, vol. 3, pp. 23-113. Mexico City: Universidad Nacional Autónoma de México, Instituto de Investigaciones Históricas, Etnohistoria, Serie Antropológica 70.

Ponce de León, Arturo
  1983 Fechamiento arqueoastronómico en el altiplano de México. In: Anthony F. Aveni and Gordon Brotherston, eds., *Calendars in Mesoamerica and Peru: Native American Computations of Time*, pp. 73-99. Oxford: British Archaeological Reports (BAR International Series 174).

  1991 Propiedades geométrico-astronómicas en la arquitectura prehispánica. In: Johanna Broda, Stanislaw Iwaniszewski, and Lucrecia Maupomé, eds., *Arqueoastronomía y etnoastronomía en Mesoamérica*, pp. 413-446. Universidad Nacional Autónoma de México, Instituto de Investigaciones Históricas, Serie de Historia de la Ciencia y la Tecnología 4.

Proceso Inquisitorial del Cacique de Tetzcoco
  1910 *Publicaciones de La Comisión Reorganizadora del Archivo General y Público de la Nación*, Eusebio Gómez de la Puente, ed. Mexico City: Estados Unidos Mexicanos, Secretaría de Relaciones Exteriores. Republished, in facsimile, with new introduction and different title, *Proceso inquisitorial del Cacique de Tetzcoco Don Carlos Ometochtzin (Chichimecatecotl)*, as Biblioteca Enciclopedica del Estado de México XCI. Mexico City, 1980.

Rickards, Constantine G.
  1929 The Ruins of Tlaloc, State of Mexico. *Journal de la Société des Américanistes* 21:197-199. Paris.

Sahagún, Fray Bernardino de
  1950-1982 *Florentine Codex. General History of the Things of New Spain, Fray Bernardino de Sahagún*. Translated from the Aztec into English, with notes and illustrations, by Arthur J. O. Anderson and Charles E. Dibble. In 13 parts. Monographs of the School of American Research, no. 14, parts I-XIII. Santa Fe: The School of American Research and the University of Utah Press.

  1982 *Historia general de las cosas de Nueva España. Primera version integra del texto castellano del manuscrito conocido como Códice Florentino*. Introducción, paleografía, glosario y notas por Alfredo López Austin y Josefina García Quintana. 2 vols. Mexico City: Fomento Cultural Banamex.

  1993 *Primeros Memoriales*. By Fray Bernardino de Sahagún. Facsimile edition. Photographed by Ferdinand Anders. Norman: University of Oklahoma Press, in cooperation with the Patrimonio Nacional and the Real Academia de la Historia, Madrid, Civilization of the American Indian Series 200, pt. 1.

  1997 *Primeros Memoriales*. By Fray Bernardino de Sahagún. Paleography of Nahuatl text and English translation by Thelma D. Sullivan. Completed and revised, with additions, by H. B. Nicholson, Arthur J. O. Anderson, Charles E. Dibble, Eloise Quiñones Keber, and Wayne Ruwet. Norman: University of Oklahoma Press, in cooperation with the Patrimonial Nacional and the Real Academia de la Historia, Madrid, Civilization of the American Indian Series 200, pt. 2.

Sullivan, Thelma D.
  1974 Tlaloc: A New Etymological Interpretation of the God's Name and What It Reveals of His Essence and Nature. In: *Atti del XL Congresso Internazionale degli Americanisti, Roma–Genova, 3-10 Settembre 1972*, vol. II, pp. 213-219. Genoa, Italy.

Tichy, Franz
  1991 Los cerros sagrados de la cuenca de México en el sistema de ordenamiento del espacio y de la planeación de los poblados. El sistema ceque de los Andes en Mesoamérica? In: Johanna Broda, Stanislaw Iwaniszewski, and Lucrecia Maupomé, eds., *Arqueoastronomía y etnoastronomía en Mesoamérica*, pp. 447-459. Universidad Nacional Autónoma de México, Instituto de Investigaciones Históricas, Serie Historia de la Ciencia y la Tecnología 4.

Torquemada, Fray Juan de
  1975-1983 *Monarquía Indiana*. Edición preparada por el Seminario para el estudio de fuentes de tradición indígena, bajo la Coordinación de Miguel León-Portilla. 7 vols. Mexico City: Universidad Nacional Autónoma de México, Instituto de Investigaciones Históricas, Serie de historiadores y cronistas de Indias 5.

Townsend, Richard F.
  1991 The Mt. Tlaloc Project. In: David Carrasco, ed., *To Change Place: Aztec Ceremonial Landscapes*, pp. 26-30. Wiyot, Colorado: University Press of Colorado.

  1992a *The Aztecs*. Ancient Peoples and Places, Glyn Daniel, Founding Editor. London: Thames and Hudson.

  1992b The Renewal of Nature at the Temple of Tlaloc. In: Richard Townsend, General editor, *The Ancient Americas: Art from Sacred Landscapes*, pp. 171-185. Chicago: The Art Institute of Chicago.

Wicke, Charles, and Fernando Horcasitas
  1957 Archaeological Investigations on Monte Tlaloc, Mexico. *Mesoamerican Notes* 5:83-96.

Sacred Mountains and Miniature Worlds: Altar Design Among the Nahua of Northern Veracruz, Mexico

Alan R. Sandstrom

Introduction

Nahua ritual specialists from the Huasteca region of northern Veracruz spend a great deal of time and effort constructing altars and dedicating offerings upon them in a heartfelt attempt to establish balance and harmony between the human and spirit worlds in our precarious and uncertain universe (see Burkhart 1989 for a discussion of similar ideas in 16th-century Nahua world view). In this article, I would like to outline some of the principles that underlie Nahua altar design and show how altars provide insight into Nahua religious thought and ritual behavior. I base my findings on more than 30 years of ethnographic field research in a single Nahua community. Over this period, I interviewed ritual specialists and laymen and witnessed many ritual occasions that ranged from simple divinations lasting only 20 minutes to elaborate blood offerings associated with pilgrimages to sacred mountains taking place over many days and nights. My purpose is to discuss altars not as mere static constructions but as the key dynamic element of an ancient, complex religion and the embodiment of Nahua conceptions about the nature of human beings, spirit entities, and the universe they inhabit. For additional information on the world view of the Nahua of northern Veracruz and nearby regions, see Williams García (1957), Signorini and Lupo (1989), Baéz-Jorge and Gómez Martínez (1998, 2000, 2001), and Gómez Martínez (1999a).

I will examine Nahua altars as concrete expressions of abstract ideas rarely articulated by the ritual specialists. Most Nahua learn about their religion by participating in rituals and by helping to prepare altars and the sacred paraphernalia and offerings for sacrifice (Sandstrom and Sandstrom n.d.). Among the Nahua of northern Veracruz, there is no tradition of systematic explication of esoteric points of theology and so altars and associated sacred items are important mnemonic devices that orient thought and affirm the truth of basic religious ideas. I will analyze altar design in the context of Nahua ideas about the sacred nature of the landscape in which they live. People all over the world incorporate elements of their natural surroundings into a conception of the sacred, producing what Roy Rappaport (1984[1968]) characterized as a "cognized model of the environment." I will also discuss altars as an example of the practice, widespread throughout ancient and contemporary Mesoamerica, of what Evon Vogt (1976) called "scaling." In the process of scaling, large cultural categories are miniaturized and small categories are projected onto large structures. Finally, I would like to link certain ritual behaviors associated with Nahua altars to their productive activities and hopefully provide insight into factors that account for the origin and continuance of Nahua rituals.

Over 430,000 Nahua (five years old and above) live in the tropical forests of northern Veracruz and the surrounding Huasteca region.

Most families make their living through slash-and-burn horticulture coupled with temporary wage labor on neighboring cattle ranches or in cities (Sandstrom 1995:184); see Guy Stresser-Péan (1979) for information on the Huasteca region. The people speak the Nahuatl language in everyday interaction although the majority also speak Spanish or another indigenous language. Most Nahua identify as Catholics but their beliefs and ritual behavior range from the fairly orthodox among people who live in or near large towns or cities to predominantly Native American beliefs and practices that have been little influenced by Christianity. James Dow (2001a:2) has labeled the syncretic system of beliefs found throughout Mesoamerica "Catholic affiliated" religion. Since the early 1980s, a significant number of Nahua from the region have converted to Protestantism, mainly to one of several sects identified with Pentecostalism. The new Protestants reject all forms of Catholicism as well as the Native American practices so widespread throughout the region. Despite the hostility of Protestants and the more orthodox Catholics among them, many people continue to observe the syncretic Native American religion, elements of which are deeply rooted in the pre-Hispanic past.

The Nahua ritual specialist is called by the general term *tlamatiquetl*, meaning "person of knowledge." Some anthropologists (see Vogt 1976) call these specialists "shamans," while others object to using a term from the Tungus people of Siberia in the Mesoamerican context (see Kehoe 2000) or debate the use of the term (see Dow 2001b, Lipp 2001, and Sandstrom 2000a). Other specialists such as midwives or prayer leaders may also possess sacred power but it is the person of knowledge who leads rituals and constructs altars. The role is open to males and females and individuals are usually called to the profession through dreams or miraculous recovery from a serious illness. Ritual specialists learn their profession by apprenticing to an established master. They assist the master and, as their knowledge slowly increases, begin to conduct rituals and eventually develop a clientele of their own. It is important to note that training in ritual techniques alone is not enough to make a successful ritual specialist. Their cures must be effective and their offerings must produce results before they are accepted by the community. Ritual specialists conduct a range of religious observances from brief divinations and curings for individual clients to extensive offerings involving participants from several communities and even different Native American ethnic groups.

Every religious observance requires ritual specialists to construct an altar. Altars range from elaborate installations involving long tables with an arch extending over them, to a single lighted beeswax candle placed alongside a simple offering of a soft drink. As I will discuss, a natural land form that is part of the Nahua sacred environment may also serve as an altar. Regardless of its dimensions and complexity, the altar and the sacralized items that make up the altar are together called in Spanish a *mesa* (literally, "table"). In Nahuatl, the word for altar is *tlaixpamitl,* which refers to something one "stands before or in front of" (see Sharon 1976 for a comprehensive discussion of *mesas* throughout Latin America). I will refer to altars and *mesas* interchangeably throughout this chapter. In the typical raised, table-type altar design, an arch made from a bent tree branch is fixed over one or more wooden tables. The arch is decorated with sprigs of green leaves, flowers, pinwheel-like ornaments representing stars made from palm and marigold blossoms, symbolic incense braziers woven from palm leaves, and other items. The table top itself is covered with various objects that will be used in the ritual offering, including palm and marigold adornments, candles, cut-paper figures (which I will describe shortly), statues of Catholic saints whose identities are syncretized with Native American spirits, and small dishes holding various items such as a bell used to arouse the spirits, a tobacco offering, and the ever-present copal incense (Figures 1 and 2).

On the altars of many ritual specialists may be found a sealed wooden chest containing a permanent collection of paper figures portraying the spirits of the seeds planted in the fields. The images inside the box wear tiny cloth outfits, earrings, and necklaces, and have combs or other accouterments that are intended to adorn and comfort the spirits. I will say more about this box and its contents shortly. Beneath the table is another array of sacred objects, including paper figures, copal incense, and palm and marigold adornments. On some occasions, altars are freestanding and constructed outside in the courtyard or patio of a shrine or house. This is the case for the altar called *cruz afuera* ("outside cross") dedicated

Figure 1. A typical altar set up by members of each household for the winter solstice ritual. The arch is decorated with green leaves and red poinsettia bracts. The boxes on the table contain Catholic statues representing the Virgin of Guadalupe (*tonantsij*, "our honored mother") and Jesus and Mary (reinterpreted as *tequitl* and *tequitl isihuaj*, "work" and "work's wife"). Offering of corn and beans beneath the table complete the three-tiered design of the Nahua altar.

to the sun. The altar within a shrine or house is always positioned against a wall, usually facing the door of the building. On the wall above the altar, people often hang paper images of guardian spirits and a cross, which is symbolically linked to *tonatij*, the supreme spirit of the sun. Small decorative items such as tinsel or mass-produced pictures of Catholic saints are also common. A simple or elaborate altar and ritual occasion may also be accompanied by an additional array of paper figures that the ritual specialist carefully arranges on the ground at a source of water such as a nearby spring or stream.

A second type of altar is placed directly on the ground. The spirits to whom these altars are dedicated are often associated with the earth and the underworld. For example, small offerings are carefully arranged on the ground around a clay incense brazier and dedicated to spirits of a field just before it is planted. The owner of the field might even erect a small arch over the offerings, thus mimicking a typical three-tiered, table-type altar. Altars associated with curing rituals are laid on the earth because the Nahua link disease to spirits of the dead from the underworld. In most cures, an elaborate *mesa* is arranged directly on the floor of the patient's house. The *mesa* consists of paper figures, palm and marigold adornments, offerings of tobacco, candles, corn meal, raw egg, and prepared foods such as coffee, bread, and tortillas. The ritual specialist may spend several hours preparing this display before actually curing the patient (see Figure 3). A great deal of individuality is expressed by the specialist in the arrangement of ritual items. In some cases, pa-

Figure 2. A decorated altar for a ritual to bless the corn before planting. Red and white flowers replace the ubiquitous marigolds when these are out of season. The ritual specialist kneels before carrying basket containing seed corn. In the basket are floral adornments representing Seven-Flower and Five-Flower, male and female aspects of the corn spirit. Note the firecrackers and seed pod of the *coyol* palm, representing fertility, leaning against the back wall. The three-tiered design of the altar is evident.

per images of disease-causing spirits are arranged like the spokes of a wheel around a small hole

Figure 3. *The ritual specialist lights tallow candles representing the underworld. At the center of the* mesa *are cups containing coffee and bread, a raw egg, candles, earth from the patient's house, and palm-leaf-and-marigold brooms for sweeping the patient clean of disease-causing spirits, all placed on a display of cut-paper figures representing these spirits. The large darkened figures with lighted cigarettes in their mouths represent malevolent leaders of dead souls receiving a tobacco offering. The paper figures have been soaked with the offerings, including soft drinks and cane alcohol in the bottles. The* mesa *is encircled with poured liquid offerings and a leaf- and flower-decorated vine tied into a loop to keep the dangerous spirits confined.*

dug in the earth (Figures 4, 5, and 6). In others, the paper figures are laid out in a grid pattern. Often the ritual specialist creates a kind of boundary around the curing altar by encircling it with a vine tied in a loop, or by pouring liquid offerings in a circle around the central array (compare the curing altars constructed by ritual specialists in Peru analyzed by Joralemon and Sharon 1993).

Most participants in a ritual are familiar with the different types of altars, but it is the responsibility of the presiding ritual specialist to construct and decorate these sacred spaces. During a cure, family members help the ritual specialist obtain the plants, sacrificial chickens, tobacco, cane alcohol, flowers, and other items that are required during the ritual event. For larger communal observances, people may come from many miles away to help the ritual specialist prepare the altar and procure various items that will be used. Most participants arrive with contributions of food, gathered items such as flowers and plants, as well as money. Of equal importance is the labor that participants expend in the sometimes onerous preparations for Nahua rituals. More elaborate observances require an enormous amount of work and personal sacrifice as participants deprive themselves of sleep for days on end during which individuals busy themselves constructing floral adornments, cutting paper, dancing, playing music on violin and guitar, and assisting at lengthy dedications of offerings to spirit entities. While no formal accounts are kept of an individual's labor, people are very aware of who helped with the preparations and who did not. In 2001, when I accompanied a group of Nahua

Figure 4. *The Nahua ritual specialist rubs the seated patient with leaves while chanting during a curing. Her* mesa *of paper images of disease-causing spirits encircles a small hole in the floor. Dried corn leaves on the left contain copal incense and the feathers on the right are from a sacrificial fowl. Note the leaf and flower loop to contain the dangerous spirits. The ritual specialist and the mother of the patient are constructing an altar on the left where offerings will be dedicated to house guardian spirits. My wife, Pamela Effrein Sandstrom, is in the background taking notes on the proceedings.*

Figure 5. In a continuation of the curing ritual in Figure 4, the party has moved to the peak of a sacred hill at the edge of the community. The patient, exhausted from his illness, rests on the ruins of a prehistoric stone structure. The ritual specialist looks on as the mother of the patient arranges food wrapped in banana leaves on an altar to the hill guardian spirits. Note the arch representing the celestial realm and the upright paper images of witness spirits. These figures will observe the offering and bring word to hill spirits so that they will cure and protect the patient. The ritual specialist carries adornments that may represent the sun. One object of the curing is to transfer some of the sun's power to the patient in order to effect a cure.

Figure 6. In another curing episode, a ritual specialist arranges an altar at the top of a sacred hill preparatory to making an offering to guardian spirits on behalf of his patient. Note the marigold-covered arch with the paper image of the sun. Six images of witness spirits stand upright before four marigold-covered crosses representing the four sacred realms. Witnesses take these offerings to powerful protector spirits associated with sacred hills. The specialist arranges palm and marigold adornments on a paper bed where additional cut-paper images of witnesses have been placed. In the background are the dried remains of a previous altar.

and Otomi on a pilgrimage to a sacred mountain, someone from a distant community who did not know me asked loudly, "Why is this stranger coming with us?" People in the crowd answered back, "He helped a lot with the *mesa*." That response effectively answered the question and no more was said on the subject.

One key component of Nahua altars requires explanation. The Nahua (along with the Otomi, Tepehua, Huastec, and to a lesser extent the Totonac) of northern Veracruz and the neighboring Sierra Norte de Puebla portray key spirit entities through the medium of cut-paper figures. Paper cutting for rituals is a practice recorded throughout the Mesoamerican culture area by 16th-century chroniclers but it is only in northern Veracruz and surrounding regions that the art survives (Sandstrom and Sandstrom 1986, Dow 1986; see also Barrera Rivera et al. 2001 for a description and photographs of a recent magnificent archaeological find of Aztec paper). The images are cut with scissors by ritual specialists who portray most spirits as small anthropomorphic figures with their hands raised by the sides of the head. The images are cut with crowns and other iconographic features that identify the particular spirit. For example, a figure with leaves and corn cobs cut from the body or cut as appendages from the sides of the body might represent the corn spirit. A figure cut with animal horns and rib holes typically represents a disease-causing spirit of the dead. Nahua and Otomi ritual specialists sometimes cut the figures from paper made from the inner bark of trees from the genus *Ficus*. Specialists from all groups also use inexpensive manufactured paper for most of their cuttings.

Images are most often cut from natural, undyed newsprint paper but sometimes disease-causing spirits and seed spirits are cut from colored tissue paper or coated paper. A great deal of a ritual specialist's time is spent cutting the images. For a medium-length curing ritual, the specialist may cut only 250 images. For the blood sacrifice and pilgrimage described below, the ritual specialist and his helpers cut over 16,000 images. Paper images may be made to depict almost any conceivable thing including inanimate objects. See Figure 7 for an image of the spirit of the altar or *mesa*.

The Nahua spirit pantheon is complex and difficult to summarize. My coauthor and I have argued that the Native American religion of this part of Mexico has a pantheistic quality (Sandstrom and Sandstrom 1986:275-80; see also Monaghan 2000). For pantheists, the universe and all of the objects and beings that exist within it constitute the sacred. Whereas for most Christians God created the universe, for pantheists God is the universe. In brief, there is only one deity or source of the sacred and all of the different beings and entities in the world are manifestations or aspects of that single sacred principle. It is the great unity that underlies apparent diversity. Thus, for the Nahua (as well as their Otomi, Tepehua, Huastec, and Totonac neighbors and probably all other Mesoamerican cultures) there is one single, all-pervasive sacred principle. The Nahua call this principle *totiotsij*, literally "our honored deity." All of the various spirits are aspects of this single entity. The ritual specialist cuts images of spirits for a specific purpose such as to cure disease, increase fertility in the fields, or appeal for rain. Once the ritual is ended, the discrete spirits return to the unity from which they are temporarily extracted. The number of spirits in the Nahua pantheon is infinite, limited only by the imagination of the ritual specialist.

Ritual specialists, however, are constrained by the historical experiences of their society and by the expectations and understandings of lay ritual participants. They must operate within a certain range of variation if the religious observance is to have meaning for the community of believers and they are guided by the fact that the Nahua pantheon of spirits has been explicated in widely shared myths and is associated with specific functions or roles. Although the ritual specialist has a great deal of freedom in portraying disease-causing spirits, the images must be linked symbolically to the underworld and to the winds that are associated with illness and misfortune in order to be effective for patients and their families. Most ritual practitioners portray these pathogens with rib holes or other skeletal features to get across this meaning. The cosmos includes a number of celestial spirits such as the sun, moon, and stars. Commonly portrayed earthly spirits include hills, caves, seeds, many aspects or manifestations of the earth itself, human souls, and animals. We also find a large number of spirits corresponding to the different forms of water, including springs, water in caves, streams, lakes, rivers, the ocean, clouds, rain, fog, and dew. Underworld spirits in-

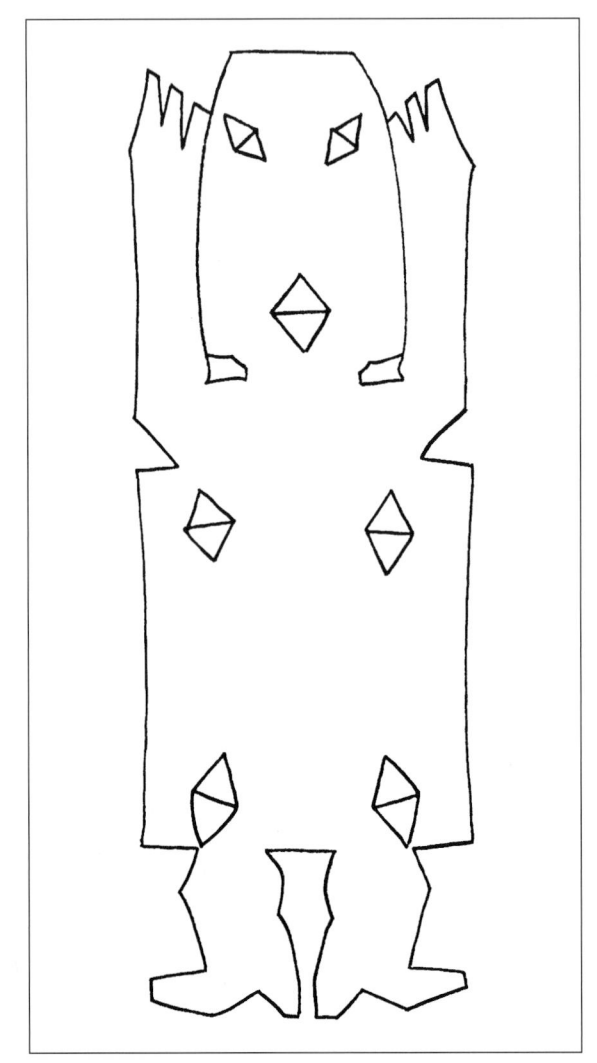

Figure 7. Paper image of the spirit of the altar or mesa cut from plain manufactured paper by ritual specialist Encarnación Téllez Hernández in Amatlán, Veracruz. Amatlán is a pseudonym to protect the privacy of the community where I have conducted extensive field research. The four cuts from the body outline the four corners of the altar table.

clude the souls of humans and a large number of dangerous figures who threaten the human community with death and destruction. Intermediaries between these four realms include witness and guardian spirits. These and other major Nahua spirits are itemized in Sandstrom (1991: 256-257).

It is no exaggeration to say that altars are the primary focus of Nahua ritual activity and attention (Figure 8). The overwhelming majority of effort in preparing and executing ritual observances of all kinds surrounds the altar. Each dwelling in a traditional Nahua community has a home altar where pictures of saints, incense braziers, and other ritual paraphernalia are kept. Household rituals are organized around the home altar, which is usually a simple table or shelf (Figure 9). During rituals, an arch may be added and decorated with leaves and flowers. In shrines or in the houses of ritual specialists, the altar is often larger and more elaborate. In general, altars are designed to be beautiful places that are attractive to spirit entities. They are places of bounty filled with an abundance of offerings, lighted beeswax candles, fresh greenery and flowers, pleasantly scented herbs, copal incense, and row upon row of neatly arranged paper images evoking the various spirits to be feted. Before the altar, people move slowly and respectfully. During moments of high emotional drama in larger ritual events, chickens and turkeys are sacrificed and their blood spread on each paper figure. In this way, participants dedicate to the spirits the gift of *chicahualistli*, the energy of life carried in the blood. For such elaborate rituals, a guitarist and violinist are contracted to play the plaintive and repetitive *xochisonis* or "flower sounds" (Provost and Sandstrom 1977, Hernández Azuara 2001). Dancers perform holding rattles and sacred walking sticks that are symbolically linked to thunder spirits who bring rain from the Gulf of Mexico to caves at the peak of a sacred hill (see below). Chanting by ritual specialists and laymen alike implores the spirits to accept the offered gifts. On several occasions during a long offering, the ritual specialist and assistants turn their attention to the smaller altars at a nearby spring or other source of water. It is interesting that during curing rituals, the floor altars dedicated to disease-causing spirits are also made to be pleasant places filled with an abundance of flowers, food, and drink. The malignant spirits assembled on the floor, however, are never given blood for fear that it would add to their strength. In general, altars are places where the Nahua exchange the best they have to offer for favors only the spirits can provide.

Figure 8. A ritual specialist (right) carrying the sacred walking stick and a participant holding a copal incense brazier dance before an altar in a crop fertility ritual. Note the miniature incense brazier made from palm leaves hanging from the arch. The altar is the typical three-tiered design. The pot on the floor holding the palm and marigold adornments contains water and represents the fourth realm. Ribbons hanging from the walking stick represent the rays of the sun at sunrise.

The Altar as Model of the Universe

In what follows, I will be discussing only the first type of Nahua altar, namely the table altar with the arch over it. The altars laid on the ground for earth-related spirits and disease-causing spirits from the underworld are, I believe, modifications of this basic design. As mentioned earlier, in this second type of altar the paper images, sacred adornments, and offerings are laid on the ground to affirm symbolically the terrestrial origin of the spirits that are addressed. The arched table altar is the basic model for other altar types but more importantly, it is the model for fundamental Nahua conceptions of the universe. This

Figure 9. A typical Nahua home altar. The cross decorated with marigold flowers represents the sun or sometimes the four sacred realms. Saints' pictures are reinterpreted as guardian spirits that protect the house. Note the lighted beeswax candles and smoking copal incense brazier indicating that the family has made some request of the spirits. The dried palm and flower adornments wrapped in the cut-paper "bed" on the lower right are remnants of a previous offering.

standard altar design is composed of four components that correspond to the four sacred realms of the Nahua. The first tier is the table top where the main offering is dedicated. The table top of the altar is a symbolic representation of *tlaltepactli*, or alternatively, *tlalticpac*, the "surface of the earth." The Nahua conceive the earth in two forms, as revealed in myths that they tell. In one form, the earth is the back of a crocodilian monster who floats in the sea. The monster is the grandmother of the corn spirit, *chicomexochitl* (literally, "seven-flower"), and her rough, plant-covered back is the earth's surface. In a second conception, the earth is seen to resemble a *comali*, or circular clay griddle for cooking tortillas, surrounded by water. The surface of the earth is where humans and animals walk and it is where the fields are laid out that supply people with life-giving food.

The second element of the altar is the arch, which symbolically represents *ilhuicactli*, the celestial realm. Nahua report that they see the sky as a gigantic curved, anthropomorphic mirror that literally arches over the earth's surface (Sandstrom 1998:69). It reflects the stars that guard people at night after the sun has gone down. During the day it is the place from which the sun, *tonatij*, casts its brilliant, life-giving rays to be received by the plants and creatures of the earth. The symbolic link between arch and sky realm is reinforced in several ways. As mentioned, common adornments attached to the arch are palm and marigold pinwheel-like constructions. These are the *sitlamej* or "stars," charged with guarding over people during the sun's absence. During some rituals a circular paper cut-out of the sun is attached to the highest point of the arch, reaffirming the link between sky and arch. In ritual appeals for rain, participants lean the decorated sacred walking sticks against the arch. The walking sticks are carried by the *pilhuehuentsitsij* (literally, "little old ones") who are dwarf-like rain or thunder spirits responsible for bringing precious water from the sea. These old men are metaphors for the rain-bearing clouds that move inland from the Gulf of Mexico. As they carry their loads across the sky, they strike their sticks, causing thunder and lightning.

On the third tier beneath the altar, ritual specialists lay out an array of paper images, adornments, and offerings to the more benign earth-related spirits. This realm is called *tlali* ("earth") and it represents the earth as a whole. Paper figures laid here are not disease-causing spirits of the wind or the fearsome leaders of dead souls mentioned earlier. Instead they represent salutary earth spirits related to crop fertility and the sacred landscape. The earth also contains the underworld, called *mictlan*, "place of the dead." The Nahua conceive *mictlan* to be similar to the earth's surface except that the sun does not shine or shines weakly and it is inhabited by the dead. These spirits are said to marry, live in villages, and farm just like people on the surface, but *mictlan* is a bleak, somber land of scarcity and want. The leaders of dead souls are powerful monsters that appear as skeletons, blackened figures, or owls, all of which must be kept at bay. In short, the underworld is viewed by the Nahua with deep ambivalence. It is the home of ancestors who will watch over their living kinsmen but these spirits of the dead often do not realize their own power and can cause harm as well. It is also the home of the souls of people who died violent or unpleasant deaths who wander the earth as disease-causing wind spirits. The *mesa* assembled on the earthen floor for curing rituals is composed of paper images of these wind spirits along with their terrifying leaders in the underworld. The curing *mesa* is really an abbreviated altar in which the sky, earth's surface, beneficent earth, and water realms are left out.

The fourth realm is the water, represented by the small altar and offering set up by the spring or stream. Water is a crucial element in Nahua world view, which is not surprising given their horticultural mode of production. There are a number of water spirits in the pantheon, although they all seem to be aspects of a single powerful deity. Chained to the bottom of the ocean because of his uncontrolled temper is a major water spirit syncretized with the Christian figure Saint John the Baptist (*San Juan Bautista*). One of his minions or perhaps his alter-ego is *apanchanej* ("water dweller"), a female spirit who lives in springs, lakes, and caves and who is responsible for the fish and the rain that falls on the fields. She oversees a watery realm in which sea creatures live and that serves as the destination of the souls of people who die from certain catastrophic causes such as being struck by lightning. Her minions include the dwarf-like old men who carry water from the sea to her abode in caves at the top of a sacred mountain. In some rituals, the water realm is represented by a pot filled with water from which a lighted candle protrudes. This symbolic element is set upon the altar table or the floor to connect it to the earthly realm. Sometimes participants place a container of water before the box housing the seed images as an offering and to link water to crop fertility (see Baéz-Jorge 1992, Gómez Martínez 1999b, and Martínez de la Cruz 2000).

In constructing and adorning an altar, the ritual specialist is creating a model of the Nahua universe for all participants to behold. The four basic realms of sky, earth's surface, earth as a whole (including underworld), and water are clearly represented and enlisted to create harmony and balance between the spirit world and the human community. Paper images of earthly, celestial, and water-related spirits are placed on their corresponding sections of the altar and receive the offerings of food, drink, incense, music, dance, and tobacco. Before such an offering is made, specialists hold a curing ritual in which offerings are dedicated to wind spirits and their leaders in the underworld. The ritual sequence is identical to a regular curing except that there is no patient. The purpose of this preliminary curing is to prevent dangerous spirits from being attracted to the area and partaking of offerings meant for the more salutary spirits. In short, while disease-causing spirits are part of the earth realm, they are symbolically distinguished from other earth spirits by the separate *mesa* and offerings.

Once the preliminary offering has been dedicated, the ritual specialist carefully gathers all paper images of the disease spirits and forms them into a bundle. The specialist then instructs a helper to place the bundle deep in the forest where no one will accidently come into contact with it and risk possible infection. During the main ritual, spirit entities from all realms are attracted to their corresponding images and partake of the offerings. Ritual specialists symbolically feed the spirits by spreading the offerings on each paper image. Remaining food and drink are then consumed by the people in attendance. Images of the salutary spirits that form the altar array are left in place after the ritual is over, along with all of the adornments. They are not discarded until the altar is cleaned in preparation for the next ritual offering, perhaps months later.

The Nahua practice of modeling the structure of the universe in their altar designs is part of a larger cultural complex in which elements of the landscape are seen to be part of a sacred order. It is sometimes difficult for outsiders to understand the Nahua view of their natural environment because it differs so radically from the Euro-American perspective. The landscape is literally alive with meaning. Each hill has a name and associated spirit entity that plays a part in local myth. But it is not just hills that are treated in this manner. Every aspect of the landscape including holes, clefts in a rock face, caves, flat places, muddy places, rocky places, protuberances and every kind of oddity in the physical environment has a name and place in the spirit pantheon. If you ask a Nahua to draw a map, he or she will usually make a series of dots on a piece of paper indicating the significant geographic features of the area. Rarely does a person draw a boundary line surrounding the mapped area. Each house in a Nahua community has a name based on some local geographical feature or abundant plant. In a practice anthropologists call "toponymy," people may actually take the house name as their own surname (Sandstrom 2000b). For example, Juan Hernández may take the name Juan Atlalco (literally, "Juan Muddy Place") because that is the area where he has his house. People identify with the environment to a remarkable degree and it is not an exaggeration to say that the landscape is a model for the Nahua sacred realm. The Nahua are particularly interested in geographic anomalies such as a pond on a mountainside or a cave at the peak of a hill. Because these places become identified with spirit entities, it is common for geographical locations to be depicted in paper during rituals. The intimate relation that the Nahua have with the environment is consonant with a pantheistic world view.

The moral quality that permeates Nahua relations with the environment is common in cultures all over the world. In explaining the ecological basis of religious ritual among the Tsembaga in highland New Guinea, Roy Rappaport uses the phrase "cognized model of the environment" to refer to "the model of the environment conceived by the people who act in it" (Rappaport 1984 [1968]:238, 1979:97-144). He distinguishes this perspective from what he calls "operational models of the environment," defined as the "attempt to represent nature in the terms of Western science" (Rappaport 1984[1968]:342). Cognized versus operational models correspond to the anthropological emic-etic distinction developed and elaborated by Marvin Harris (Headland, Pike, and Harris 1990). These two models usually differ from each other and it is almost certain that cognized models will contain reference to spirit entities and other cultural constructions that have no place in an etic operational model. According to Rappaport "[t]he discrepancy between cultural images of nature and the actual organization of nature is a critical problem for mankind and one of the central problems of any ecologically oriented anthropology" (1979:97). Rappaport is careful to point out that a cognized model of the environment may in fact be maladaptive and lead to the extinction of the group. However, he also states that the operational (scientific) model could ultimately lead to greater ecological devastation and human extinction because it is not based on "respect as a guiding principle" (Rappaport 1979:100). Neither scientific knowledge nor belief systems provide any guarantees. All evidence suggests, however, that the Nahua cognized model of the environment is part of a Native American world view that is ancient in Mesoamerica (Mönnich 1976; see also Reyes García and Christensen 1976). We can assume, therefore, that Nahua religious beliefs and practices—so closely based on their observations of and interaction with the natural environment—have contributed significantly to their physical survival. In this sense, their cognized model of the environment has proven itself over the centuries to hold a high degree of truth value.

The Nahua Altar as a Seat of Exchange

Ritual activity among the Nahua always focuses on the altar or one of its variations. As suggested, the altar may be abbreviated or modified depending on the ritual occasion, but it always remains at the center of action. Important calendrical ritual observances include the winter solstice, the new year, a variety of crop fertility rituals usually held in late winter or early spring, and the Day of the Dead. There are also a number of rituals such as curings to deal with life crises and rites of passage. For a list of rituals from this community, see Sandstrom (1991:294-295). The key feature of all Nahua rituals is the offering. The Nahuatl word for ritual is *xochitlalia*, meaning "to place flowers on the earth" or "to put down flowers." The word *tlamanilistli* (literally, "something spread out") is used to signify "offering" (in Spanish *ofrenda* or *promesa*) and because this activity essentially defines Nahua religious observances, it can be used as a general term to refer to any ritual occasion. For the Nahua, rituals are an important form of exchange with spirit entities. In funerals, they offer food to the dead soul. During the winter solstice, ritual specialists orchestrate an extensive offering to *tonantsij*, the female fertility spirit associated with the Virgin of Guadalupe, in order to promote human and crop fertility. During the Day of the Dead, family members construct an altar in their house and make three food offerings each day to the souls of departed kinsmen (Figures 10, 11, and 12). Even feared and dangerous disease-causing spirits of the dead are given food and drink during the rituals designed to remove them from the patient's body and surroundings. Spirits, for the Nahua, are social beings who respond to the nor-

Sacred Mountains and Miniature Worlds: Altar Design Among the Nahua of Northern Veracruz 61

Figure 10. A typical home altar for the Day of the Dead commemoration. Note the pinwheel-like adornments on the arch representing guardian stars and the palm-and-flower symbolic incense brazier. The altar arch is decorated with fruit, leaves, and bread. Food is placed on the table for the spirits of dead kinsmen to consume. The house altar is behind the arch.

mal exchanges that lie at the heart of all human interaction. To give a gift is to obligate the receiver.

Altars are thus seats of exchange, sacred places where spirits receive offerings. Because they are designed to be beautiful bowers with greenery, flowers, incense smoke, music, and abundant food and drink, they are attractive to people as well as the spirits. During fertility rituals such as the one held for winter solstice, the altar table becomes a direct analog of the *milpa* or horticultural field. Although I reported that the people call the altar table top *tlaltepactli,* "surface of the earth," a more precise description might be the culturally significant *milpa* (see Wisdom 1940:430 and Vogt 1976:132 for similar symbolic connections among the Ch'orti' and Tzotzil Maya). The *milpa* is where rain, soil, sun, and human labor conjoin to produce the life-sustaining corn, beans, chilies, and other crops. The spirits provide the raw produce in the fields and the people keep up their side of the exchange by offering prepared food in return. This exchange of cooked food for raw produce symbolically bridges the gap between Nahua culture and the gifts of nature, between the human community and natural environment. The altar serves as a kind of portal that links the Nahua with the spirit world and is a concrete expression of their dependence on the forces of nature represented by the spirits of earth, water, sun, and seeds.

An interesting feature of Nahua altar design, as well as the ritual behavior that surrounds altars, is the key role played by repetitive actions in the preparation and dedication of offerings. As an example, Nahua ritual music is played on the guitar and violin and the melodies are highly repetitive. During larger rituals, music is played

Figure 11. An elaborate arch with star adornments set up at the outskirts of the village during Day of the Dead to give food to the wandering souls of those whose relatives have neglected them. Its purpose is to keep potential harm from entering the community. Candles are placed in the green heart of a banana stalk that has been set up in front of the altar. (Photograph courtesy of Paul J. Provost.)

Figure 12. A widow places food offerings on an altar that has been constructed over the grave of her husband. Such offerings are made during Day of the Dead and at other times during the first several years after a death. Note the crosses beneath the arch and the use of cut-paper flowers for adornments.

continuously day and night and the music has a hypnotic effect on participants. A variety of fresh-flower adornments are used to beautify the altar, all of which require manufacture over a short period of time to keep them from drying out. Participants spend many intensive hours preparing thousands of the different types of floral decorations. Helpers tie these adornments in bundles of twenty, stack them neatly in carrying baskets, and then carefully lay them on the altars during the course of the ritual. I have already mentioned the paper figures that are cut in the hundreds and even thousands for each ritual. These figures are counted, laid out on special cut-paper "beds," and stacked up so that they look like thick books. In the course of the ritual, the specialist and helpers carefully lay out the beds on the appropriate levels of the altar. Before cutting, specialists fold the paper in such a way that eight images at a time are produced. This practice helps speed up production but cutting paper still takes many hours of work for an offering of any size. In addition, chanting is repeated over and over again by ritual specialists and laymen alike as they stand before the altar holding a sacred walking stick or smoking incense brazier. Nahua sacred dances are also highly repetitive and may be performed day and night. Rituals require a great deal of patience and there is never an attempt to rush the proceedings.

It is difficult to explain why Nahua rituals exhibit so much repetition. Of course, in any society rituals are composed of repeated segments, but the Nahua carry this universal feature to an extreme. I was never able to elicit an explanation for why repetition was so important. Specialists and laymen simply comment that rituals have always been done in this way. Based on the previous analysis of the role of altars as places of exchange between people and spirits, I would like to offer a tentative explanation for why repetition is so important for the Nahua. I believe that the answer lies in the horticultural mode of production. Slash-and-burn horticulture is characterized by highly repetitive sequences of acts. In fact, the assembly-line quality of this type of cultivation is striking for people who first witness it. Clearing the trees and brush and stacking the material for burning is an arduous and repetitive task. Planting is done by a group of men who walk the fields in a row and repeatedly plunge their digging sticks into the ground and place seeds in the hole they make. Harvesting of corn, beans, and sugarcane is accomplished by thousands of repeated actions that extend over days and weeks. Even the preparation of food is repetitive in the extreme. The staple crop is corn and family members must shuck, shell, and grind the ears by the thousands throughout the year. All of this work is done by hand. Here, then, may be an insight into Nahua ritual behavior. Just as the gifts from the spirits in the form of crops in the fields require much repetitive labor to be of use to human beings, so an equivalent type of labor is appropriate and perhaps even necessary in preparing altars and offerings for the spirit benefactors. Tasks associated with the ritual are thus symbolically linked to the chores performed by farmers in their fields, and a kind of equivalence is established between altar and *milpa.* Repetitive effort creates a symmetry in the perpetual exchange between the Nahua and the sacralized forces of nature that make life possible and worth living.

Scaling in Nahua Ritual and Altar Design

In his analysis of Tzotzil ritual in Chiapas, Evon Vogt coined the term "scaling" to describe the practice of making large- or small-scale models of "culturally perceived realities or categories" (Vogt 1976:11). The Nahua clearly share in this activity and I will begin by discussing their practice of creating miniature versions of larger structures and processes (see Sharon 1978 for an extensive discussion of altars in Peru and other areas of Latin America). We have seen that the altar is a model of the universe and that the repetition in rituals is a kind of compressed version of the tasks associated with slash-and-burn horticulture. There are several other areas where the Nahua create tiny worlds. One of the clearest examples is the box found on the altars of many ritual specialists. The box is made from tropical cedar, called *teocuahuitl,* "sacred wood," in Nahuatl. Inside, as already indicated, are a collection of paper figures representing the spirits of the seeds that are planted in the fields, although in the boxes I have seen most images simply portray varieties of corn. The figures are approximately 12 inches tall cut from a coated paper that is designed to last longer than the normal tissue paper used for offerings. According to Nahua myth, the seed spirits originated in a cave at the top of a sacred mountain called Postectli (or alternatively, Postectitla). The cave is the home of our sacred mother *tonantsij,* and the water spirit *apanchanej.* It is possible that these two female spirit entities are one and the same or perhaps different aspects of a single deity. The seeds were born in this cave and cared for by their mother. The Nahua view the seeds as children who must be nurtured, just as real seeds require care in the *milpa.* At some point in the mythical past, the seeds were lured from their home and placed in the sacred box, which is an analog of the original cave. The figures are carefully stored standing upright and facing forward. The ritual specialist provides them with a miniature world and the cloth outfits and personal adornments mentioned earlier, as well as tiny furnishings such as grinding stones, carrying bags, and chairs. As long as the community is a happy place where people are generous and where there is no violence, lying, or stealing, the seeds will remain in the community to feed the people. When people become complacent or engage in antisocial behavior, the seeds will be motivated to return to their mountain home and leave the people to starve.

Another example of miniaturization in Nahua religious practice is the paper image complex itself. The paper figures symbolically represent the forces of nature, sacred aspects of the landscape, human souls, and the multitude of spirit entities in the pantheon. When laid on altars, these figures reproduce in miniature the spirit realm, which essentially encompasses the entire universe. The number and range of spirits is unlimited and one function of altar construction is to reduce this infinity to a manageable size. The practice of miniaturizing has been well documented among the Maya and was apparently pursued by prehistoric populations throughout Mesoamerica (Gillespie 2000:135-160). For example, in many archaeological sites, researchers have found large numbers of clay figurines that appear to be miniature versions of ancestors, spirit entities, or political leaders (Marcus 1998). We also know that ritual paper cutting traces to the pre-Hispanic period (Sandstrom and Sandstrom 1986:3-34). But we are not certain if the current focus on creating paper images of spirit entities is pre-Hispanic or a response to colonial pressures. It is possible that ritual specialists changed from making clay figurines to cutting paper images in order to escape detection by missionaries and Spanish authorities. Finally, as a point of interest, there is even a trend in contemporary tourist art production in Mexico toward miniaturization, although it has not been possible to trace it to the pre-Hispanic period.

The Nahua also scale in the opposite direction, projecting a smaller object symbolically onto a larger format. The human body is one of their key symbols that illustrates this form of projection. The body is a rich source of symbols in all cultures of the world but it is a particularly powerful metaphor for the indigenous people of Mesoamerica, and particularly the Nahua (Douglas 1978[1970]:101, Turner 1967:90; see also López-Austín 1988[1980]). I have shown elsewhere that the human body is the symbol for life or the animating principle of the universe among the Nahua (Sandstrom 1998). An excellent example of the symbolism of the body can be found in the paper figures. Ritual specialists use anthropomorphic images to portray all types of spirit entities ranging from disease-causing winds to seeds and sacred mountains. Body symbolism communicates that the entity portrayed is alive or that it plays an active role in human existence. Use of the body in this way is consonant with a pantheistic world view, where all entities and beings are conceived as aspects of a single sacred living principle.

As we have seen, the Nahua conceive the sky as a gigantic curved anthropomorphic mirror that reflects starlight down to earth. The head of this enveloping form lies in the west and the feet lie in the east. In this example, the Nahua have projected the human body onto the celestial plane. They also view the earth as existing in the huge form of a human body. People told me that the mountains are the body's head and its feet are in the underworld. They also say that the soil is the earth's flesh, the rocks are its bones, and the water is its blood. One reason that an offering is dedicated to a field before planting is to compensate for annoying the earth by digging into its flesh. Here again, the Nahua project the human form onto the enormity of the entire earth. As a final example of projection from small to large, the sun, which the Nahua believe to be the source of all animating energy in the universe, is portrayed in paper figures as a face gazing down from the celestial realm. During periods of little rain or drought, I have seen families draw a large circular face on the ground using ashes from the fireplace in an effort to influence the sun to moderate its burning rays. In these examples, we can see the Nahua mapping the smaller human body onto the largest structures in their universe. In the following description of a pilgrimage and blood sacrifice to appeal for rain, I will show that the practice of scaling from small to large is found in surprising contexts.

In June 1998 and again in June 2001, my family and I were privileged to be invited by the Nahua to participate in a massive offering and a pilgrimage to the sacred mountain Postectli. Postectli, the heart of Nahua territory, is the famous mountain where *tonantsij* and her seed children originated and from which *apanchanej*, the water spirit, sends her life-giving rain (see Figure 13 for a paper image of this significant geological feature). The preparations lasted more than a week as participants made thousands of floral adornments and a number of ritual specialists cut the more than 16,000 paper figures nec-

Figure 13. Paper image of the spirit of Postectli cut by a ritual specialist in the community of Ichcacuatitla, Veracruz. The image is cut from coated green paper and has a crown that may represent plants. The shape cut from the body represents the sacred mountain. The image was collected by Lic. Arturo Gómez Martínez.

essary for this major offering (Figure 14). When all was ready, the ritual specialists held a curing to insure that disease-causing winds would not be attracted to offerings intended for salutary spirits. Afterwards, several major offerings were dedicated on the altars in the shrine near the house of the ritual specialist who had organized the event, at the outside altar to the sun, and at a nearby spring, one of the many homes of the water spirit (Figure 15). The main offering in the shrine began when practitioners carefully laid out hundreds of paper images on top of and beneath

Sacred Mountains and Miniature Worlds: Altar Design Among the Nahua of Northern Veracruz 65

Figure 14. The ritual specialist removes the paper images of seed spirits from the box on his altar in preparation for a major offering to increase crop fertility. He places the dressed and decorated images in a basket. The woman in the foreground is undressing each image. The clothes will be washed and the box thoroughly cleaned before the images are dressed again and returned to their miniature home. One of the purposes of this type of ritual offering is to create a happy atmosphere for the seed spirits so that they will continue to supply crops to the community.

Figure 15. As part of major rituals, a small altar is set up at a nearby source of water. Here ritual specialists dedicate an offering to a spring that emerges from beneath a huge ceiba (silk cotton or kapok) tree. The specialist (right) holds a sacred walking stick decorated with ribbons representing the colorful rays of the sun at dawn. A helper (second from right) pours out a soft drink offering to the water spirit. A man dressed in white standing above the spring holds a lighted beeswax candle while shaking a rattle. The man next to him rings a small bell to alert the water spirit that offerings are being made.

the altar table. Next, the throats of several chickens and turkeys were slashed using scissors and the blood carefully dripped or spread on each paper figure. All the while the sacred music played and people danced, shaking rattles and parading walking sticks, floral adornments, pots of water, and other items.

Early in the morning, after days of preparations and almost continuous ritual activity, people loaded carrying baskets and set off on the pilgrimage to Postectli. We walked for almost 12 hours through the sweltering heat of the tropical forest before arriving at the foot of this unusual and magnificent geological feature (Figure 16). The mountain is a basaltic core that juts almost 2,000 feet vertically from the surrounding countryside. It is a bullet-shaped rock covered with tropical growth overlooking the Nahua town of Ichcacuatitla, Veracruz. At the base of this huge monolith is a shrine where the group of pilgrims first stopped. After resting for a while, the participants began final preparations for the climb up the mountain early the next morning. During the night, the specialists held another curing ritual to make sure that disease-causing spirits were removed from the immediate vicinity. They spent the whole night dedicating an offering at the shrine and at dawn shouldered the adornments, sacrificial fowl, and offerings and began their approach to the mountain (Figure 17).

The climb was arduous but all of the nearly 70 participants, both males and females ranging in age from 10 to probably 75 years old, were eager to complete the ascent. About one-third of the

Figure 16. The pilgrims, carrying offerings and adornments, walk towards Postectli looming on the horizon.

Figure 17. After arriving at the shrine at the base of Postectli, the pilgrims dedicate an offering. Note the square arch over the altar table with the images of guardian stars made from palm leaves and marigolds. Offerings on the altar table and beneath it are clearly visible. Under the table on the right is a pot with water and flowers representing the water realm. People at the right kneel and hold sacred walking sticks. Note the opened boxes at the back of the altar containing the seed spirits.

way up we stopped at a wide spot in the trail and rested as the ritual specialists unpacked items and began to create another altar. There was an old narrow platform made from poles leaned against the rock wall and participants cleared brush and strengthened the structure by renewing the lashings that held it together. After yet another curing sequence, they laid out hundreds of paper figures, sacrificed several birds, and dripped the blood on each of the images (Figure 18). In an unusual episode that I had never before witnessed, the participants trapped a living white chicken in a small crevice in the rock face, along with some floral adornments. This offering was to *mixtli*, the cloud spirit. After shouldering their load once again, the pilgrims began the more difficult part of the climb. The trail went nearly straight up and in several locations required hand-over-hand rock climbing. At two particularly difficult sections, participants had to hold on to 75-foot ropes to scramble up the steep face of the mountain.

At about two-thirds of the way to the summit, we stopped at a flat place and set up another complex altar. Ritual specialists and helpers cleaned a weathered altar table left behind by earlier pilgrims and laid out hundreds more of the paper images. Again, they sacrificed fowl and carefully spread the blood on all of the images (Figure 19). A small number of helpers then followed the ritual specialists for about 100 yards on a narrow trail that led to two small caves in the rock face. The first of these was the home of *apanchanej*, *tonantsij*, and the seeds. With participants perched precariously on the edge of the densely overgrown trail leading up the mountain, the ritual specialists left offerings, including sacrificed fowl,

Sacred Mountains and Miniature Worlds: Altar Design Among the Nahua of Northern Veracruz 67

Figure 18. One-third of the way to the summit of Postectli, pilgrims construct an altar. The man in the background holds candles and a sacred walking stick as helpers place offerings both on the altar table and beneath it. Underneath the adornments and offerings are paper images covered with the blood of sacrificial fowl.

Figure 19. Two-thirds of the way to the summit of Postectli, pilgrims construct an altar. Musicians play as exhausted participants rest in the background. The typical three-tiered altar with the leaf-covered arch is plainly visible on the right. Bloody paper images beneath the table are from an earlier sacrifice.

in the cave entrance. A short distance away was a second cave that was home to the thunder spirits who carry water from the sea. Here yet another smaller offering was dedicated.

The now-exhausted pilgrims climbed for about 30 minutes longer to reach the barren and wind-swept summit. Once there, they began to set up altars to the cross—representing an aspect of the sun—the moon, and, most remarkable of all, a circular altar directly dedicated to the sun spirit, *tonatij*. This altar was made of a hoop, about three feet in diameter that had been fixed to a pole about eight feet high. Palm fiber woven over the hoop made a kind of platform on which numerous offerings were placed. Helpers tied paper streamers to the hoop and led them away in all directions, like spokes in a wheel, nearly covering the peak. What they had created was an image of the sun with the paper streamers representing the rays of life-giving light emanating from the center (Figure 20).

This abbreviated description of one of the most lengthy and complex rituals I have seen among the Nahua represents a most remarkable example of scaling. Because I was able to witness the whole event on two different occasions, I could formulate questions and pay attention to details to a degree that would have been impossible had I seen it only one time. I was puzzled by the structure of the ritual and by the construction of altars at one-third and two-thirds of the way up the summit. In response to my repeated questions, one of the ritual specialists told me what probably should have been obvious. The pilgrimage to Postectli to appeal for rain reproduced on a gigantic scale the simple table altar found in the little shrine back in the community. Offerings at the first altar are analogous to the offerings beneath the table altar. The paper images cut for this part of the offering are the same as those placed beneath the altar. The second altar was the analog of the table top and the paper

Figure 20. At the summit of Postectli, pilgrims dedicate a circular altar to the sun. Note the paper streamers representing light rays. Helpers prepare an altar on the right that will be dedicated to the cross, an aspect of the sun spirit, tonatij.

images arrayed there reflected this position. Finally, at the summit, altars to celestial spirits were constructed, including the magnificent offering to the sun. In addition, the offering made to the two small caves are equivalent to the offerings made by the spring or stream back at the shrine. In sum, the ritual turned Postectli into a huge altar that, like its smaller counterpart, represents all four sacred sectors of the Nahua universe: earth's surface, earth as a whole, celestial, and watery realms. Of course scale is relative. Postectli may be an enormous altar but it is still a miniature version of the universe.

Summary and Conclusion

In this brief article, I have tried to show that much ritual activity among the Nahua of northern Veracruz, Mexico, takes place on and around altars. These religious constructions vary in design according to the rituals in which they are used, but they all seem to be modifications of a single basic structure. The simple table to which an arch is affixed coupled with offerings at a nearby source of water model the sacred realms of the Nahua universe. To use the terms of Clifford Geertz (1973), altars are models of and models for Nahua conceptions about the fundamental nature of the cosmos. Nahua religion is based on a cognized model of the environment wherein geographic features take on sacred attributes. The Nahua conception of the sacred is pantheistic in that everything in the universe is part of an indivisible divinity that underlies all apparent diversity. The rituals and associated altars must be understood in the context of the slash-and-burn horticultural production system and much ritual behavior reflects the highly repetitive activities associated with this form of cultivation. Like other indigenous peoples in Mesoamerica, the Nahua scale down and create miniature worlds as part of their religious practices. They also scale up imposing smaller structures on larger realities, even turning mountains into altars. Finally, the use of the human body as a metaphor for understanding large structures and processes, as well as smaller ones, permeates Nahua thought.

The Nahua altar is a center of activity and seat of exchange where people sacrifice what is of value to them in order to establish balance and harmony in a universe filled with unpredictable forces and events. It reveals many important features of the people's world view and says a great deal about what it means to be Nahua. Finally, it is a concrete expression of abstract and philosophically profound ideas that trace to the ancient religions of Mesoamerican civilization.

References Cited

Baéz-Jorge, Félix
 1992 *Las voces del agua: El simbolismo de las sirenas y las mitologías americanas.* Xalapa: Universidad Veracruzana.

Baéz-Jorge, Félix, and Arturo Gómez Martínez
 2001 Tlacatecolotl, señor del bien y del mal (dualidad en la cosmovisión de los nahuas de Chicontepec). In: Johanna Broda and Félix Báez-Jorge, eds., *Cosmovisión, ritual e identidad de los pueblos indígenas de México,* pp. 391-451. México, D.F.: Consejo Nacional para la Cultura y las Artes and Fondo de Cultura Económica.

2000 Los equilibrios del cielo y de la tierra: Cosmovisión de los nahuas de Chicontepec. Desacatos: *Revista de Antropología Social* 5:79-94.

1998 *Tlacatecolotl y el diablo: La cosmovisión de los nahuas de Chicontepec*. Xalapa, Veracruz: Secretaria de Educación y Cultura.

Barrera Rivera, José Álvaro, Ma. de Lourdes, Gallardo Parrodi, and Aurora Montúfor López
2001 La Ofrenda 102 del Templo Mayor. *Arqueología Mexicana* no. 48:70-77.

Burkhart, Louise
1989 *The Slippery Earth: Nahua-Christian Moral Dialogue in Sixteenth-Century Mexico*. Tucson: University of Arizona Press.

Douglas, Mary
1978[1970] *Natural Symbols: Explorations in Cosmology*. London: Barrie and Jenkins.

Dow, James W.
1986 *The Shaman's Touch: Otomí Indian Symbolic Healing*. Salt Lake City: University of Utah Press.

2001a Protestantism in Mesoamerica: The Old within the New. In: James W. Dow and Alan R. Sandstrom, eds., *Holy Saints and Fiery Preachers: The Anthropology of Protestantism in Mexico and Central America*, pp. 1-23. Westport, Conn.: Praeger.

2001b Central and North Mexican Shamans. In: Brad R. Huber and Alan R. Sandstrom, eds., *Mesoamerican Healers*, pp. 66-94. Austin: University of Texas Press.

Geertz, Clifford
1973 Religion as a Cultural System. In: Clifford Geertz, *Interpretation of Cultures*, pp. 87-125. New York: Basic Books.

Gillespie, Susan
2000 Maya "Nested Houses": The Ritual Construction of Place. In: Rosemary A. Joyce and Susan D. Gillespie, eds., *Beyond Kinship: Social and Material Reproduction in House Societies*, pp. 135-160. Philadelphia: University of Pennsylvania Press.

Gómez Martínez, Arturo
1999a *Tlaneltokilli: La espiritualidad de los nahuas chicontepecanos*. Tesis para licenciatura, Universidad Veracruzana.

1999b *El agua y sus manifestaciones sagradas: Mitología y ritual entre los nahuas de Chicontepec*. Chicontepec, Ver., México: H. Ayuntamiento Constitucional de Chicontepec, Veracruz.

Headland, Thomas N., Kenneth L. Pike, and Marvin Harris
1990 *Emics and Etics: The Insider/Outsider Debate*. Newbury Park, Calif.: Sage Publications.

Hernández Azuara, César
2001 *Son Huasteco y sus instrumentos en los siglos xix y xx*. Tesis para licenciatura, Escuela Nacional de Antropología e Historia.

Joralemon, Donald, and Douglas Sharon
1993 *Sorcery and Shamanism: Curanderos and Clients in Northern Peru*. Salt Lake City: University of Utah Press.

Kehoe, Alice
2000 *Shamans and Religion: An Anthropological Exploration into Critical Thinking*. Prospect Heights: Waveland Press.

Lipp, Frank
2001 A Comparative Analysis of Southern Mexican and Guatemalan Shamans. In: Brad R. Huber and Alan R. Sandstrom, eds. *Mesoamerican Healers*, pp. 95-116. Austin: University of Texas Press.

López-Austin, Alfredo
1988[1980] *The Human Body and Ideology: Concepts of the Ancient Nahuas*. Thelma Ortiz de Montellano and Bernard Ortiz de Montellano, transl. Salt Lake City: University of Utah Press.

Marcus, Joyce
1998 *Women's Ritual in Formative Oaxaca: Figurine-making, Divination, Death and the Ancestors*. Memoirs of the Museum of Anthropology, University of Michigan, Number 33. Ann Arbor: University of Michigan Museum of Anthropology.

Martínez de la Cruz, Rafael
2000 *Apanchaneh, señora del agua: Ritual y cosmovisión entre los nahuas de Chicontepec*. Tesis para licenciatura, Universidad Veracruzana.

Mönnich, Anneliese
1976 La supervivencia de antiguas representaciones indígenas en la religión popular de los nawas de Veracruz y Puebla. In: Luis Reyes García and Dieter Christensen, eds., *Das Ring aus Tlalocan: Mythen und Gabete, Lieder und Erzahlungen der heutigen Nahua in Veracruz und Puebla, Mexiko; El anillo de Tlalocan: Mitos, oraciones, cantos y cuentos de los nawas actuales de los estados de Veracruz y Puebla, México*, pp. 139-143. Quellenwerke zur alten Geschichte Amerikas aufgezeichnet in den Sprachen der Eingeborenen, Bd. 12. Berlin: Gebr. Mann Verlag.

Monaghan, John
2000 Theology and History in the Study of Mesoamerican Religions. In: John Monaghan, volume ed, *Supplement to the Handbook of Middle American Indians, Ethnology, Volume. 6*, pp. 24-49. Victoria R. Bricker, general ed. Austin: University of Texas Press.

Provost, Paul J., and Alan R. Sandstrom
1977 *Sacred Guitar and Violin Music of the Modern Aztecs* (including ethnographic notes). Ethnic Folkways Records, No. FE 4358. New York: Folkways Records distributed by Smithsonian Folkways Recordings.

Rappaport, Roy A.
1979 *Ecology, Meaning, and Religion*. Richmond, Calif.: North Atlantic Books.

1984 [1968] *Pigs for the Ancestors: Ritual in the Ecology of a New Guinea People.* Enlarged Edition. New Haven: Yale University Press.

Reyes García, Luis, and Dieter Christensen, eds.
1976 *Das Ring aus Tlalocan: Mythen und Gabete, Lieder und Erzahlungen der heutigen Nahua in Veracruz und Puebla, Mexiko; El anillo de Tlalocan: Mitos, oraciones, cantos y cuentos de los nawas actuales de los Estados de Veracruz y Puebla, México.* Quellenwerke zur alten Geschichte Amerikas aufgezeichnet in den Sprachen der Eingeborenen, Bd. 12. Berlin: Gebr. Mann Verlag.

Sandstrom, Alan R.
1991 Corn is Our Blood: Culture and Ethnic Identity in a Contemporary Aztec Indian Village. Civilization of the American Indian Series, vol. 206. Norman: University of Oklahoma Press.

1995 Nahuas of the Huasteca. In: James Dow and Robert V. Kemper, eds., Encyclopedia of World Cultures, pp.184-187. Boston: G. K. Hall.

1998 El nene lloroso y el espíritu nahua del maíz: El cuerpo humano como símbolo clave en la Huasteca veracruzana = The Weeping Baby and the Nahua Corn Spirit: The Human Body as Key Symbol in the Huasteca Veracruzana. In: Jesús Ruvalcaba Mercado, ed., *Nuevos aportes al conocimiento de la Huasteca,* pp. 59-94. Selección de trabajos pertenecientes al VIII encuentro de investigadores de la Huasteca. México, D.F.: Centro de Investigaciones y Estudios Superiores en Antropología Social.

2000a Shamanism. In: David Carrasco, general ed., *Encyclopedia of Mesoamerican Cultures,* pp. 142-44. New York: Oxford University Press.

2000b Toponymic Groups and House Organization: The Nahuas of Northern Veracruz, Mexico. In: Rosemary Joyce and Susan Gillespie, eds., *Beyond Kinship: Social and Material Reproduction in House Societies,* pp. 53-72. Philadelphia: University of Pennsylvania Press.

Sandstrom, Alan R., and Paul J. Provost
1977 *Sacred Guitar and Violin Music of the Modern Aztecs.* Ethnic Folkways Records, no. FE 4358. New York: Folkways Records distributed by Smithsonian Folkways Recordings.

Sandstrom, Alan R., and Pamela Effrein Sandstrom
n.d. The Shaman's Art: Sacred Paper Cuttings among Nahua Indians of Northern Veracruz, Mexico. In: Linda Walbridge and April K. Sievert, eds., *Personal Encounters: A Reader in Cultural Anthropology.* McGraw-Hill Publishing (forthcoming).

1986 *Traditional Papermaking and Paper Cult Figures of Mexico.* Norman: University of Oklahoma Press.

Sharon, Douglas
1976 Distribution of the Mesa in Latin America. *Journal of Latin American Lore* 2(1):71-95.

1978 *Wizard of the Four Winds.* New York: Free Press.

Signorini, Italo and Alessandro Lupo
1989 *Los tres ejes de la vida: Almas, cuerpo, enfermedad entre los nahuas de la Sierra de Puebla.* Xalapa: Universidad Veracruzana.

Stresser-Péan, Guy, ed.
1979 *La Huasteca et la frontière nord-est de la Mesoamérique.* Actes de XLIIe Congrès International des Americanistes (Paris, 2-9 Septembre 1976) 9B:9-157.

Turner, Victor
1967 *The Forest of Symbols: Aspects of Ndembu Ritual.* Ithaca: Cornell University Press.

Vogt, Evon Z.
1976 *Tortillas for the Gods: A Symbolic Analysis of Zinacanteco Rituals.* Cambridge: Harvard University Press.

Williams García, Roberto
1957 Ichcacuatitla. *La Palabra y el Hombre* 3:51-63.

Wisdom, Charles
1940 *The Chorti Indians of Guatemala.* Chicago: University of Chicago Press.

Central and Northern Mexico

The Wixárika (Huichol) Altar: Place of the Souls, Stairway of the Sun

Stacy B. Schaefer

The altar, or *niwetari*[1] as it is called by the Wixárika (Huichol) of the Sierra Madre of Jalisco, Mexico is construed as a space where the layers of the universe—the underworld, the middle world of the living, and the upper world—converge. It serves as an *axis-mundi*, a focal point within Wixárika culture, where basic elements of life, health, sustenance, family, and the soul are symbolically expressed in the objects placed upon it and in the ritual actions that occur around it. Wixárika altars are located in traditional temples (*tuki, tukite* pl.), family god houses (*xiriki, xirikite* pl.), and inside the Catholic church (*teyeupáni*). Generations of Wixáritari (pl.) have painstakingly maintained these altar traditions, embellishing them with ancient and newly introduced objects and ideas relevant to their lives. Slight variations exist in Wixárika altars from one community to the next and from one family to another.

The information provided in this paper comes from a number of sources. These include my observations of *niwetarite* (pl.) in a number of Wixárika ranches and temples and in the church in San Andrés Cohamiata, the discussions I have had over the years with several shamans and their families from the San Andrés Cohamiata community, and my participation with these families in ritual activities where the *niwetari* features prominently. I present here a description of a number of altars recognized by Wixáritari as *niwetarite* and my experiences surrounding them during Wixárika rituals and ceremonies, as well as the information I learned from my Wixárika consultants supplemented with information gleaned from the literature on Wixáritari.[2]

The term "*niwetari*" comes from the word "*niwe*" meaning son or daughter. The importance of family members and the intertwining of their souls with their living and deceased relatives are inscribed into the essential meaning of the altar as a resting place for souls. The *niwetari* is referred to as the stairway of the sun; the crucial role of the soul and the sun in altar traditions in the temple, the church, the family ancestor house, and the pilgrimage to Wirikuta, the peyote desert of San Luis Potosí, are themes I explore in this paper.

Description of *Niwetarite*

The Temple—The *Tuki*

In the sierra community of San Andrés Cohamiata, in the state of Jalisco, there are a number of temple districts based on lineage affiliation that are comprised of dispersed ranches of related Wixárika families dotting the regional landscape. Each temple district is defined by a large circular temple with a central fireplace in the outdoor dirt patio and ancillary god houses. The Wixárika families with whom I work are associated with five major temple districts, San Andrés (*Tunuwamet+a*—Temple of the Morning Star), San José (*Ta Werikt+a*—Temple of the Eagle of the Sun), Cohamiata (*Tsierikamet+a*—Temple of the Rattle Snake), Las Guayabas (*Kuyuwanemet+a*—Temple of the Rain Serpent) and Las Pitayas (*'+r+ Tsut+a*—Temple of the Arrow). This last temple,

Douglas Sharon, ed., *Mesas & Cosmologies in Mesoamerica*. San Diego Museum Papers 42, 2003.

Las Pitayas, has merged its cargo members with the San Andrés temple.

One enters the circular Wixárika temple at each compound through the doorway oriented to the east; inside, the *niwetari* is situated on the west wall facing the doorway. It is fashioned in the form of a table, or *mesa*, with four wooden posts that sustain a rectangular horizontal upper structure made from the canes of *haku (Otatea acuminata* var. *aztecorum)* or *haka (Arundo donax)* tied together with fibers. A variant of this, which I am told is a more ancient altar form, is made from rocks and adobe, and is built in tiers, like a stairway, reaching from the dirt floor to around 3.5 to 4 feet in height. Below the altar is a sacred hole in the dirt floor, covered with a carved stone disk decorated with symbols of deer, eagles, and peyote. During ceremonies the stone disk is removed, candles are lit, and offerings, the fervent prayers of participants, as well as the music of the guitar and violin players who sit below the altar fill this sacred hole for the earth goddess, *Yurienaka* (Figure 1).

Figure 1. Guitar and violin players carrying out their cargo sit under the altar in the San Andrés temple while they play music. To the side is one of the large Christ figures that has been bought to the temple for the ceremony (photo by James A. Bauml).

Temple members are given special roles, *cargos*, requiring them to care for specific gods or goddesses in the temple; they must also complete associated ritual obligations for five years. Upon arriving at the temple for ceremonial occasions, the cargo holders place on top of the altar woven and embroidered bags filled with a multitude of offerings; in the case of *mesa*-style altars, these bags are hung from the altar's wood and bamboo frame. The ceremonial calendar determines the kinds of offerings brought to the temple altar; Wixáritari recognize two main seasons, the dry season with the performance of the harvest ceremony and the rainy season ceremony for calling on the rains and preparing the earth for planting. In the fall, freshly harvested young corn and squash adorned with marigold *(Tagetes erecta)* flowers are placed in offering bags and upon the altar, along with thread crosses *(tsikurite* pl., commonly referred to in English as "god's eyes") and gourd rattles that will be held by children and their parents when the leading shaman of the temple performs the harvest and drum ceremony known as *Tatei Neixa* (Dance of our Mother) (Bauml 1994). At the end of the dry season, with the beginning of the rains in May or June, the altar is the resting place for bags filled with peyote, votive gourd bowls pertaining to the numerous gods in the temple, dried deer meat and dried deer faces, one of which has a small woven pouch *(wainuri)* with a prayer arrow attached to the forehead and contains the sacred tobacco *makutse (Nicotiana rustica)* (Schaefer 2002:244-248). This ceremonial occasion, *Hikuri Neixa* (Dance of the Peyote), marks the completion of the dry season activities of deer hunting and the peyote pilgrimage. Family members also bring their sacred ears of *maíz* and the dried stalks and leaves of the *maíz* to the temple altar to initiate the planting season.

Except for ceremonial events, the temple altar remains bare, save for a few objects that individuals may have placed upon it for personal prayers. When one of my Wixárika families was completing the leading five-year cargo role of *'+r+ kwekame*, the keeper of the temple and the sacred offerings, at the San José temple, I had the opportunity to join them for three years in the ceremonial activities of the *Hikuri Neixa* ceremony. The family of the cargo holder *'+r+ kwekame* assumes the position in the temple looking inward, directly to the right of the altar. From this location I was able to observe the temple *niwetari* as an active part of the sacred time and space invoked during the period of two days and nights (sometimes more) that each ceremony lasted. I have had the good fortune to participate in additional *Hikuri Neixa* ceremonies in the temples of Cohamiata, San Andrés, and Las Guayabas. In the San Andrés temple I also participated in two *Tatei Neixa* ceremonies, part of the weaving of the *wainuri* (sacred tobacco bag) ceremony, and the ceremony to keep horses and other domestic animals away from the *milpa*. Seeing and participating in these events prompted me to formulate questions about the temple and its *niwetari* that I later asked my Wixárika consultants.

God House of the Family Ranch—The *Xiriki*

Within the temple districts most Wixáritari live in ranches of multiple houses constructed from adobe, stone, or bamboo with grass-thatched roofs scattered throughout the rugged countryside. The ranch of the principal shaman or elder of an extended family is most commonly where the god house, *xiriki*, is located; this house also serves as the family ancestor shrine. Many of the same types of ceremonies that occur in the temple take place at the family level in the *xiriki*. Members of the extended family are also given five-year cargos to complete, such as *tsaulixika*, the shaman singer, '+r+ kekame, the keeper of the *xiriki* and sacred offerings, and *Niwetsika*, the corn goddess. *Xiriki* structures are made from the same materials as the houses and storage structures; most of them are built like a small house with four walls, however some are circular like miniature versions of the temple. Judging by these similarities, it is quite plausible that the circular and more traditional family god house may have been a prototype for the Wixárika temple because both have the same circular architectural style, the same form and placement of the *niwetari*, and in both the temple and the *xiriki* major cargo roles caring for the gods and performing the annual ceremonies are fulfilled over five-year cycles.

The altar in the *xiriki* is located on the west wall facing east towards the doorway and takes the same form as in the temple, a *mesa*-like shape made of bamboo canes, or in some instances levels of stone and adobe arranged in tiers (Figure 2). One major difference between the temple and *xiriki* altars is that the *xiriki* altar is a more permanent space for placing sacred objects pertaining to the extended family relating to its health and well-being. Some of these specific items are the family's sacred ears of *maíz* bundled together with a woven belt and situated in a votive gourd bowl decorated in its interior with miniature wax figures representing all of the family members. This gourd bowl is specifically for the *maíz* goddess *Niwetsika*. Accompanying the ears of *maíz*, which are considered to be female, are bundled dried canes and leaves that once held young ears of corn; these are seen by Wixáritari as the corn's male counterpart known as *Saulixika*, the name also given to the cargo of the leading shaman of the temple or the *xiriki*. Also resting on the altar are the family ancestors in the form of rock crystals, '+r+kate, wrapped in cotton and woven fabric and attached to votive arrows that are placed in a special woven or embroidered bag designed to carry offerings. Blessed water from sacred springs, rivers, or the ocean captured in glass and plastic bottles are kept directly on the *niwetari* or in offering bags that rest on it, as are collections of soils from sacred places and other objects collected from various pilgrimages and hunts. Fresh and dried peyotes brought from the San Luis Potosí desert are temporarily situated on the *niwetari* or underneath it until they are needed for ceremonies or planted in pots and small gardens in the ranch. Pieces of dried meat from hunted deer and sacrificed cattle strung on braided rope,

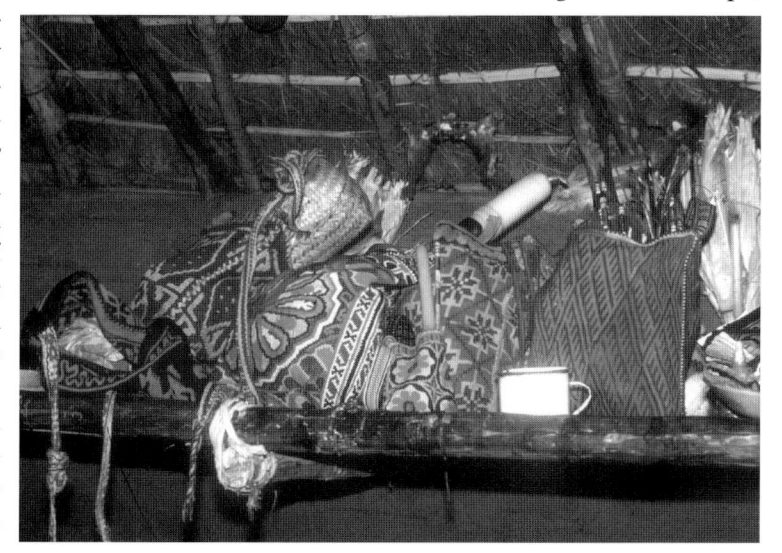

Figure 2. *Niwetari* with offerings in a family *xiriki* (photo by Stacy B. Schaefer).

as well as containers filled with the blood from these animals sit on the altar as do dried fish skewered on thin wooden sticks. Bags are hung from the *niwetari* with offerings and sacred objects, and other ritual paraphernalia, such as candles, the gourd rattles used for the children's drum ritual at harvest time, the woven basket, *takwatsi*, of individual shamans in the family containing feathered wands (*muwierite*, pl.), other power objects, and rifles used for hunting (Figure 3).

Figure 3. The *niwetari* in the family *xiriki* with offerings and lit candles during a ceremony held at the ranch. The bag hanging from the altar that the woman is handling contains a shaman's basket, *takwatsi* (photo by Stacy B. Schaefer).

Early in my field work, I lived with one of my Wixárika families and was invited to participate in the ranch ceremony to inaugurate its newly built *xiriki*. Oftentimes I slept in the *xiriki* and was able to glimpse into the daily and ritual activities related to the family god house and its altar. During my visits I participated several times in the family's *Hikuri Neixa* ceremonies, their *Tatei Neixa* ceremony, and the ceremony to welcome the return of family members, *peyoteros*, who had gone on the peyote pilgrimage. When the family pilgrims returned to the ranch, everyone crowded into the *xiriki* and peyotes that had been collected specifically for every individual in the ranch were removed from bags that the returning pilgrims had placed on the altar. These designated peyotes were blessed by prayer and the feathered power wand (*muwiere*) of the family shaman and ritually consumed by the family members who had prayed and waited for the safe return of the *peyoteros*.

On another occasion when other members in the family had returned from the peyote pilgrimage, bags and boxes filled with peyote were stored on the altar and beneath it. I was sleeping in the *xiriki* and awoke to the opening of the door by the elder shaman of the ranch. She proceeded to gaze upon the numerous peyote tops surrounding the altar, examining their sizes and shapes, and broke into a spontaneous song. I asked her what song she was singing, and she answered that she was just repeating what the peyotes were singing to her. This shaman is also renowned for her healing powers, particularly with infertile couples. During her curing sessions she also placed special offerings on the *niwetari* in the god house before instructing visiting couples to leave their offerings in sacred places as prayers directed to specific gods.

The death of a family member prompts the construction of a temporary west-facing altar in the ranch, either in the outdoor patio or in one of the other houses. A ceremony is performed to see the soul off to the other world (Anguiano 1996). According to general Wixáritari beliefs, the soul of the deceased retraces its life and then travels along the path of the sun, visiting specific locations, until it reaches the west and the ocean. The shaman performs the mortuary ceremony, singing to locate the soul on its journey and to call it back to the ranch so that living family members can bid farewell. Once the shaman has accomplished this, he sends the soul to the sky above the peyote desert where it will join other souls awaiting its arrival (Furst 1967). These altars are made specifically for the funeral ceremony. They take the form of a table; the objects placed on it are the belongings of the defunct member. If the person owned cattle or other livestock, these are oftentimes tied to the altar or nearby in the *rancho*. With the completion of the ceremony, the altar is taken down and the deceased person's most personal possessions that might be needed in the other world are buried with him or her. Another reason the altar is taken apart is as a precautionary measure to prevent the soul from returning, hungry and dangerous, bringing sickness and disease to the *rancho*, especially to children who are highly vulnerable to contracting debilitating illnesses.

The Church—The *Teyeupáni*

The Catholic church in San Andrés stands on the eastern edge of the main dirt plaza across from the local government house and jail. Originally constructed of adobe bricks in the 1700s, its outer walls were rebuilt by the community more than 15 years ago with oven-fired bricks covered with plaster and white paint. The doorway of the church faces west onto the plaza; however, most of the year, the church remains vacant with its doors closed. The major events that take place inside the church revolve around: the changing of the tribal government beginning in early January, the initiation of Lent with the ceremony of *"Las Pachitas,"* and Holy Week, *Semana Santa*.

The altar in the Church is located on the east wall facing west, and is tiered with several levels extending from the dirt floor up to around 12 feet in height; individuals climb up these tier-like steps during ritual events (Figure 4). Two large carved wooden images of Jesus Christ on the cross rest on the top tier of the altar. One of the figures is called *Tanana* (Our Godmother) and pertains to the community of San Andrés Cohamiata, while the other is named *Tatata* (Our Godfather) and belongs to the community the next mesa top over called San Miguel Waixtita, a community incorporated into the political jurisdiction of San Andrés. Each Christ figure has a caretaker—*mayordomo* in Spanish, *xaturi* in Wixárika—and numerous families assist the *xaturi* with this charge (Schaefer 2002:60, 65-69). The role of *xaturi* is a five-year cargo position. Members of a temple or ranch group may request the presence of one of these figures for a particular ceremony, and then the *xaturi* fulfills the request carrying the figure to its destination and participating in the ceremony.

There are a number of other saints that pertain to the church, including *San José* of the San José temple district; *San Andrés,* the patron saint for the temple district of the same name; *Tatsunats*i for the community of San Miguel Waixtita; *Tutukwiy+* for the temple district of Cohamiata; and *Hapaxuki,* a small Christ figure considered to be the same personage as *Partisika,* god of deer, the hunt, and scorpions. These carved wooden figures are much smaller than the two large Christs; they are usually stored and displayed in their own special boxes and cared for in the house or family shrine of their caretaker who also holds this specific cargo for five years. When ritual activities require their presence in the church, the saints are placed on the church altar; for other occasions ranch and temple members may also invite one or more of the saints along with their caretakers to other ceremonies farther away. A picture of the Virgin of Guadalupe adorns the wall above the altar, however, she is not part of the cargo system, no person is in charge of caring for her, and she does not feature predominantly in the community rituals as do all the Christs and saint figures.

My familiarity with the altar in the church and the associated Christ and saint figures began when I participated in the *Semana Santa* celebrations over a six-year period of time with my Wixárika family who were helping me complete my training to become a master weaver (see Schaefer 2002:161-163). During Holy Week these figures were removed from the altar to greet the arriving *peyoteros* at the government table of authority and given offering bowls filled with peyote (Figure 5). Later they were ritually washed, completely covered with cloths, and placed on the dirt floor of the Church where they were prayed over with burning candles and incense during the Wednesday,

Figure 4. View inside the church in San Andrés Cohamiata. There are a series of steps that lead up to the altar (photo by Antonio Vizcaino).

Thursday, and Friday of *Semana Santa.* On Saturday morning before Easter Sunday, the cloths were removed from the saints and the figures of Christ, and they were once again placed upon the Church altar.

Easter Sunday is a propitious day for shamans to lead baptism rituals for Wixárika children, and I was privy to these events on a number of occasions when, over the years, I became a godmother to six children. It was during these times that I had the best vantage point for examining the church altar. Holy water and fresh-picked flowers are left in bowls by the Christ and saint figures, as are any number of burning candles and copal incense billowing from low-fired clay incense burners or emptied sardine cans with perforated holes used for the same purpose. During the baptism, the shaman leads the godparent(s) carrying the child into the church and up the steps of the altar to stand in front of the large Christ figures and the saints. As the shaman prays, he sweeps the participants with his feathered power wand *(muwieri).* Then he anoints the child's head, followed by the godparent(s)' using holy water from the altar. The shaman requests a few coins from the godparent(s), which he passes over everyone's head and places in a niche located near the ribs of the Christ figures. I noticed that the exposed parts of the bodies of these large figures are covered with a multitude of miniature beeswax figures in human form representing Wixárika children and their parents' prayers that they may have a long life and good health.

The *Niwetari* as Resting Place for the Souls

The *niwetari,* particularly the one in the family god house, is an integral part of the beliefs and traditions of Wixárika families. The Wixárika word *"niwetari"* itself refers to the place of sons and daughters. The souls of the living, the deceased, and the yet-to-be-born rest upon the altar. It is the place, as one shaman put it "where all of the souls are presented." When a new member in the family is born there is a ceremony; the shaman, parents, and close kin gather before the fire in the outdoor patio and pray. The newborn is carried into the *xiriki.* Carefully holding the baby outstretched, its face looking toward the ceiling with the head almost touching the altar, the shaman presents this new family member to the gods and the ancestors (Figure 6).

Wixárika conceptions of the soul are multifaceted (Furst 1967). According to their ontological reasoning, there are three major components that make up the Wixárika "self." One is the *"k+puri,"* the vital essence that animates the body. The *k+puri* enters the body right before birth and departs when the body dies. The *tukari* is associated with one's life path and the process of living that life during the time of its bodily existence. The third principle, which has an eternal lifespan and most closely resembles the Western concept of soul is the *'iyari,* the "heart memory," which is seated within the heart of a person. It carries the collective memory of the ancestors and is understood to be a kind of inherited memory that can evolve and become more crystallized by following Wixárika traditions. Family members who have completed religious *cargos,* followed a shamanic path, participated in many deer hunts, traveled to Wirikuta numerous times, or sought personal esoteric knowledge have an *'iyari* that is much more greatly developed than that of others.

By middle age or older, one has accumulated enough knowledge and experience that his or her soul is very powerful and dangerous and must be neutralized into the form of an *'+r+kame,* a small shiny stone or rock crystal. Deceased

Figure 5. Wixárika government official with staffs of power in hand stands in front of the table of authority upon which rests the box containing one of the saints from the church (photo by James A. Bauml).

family members also become '+r+kame. In total, a person may have up to five '+r+kame while alive and five '+r+kame after death (Perrin 1996:417, 423-424). To neutralize the soul, a ceremony is performed by a shaman specializing in these matters; he catches the '+r+kame of the living or deceased member and presents it to the family for its care. Wrapped in cotton and fabric and attached to a votive arrow, the '+r+kame is placed in the shaman's basket, *takwatsi*, or in one's bag for offerings and rests on the altar in the *xiriki*. During ceremonies at the ranch, ritual food consisting of broth from fish, deer, sacrificed cattle or chickens is placed in bowls upon the altar for the '+r+kame. Blood from these sacrificial animals, native *maíz* beer *(nawa)*, and holy water from sacred springs and water holes are also considered food for the '+r+kame, and they are anointed with these substances. A designated member of the family takes the '+r+kame to temple ceremonies, on deer hunts, and pilgrimages. After such events, they are returned to the family altar where they will remain until power no longer emanates from them, at which time they are removed and placed in caves to join the gods. The souls contained in '+r+kame are thought to be active until they disappear; some say they travel with the sun and "regenerate matter," others say they detach from the sun causing the sun to "lose its own substance"(Perrin 1996:412, 414, 425).

The *niwetari* in the family *xiriki* is also a place where souls of the yet-to-be-born can be found. Couples having difficulty conceiving a child may seek a shaman who specializes in fertility and birthing. The shaman discusses the situation with the couple, performs a series of healing rituals, and requests they bring a votive bowl containing a piece of cotton to be placed on the altar. The cotton represents the soul of the desired child, while the bowl, I have been told by one shaman, symbolizes the womb of the mother. Throughout the curing, which may last a few days or more, the shaman communicates with the gods and pays close attention to his or her dreams. At the time of birth, the shaman often takes the role of midwife. Shortly before the baby is born, he calls on *Niwet+kame*, the goddess of souls-to-be-born and also the goddess of weaving, to provide a soul, which the shaman places inside the baby's body. This goddess' name means "the splendor of the sun." The shaman in the role of midwife is called *tiniwet+wame*, a term that conveys the idea of bringing light into the world, like the rays of the sun (Schaefer 2002:250-251).

Marking the Sun's Path

The path of the sun is of fundamental importance to *niwetari* traditions. The sun, known as *"tau"* in secular terms and *"Wexik+a"* when in reference to the sun deity, is considered to be life's essence. Wixáritari intentionally orient the *niwetari* in the *tuki* and in the *xiriki* to mark its luminous path. The shamans who spoke to me about the sun's path explained that the sun has five locations or stations that it passes in the daytime and the same number of stations when it travels through the underworld at night. These day-time segments are dawn, mid-morning, noon, mid-afternoon and sunset. The nighttime markers are dusk, mid-evening, midnight, early morning around 2 or 3 a.m., and the period of darkness before dawn, around 5 a.m. On its daily journey, the sun illuminates the *niwetari* in the *xiriki* or *tuki* through the east-facing doorway as it rises during the morning. From noon until sunset, rays of sunlight enter the structure through the beams and thatching of the roof. In ceremonies that occur at night, the shaman will sing the entire night. Sitting by the fire with his special

Figure 6. Shaman of the family ranch presents her newborn grandchild in front of the altar of the xiriki (photo by Stacy B. Schaefer).

mat, *'itari*, close by, he places on the mat a circular mirror, which he uses to view the sun's nocturnal path through the underworld. To one side of the mat is a sacred hole in the outdoor dirt patio of the temple or ranch compound or inside the temple into which the shaman's song is transported. When the sun has reached one of its stations in the underworld, the shaman indicates this to the participants and they take their offerings from the *niwetari*, circle the fire and the shaman, and then return these back to the altar and resume their sitting positions. One shaman and her son explained the nocturnal journey of the sun in this way:

> [The gods] know everything that is happening during the night, everything below. Below [the sun] is walking, and all the *mara'akate* [shamans] when they are performing a ceremony, when they sing, they know everything that is happening below the earth. When the sun is rising they sing a very beautiful song. When it has made five passes under the ground to reach Reu'unaxi, sometimes the *mara'akame* sees it. *Kauyumarie* [the messenger god] sees it as if it were a sunflower that closes and afterwards when [the sun] rises, the flower awakens and opens up. When it opens up this means that the sun is awake to travel once again to the ocean [Schaefer 2002:220].

The Temple

The annual movement of the sun is reflected in the architecture of the temple and the placement of the *niwetari* against its back wall where it is illuminated by the rays of the morning sun entering through the doorway of the structure (the doorway and windows in some temples are located between 70-80° NE) (Figure 7). A comprehensive study of the Wixárika *tuki* and ethnoastronomy can be found in "The Cosmos Contained: The Place Where Sun and Moon Meet" (Schaefer 1996b). My focus for this paper is specifi-

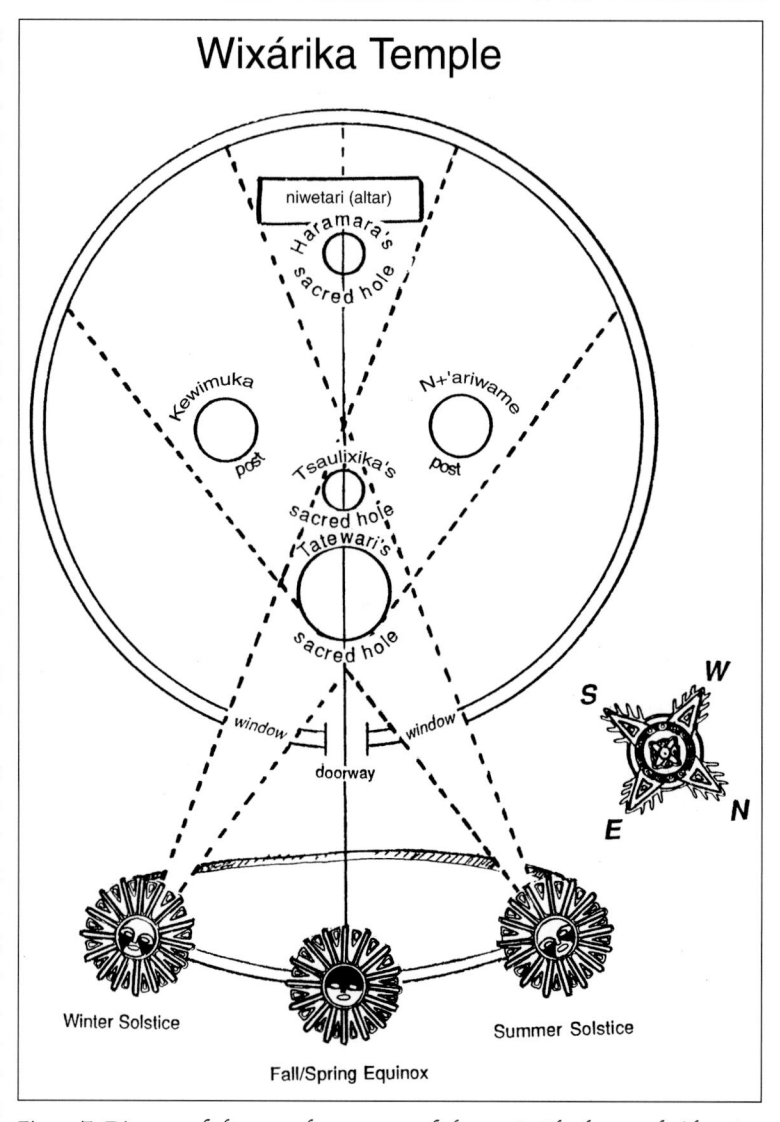

Figure 7. Diagram of the annual movement of the sun inside the temple (drawing by Nancy Moyer).

cally on the altar, its location in the temple, and the objects placed upon it that correspond to particular rituals performed throughout the annual cycle.

The temple is divided in half along an east-west axis from the doorway across the fireplace, between the two large posts that hold up the roof, to the altar lining the back wall. The temple members who are the cargo holders are also divided into two groups; the members in charge of the rainy season rituals are seated inside along the south side of the temple from the doorway to the altar, while the dry season cargo holders sit along the north side of the temple wall between the entrance and the altar.

Throughout the year the light from the sun enters the temple and moves along the back wall of the altar marking the annual solar cycle. At the time of the fall equinox, the sun shines straight into the temple, illuminating in succession the steps of the altar as it ascends into the sky. Tender young *maíz* and squash are placed on the altar marking the commencement of *Tatei Neixa*, the harvest ceremony, also known as the drum ceremony with young Wixárika children as a central focus (Furst and Anguiano 1976). The winter solstice in December is the time when the sun has reached its southernmost position; the rays of the sun enter the temple lighting the northwest part of the back wall. The harvest has been completed and temple members bring for the *maíz* goddess, *Niwetsika*, their sacred ears of mature *maíz* bundled with woven belts. These bundles of *maíz* are placed on the altar so that they may greet the sun.

By the time of the spring equinox, the rays of the sun have returned to enter directly into the temple and climb up the altar. Deer masks and other ritual paraphernalia made from deer or associated with deer hunting such as rifles and deer snares and bowls of fresh peyote recently harvested in the peyote desert may be situated on the altar or placed in bags hung from the *niwetari*. Around this time, temple members ceremoniously welcome the return of the peyote pilgrims, who are also the deer hunters. Wixáritari consider this time as the beginning of another year, the time of light, and they refer to this part of the annual cycle as daytime. In June, with the arrival of the summer solstice, the sun has reached its most northerly position, and it shines into the temple illuminating the southwest part of the wall to the left of the altar. This marks the rainy season when ritual activities revolve around rain-making, preparing the soil, and planting *maíz* and associated field crops. Community members arrive at the temple, their offering bags filled with bundles of sacred ears of *maíz* as well as dried stalks and leaves from the harvested *maíz*. Fresh and dried peyote, dried deer meat, and dried fish are also slipped into bags, all of which are hung from the altar. The *Hikuri Neixa* ceremony takes place during this time marking the end of the dry season, the beginning of the planting season, and the initiation of the rains and darkness; it is a time they refer to as nighttime.

Daylight also enters the temple through the openings in the roof at either side of the two large posts that hold up the ceiling frames. During certain times of the year the midday sun enters the temple through these gaps in the roofing material and shines down, casting beams of light onto the altar. An opening in the west wall of the temple above the altar enables light from the late afternoon to enter the temple before the sun descends below the mountains to the west, finally sinking into the salty waves of the ocean.

The Church

The *Semana Santa* ceremony in the church is performed, I am told, to bring in a new year, and to ensure that the sun will be renewed. As I mentioned earlier, it is also an auspicious time to baptise children. The act of removing the Christs and saint figures from the altar, covering them with cloths, and laying them to rest on the floor of the church on Wednesday afternoon of Holy Week symbolizes that a ritual time of darkness and chaos has begun. Wixárika youths assigned the cargo roles of the *"judios"* are in charge of the community and act out their fiendish, yet comic roles as the evil ones who killed Christ. Meanwhile, inside the church, the caretakers of the figures keep watch over their charges by the light of votive candles, burning copious amounts of copal incense that fill the air. Then, at dawn on Saturday morning, the Christ figures and saints are "brought back to life." Their caretakers uncover them, and leading shamans help place them upon the altar once again. While the Christ figures are positioned in their upright positions on the top tier, Wixárika violin and guitar music resounds in the church and the church doors are opened wide. In honor of this occasion cattle with their feet tethered are dragged, one by one, into the church, passing families, temple groups, and church and government cargo holders. Each animal is slid into place in the center of the dirt floor of the church, its head and neck resting above the cavity in the floor, the mouth of the earth goddess, where it is sacrificed. The throat is slit with a knife to allow blood to be spilled into the hole; the remaining blood from the animal is collected in bowls and used to anoint offerings held by the individual groups. The members of a group then climb the steps of the altar to anoint the Christ and saint figures. The sacrificial ritual lasts for many hours; during one *Semana Santa* in which I participated more than 40 bulls and cows were sacrificed that day in the church. All of this is done to give health and vigor to the sun, the saints, Christ, the gods, the people, their animals, and their future crops.

The *niwetari* in the church faces west and is opposite to the eastern orientation of the altar in the *tuki* and the *xiriki*. This observation prompted my asking one of my shaman consultants and her son about these differences, assuming that their answers would most likely address the movement of the sun. Instead, their response provided an equally intriguing mythical, historical, and geographical explanation. They explained that the reason for the two different altar orientations had to do with the origins and migrations of the gods and the church-associated divine entities. The Wixárika gods, the *kakauyarixi*, they said, were born in the ocean in the west. From there they traveled to Wirikuta, the peyote desert in the east, and eventually they arrived in the sierra. That is why the *niwetari* in the *xiriki* and in the *tuki* are situated to the west, where the *kakauyarixi* were born, facing east towards Wirikuta. The church altar is located on the east wall facing west because the deer god, *Kauyumarie* invited the little Christ figure *Hapaxuki* and *San José* to come to the sierra. They came from the east; only later on did the other Christ figures and saints follow. Interestingly, the Spanish missionaries who arrived at the end of the 17th century and early 18th century to colonize the Wixárika came from the east, from Zacatecas.

The *Niwetari* and the Sun in Wixárika Cosmography

On the path to the peyote desert, Wirikuta, there exists a sacred area called Niwetaritsie, meaning "place of the altar." Wixárika pilgrims pass here on their way to Wirikuta and on their return journey to the sierra. Niwetaritsie consists of five sacred spots; traveling east towards Wirikuta the first place is marked by a large rock that lies flat on the ground. It resembles a human form; a naturally occuring band of rock cutting across the middle of this human-shaped rock gives the appearance of a knotted rope across the middle of it. This is the place of the earth goddess '+*tuanaka* and was traditionally where everyone was purified. Since the highway does not pass this spot, few pilgrims visit it and the purification ritual is carried out at whatever location the leading shaman has dreamed. Each member on the pilgrimage confesses out loud to the group the names of the people other than one's spouse(s) with whom he or she has had sexual relations. A knot is tied by the shaman in a rope for each name and the rope is passed over the person's head and down the body. After all have confessed, the rope is then burned in the fire. Upon completing this ritual, the attending shaman anoints everyone with sacred water, and each participant is given a new name and a ritual *compañero* or *compañera*. Initiates on the pilgrimage are considered young and highly vulnerable, regardless of their age. As a protective measure, they are blindfolded with a bandana, which is not removed until they reach Tatei Matinieri, a spring in the desolate Zacatecas countryside on the edge of a small town (Furst 1969, 1972; Myerhoff 1974). From there they travel to the remaining three locations of Niwetaritsie and leave offerings.[3] Eventually the pilgrims reach Wirikuta where they pray and leave offerings, gather and ritually consume peyote. Then they travel onwards to leave offerings at the most easterly site in their sacred geography, the dormant volcano known as Reu'unaxi, the place where the sun was born.

On their return trip home, the pilgrims once again cross Niwetaritsie and become part of the diurnal path of the sun (Schaefer 1989; 2002:194-195). One shaman consultant, who completed a ten-year temple *cargo* of *Nauxa* (see Schaefer 1996a:152-153), the one who recites the myths at every sacred place and carries peyote selected by the pilgrims for the return journey through Niwetaritsie, explained to me the manner in which the pilgrims transverse this sacred place. He calls the five sacred spots steps of the sun's ladder to the sky. At dawn the pilgrims are located at the first place; each member is given one peyote to eat. Then the pilgrims begin walking the entire day across this large expanse of desert. Around mid-morning the pilgrims reach the next step of the sun and consume another peyote top. At noon, the pilgrims have reached the third step and consume a third peyote. Mid-afternoon, the pilgrims eat a fourth peyote marking the fourth step of the sun. Late afternoon, the fifth peyote is eaten as the sun is setting and the pilgrims have reached the end of this area of the desert known as Niwetaritsie which leads up to the sierra. This consultant commented that "sometimes people become inebriated after eating the first peyote, some after the third peyote, others after the fourth, the fifth... There they become inebriated and converse with god...when some are *empeyotado* they understand things, others encounter different things...not everyone is going to hear the same thing (have the same experience). And that is how it is done, that is why it is called Niwetaritsie."

Conclusion

The *niwetari*. and the traditions that surround it, inextricably link the lives of Wixáritari to their families, community, to the many dimensions of their cosmological world and their place within it. The basic elements for their physical survival, as manifest in offerings of *maíz*, deer meat, beef, fish, and water and the core of their spiritual survival, represented in candles, peyote, and family '+r+kate, are actually laid out upon the *niwetari*. Like a stairway to the sky, Wixáritari situate the altar to mark the path of the sun through time and space. The altar brings together the upper and lower worlds to the middle world of the living; it brings the Wixárika gods to the ceremonies, incorporates select syncretized Catholic ideology and draws to this resting place the souls of the living, the souls of the dead, and the souls yet-to-be-born. As with all important elements in Wixárika culture, the continuation of these altar traditions depends upon how well they are adapted by Wixáritari to changing times and needs. In closing, I offer two brief anecdotal examples that address the mutability of these altar traditions to accommodate change.

On a hill above the city of Tepic, capital of the state of Nayarit, a Wixárika community called Zitacua has been established. Its inhabitants are, for the most part, more acculturated compared to those from the sierra, and many of them are bilingual school teachers in the outlying *pueblos* or are experienced city dwellers. Here an interesting type of syncretism is taking form. These Wixáritari had been living scattered around Tepic and wanted to find land to establish their own community. They called upon a shaman-singer to perform a ceremony so that the gods would direct them to this land. The shaman identified the location as a hill overlooking the city of Tepic, which the gods had marked with a large rock in the shape of a sheep's head. Although the plot of land was already destined for development into an expensive *mestizo* neighborhood, one of the leaders of this group convinced the governor of Nayarit to grant the land to them (Schaefer 1996b:367-368, 493). The group erected a temple to mark their community, resplendent with a *mesa*-style *niwetari* (Figure 8). As part of the temple altar a large painted image of the Virgin of Guadalupe, something more likely to be found in a church in Wixárika territory and more closely associated with popular Mexican Catholicism than with traditional Wixárika religious practices, hangs from the wall behind it. A number of Wixárika traditions are practiced by some of the members of Zitacua, some of the people carry out major ceremonies in the temple, some even go on the peyote pilgrimage; nevertheless, elements from the larger Mexican culture, such as the prominence of the Virgin of Guadalupe, are making their way into the temple altar traditions of this community.

Another example of the adaptability of the *niwetari* is when my Wixárika friends, who are also my *compadres* (god-parent relations) came to

Figure 8. The niwetari inside the temple of the Wixárika community Zitacua (photo by Lourdes Pacheco).

visit me at my home in McAllen, Texas. Their visit coincided with the period of Lent leading up to Easter in the Catholic calendar. They brought with them their bags filled with their sacred objects: holy water, beeswax candles, prayer arrows, and the family's votive bowl containing deer hair and a miniature ceramic deer. At midday on Fridays during their visit they lit the candle, and, on top of the table-like crate covered with decorative fabric I had in my living room they placed their sacred objects, next to the menorah and Shabbat candle holders given to me by my mother. Before they prayed over the objects and drank sipfuls of the holy water they had brought, my *compadre* added to the altar the peyote they had gathered from our recent visit to the peyote fields of south Texas. This makeshift altar was now complete as a resting place for their sacred objects and for their communication with the gods.

End Notes

1. The orthography I use for writing the Wixárika language follows the linguistic style used by José Luis Iturrioz Leza and his colleagues at the Departamento de Estudios de Lenguas Indígenas at the Universidad de Guadalajara. The use of /+/ represents the vowel in Wixárika language that sounds very nazalized and is halfway between /i/ and /u/ and is unrounded like /i/.

2. In this paper I discuss what my consultants acknowledge to be altars, which they refer to as *niwetarite*. I learned from my Wixárika consultants that contrary to my first impressions of the shaman's mat, *'itari*, as a type of transportable altar, they did not view it in this manner. Hence, I have chosen to exclude the shaman's mat from this discussion. Interestingly the shaman's mat is more centrally related to hunting and the origins of deer hunting traditions.

3. Jim Bauml, ethnobotanist at the Arboretum of L.A. County and I have participated in three pilgrimages to Wirikuta with two shamans and their families. On the journey we have visited several of the places that are part of the sacred area known as Niwetaritse. We intend to visit all of these spots, record information on the history and mythology associated with them, as well as collect and document plant specimens.

> Stacy B. Schaefer
> Department of Anthropology
> California State University, Chico
> Chico, CA 95929-0400

References Cited

Anguiano, Marina
  1996 *Müüqui Cuevixa*: "Time to Bid the Dead Farewell." In: Stacy B. Schaefer and Peter T. Furst, eds., *People of the Peyote: Huichol Indian History, Culture and Survival*, pp. 377-388. Albuquerque: University of New Mexico Press.

Bauml, James A.
  1994 *Ethnobotany of the Huichol People of Mexico*. Ph.D. Dissertation, Claremont Graduate School.

Furst, Peter T.
  1967 Huichol Conceptions of the Soul. *Folklore Americas* 27:39-106.

  1969 *To Find Our Life: The Peyote Hunt of the Huichol Indians of Mexico*. 61-minute 16-mm film and VHS videocassette. Los Angeles: UCLA Latin American Center Media Division.

  1972 To Find Our Life: Peyote Among the Huichol Indians of Mexico. In: Peter T. Furst, ed., *Flesh of the Gods: The Ritual Use of Hallucinogens*, pp. 136-184. New York: Praeger.

Furst, Peter T., and Marina Anguiano
  1976 "To Fly As Birds": Myth and Ritual As Agents of Enculturation Among the Huichol Indians of Mexico. In: Johannes Wilbert, ed., *Enculturation in Latin America: An Anthology*, pp. 95-181. Los Angeles: UCLA Latin American Center Publications.

Furst, Peter T., and Stuart D. Scott
  1975 La escalera de Padre Sol: Un paralelo etnográfico-arqueológico desde el occidente de México. *Boletín del Instituto Nacional de Antropología e Historia de México* 12:13-20.

Myerhoff, Barbara G.
  1974 *Peyote Hunt: The Sacred Journey of the Huichol Indians*. Ithaca: Cornell University Press.

Perrin, Michel
  1996 The *Urukáme*, A Crystallization of the Soul: Death and Memory. In: Stacy B. Schaefer and Peter T. Furst, eds., *People of the Peyote: Huichol Indian History, Culture and Survival*, pp.403-428. Albuquerque: University of New Mexico Press.

Schaefer, Stacy B.
  1989 The Loom and Time in the Huichol World. *Journal of Latin American Lore* 15(2):179-194.

  1996a The Crossing of the Souls: Peyote, Perception, and Meaning among the Huichol Indians. In: Stacy B. Schaefer and Peter T. Furst, eds., *People of the Peyote: Huichol Indian History, Culture and Survival*, pp.138-168. Albuquerque: University of New Mexico Press.

  1996b The Cosmos Contained: The Temple Where Sun and Moon Meet. In: Stacy B. Schaefer and Peter T. Furst, eds., *People of the Peyote: Huichol Indian History, Culture and Survival*, pp. 332-373. Albuquerque: University of New Mexico Press.

  2002 *To Think With A Good Heart: Wixárika Women, Weavers, and Shamans*. Salt Lake City: University of Utah Press.

Southern Mexico and Guatemala

In My Hill, In My Valley: The Importance of Place in Ancient Maya Ritual

James E. Brady

As author of the only archaeological presentation in the symposium, I draw upon my background and experience to address two issues. The first is the antiquity of the *mesa* as an indigenous ritual stage. This is an important question because these tables are so universally referred to in indigenous languages by the term *mesa* that one must wonder if the word and its referent were not borrowed at the same time by native cultures that had no counterpart for either. While the *mesa* can take a variety of physical forms (see Sharon this volume), I will restrict my analysis to two types commonly reported in modern ethnography of the Maya area as possible regional variations. If archaeological evidence for the presence of the *mesa* as a material artifact can be produced then there is a solid basis for proposing that the modern indigenous cosmological associations were probably present in some form in the ancient context as well.

The first form of *mesa* is the low, one-piece platform often referred to as a *banco* or bench. This form appears most often in the Maya highlands of Chiapas and Guatemala. The second form is the simple bush table created by sticking two pairs of "Y" shaped stakes into the ground. A cross member is set in the notches of each pair and longer sticks are laid over the cross-members. This form appears to be common in ethnographic descriptions from Yucatán.

The Antiquity of the *Mesa*

The *banco* as a form is quite ancient, at least as a seat or a throne. Three individuals are shown seated on such benches on one side of Kaminaljuyu Monument 65, dating to the Late Preclassic (Figure 1). Jonathan Kaplan (1995) has shown that the table-altar/throne tradition dates back to the Middle Preclassic on the South Coast of Guatemala and probably relates to earlier Olmec altar/thrones (Grove 1973). Unfortunately, I know of no iconographic representations of *bancos* being used as altars in rituals. Thomas Gage, however, does give a mid-17th century account of finding a *banco* used as a table while investigating native rituals being carried out in a cave. He says:

> At the entrance the cave was broad, and went a little forward, but when we were in, we found it turned on the left hand toward the mountain, and not far, for within two rods we found the idol standing upon a low stool covered with a linen cloth (Gage 1958:281).

There is, however, solid archaeological evidence for the antiquity of the use of these *bancos*. Parts of four Late Classic examples were recovered from the Cueva de "Las Banquetas" in the Central Depression of Chiapas (Rodríquez Betancourt 1987:108). Brian Hayden (1987:176) suggests that they may have functioned as ritual tables in much the same way as they do today. On the other side of the Maya area, Keith Prufer (n.d.) has found two *bancos* during his work with the Maya Mountains Archaeological Project in southern Belize in 1995. The first probably dates to the Late Classic and has very much the form of a *mesa* in that it is 2 m long (Figure 2). The second was found in Bats'ub/25 Flight Cave near

Douglas Sharon, ed., *Mesas & Cosmologies in Mesoamerica*. San Diego Museum Papers 42, 2003.

Figure 1. Individual depicted on Kaminaljuyu Monument 65 seated on a *banco*.

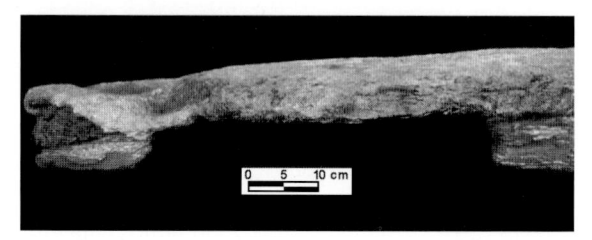

Figure 2. Large *banco* nearly 2 m long found in a cave in the Maya Mountains of Belize (photograph courtesy of Keith Prufer).

Unión Camp. The four-legged rosewood bench, 35 cm x 17 cm x 8 cm high, was found with an Early Classic burial (Figure 3). The surface of the bench had traces of red pigment, which is interesting in that I have discovered several prepared surfaces in caves that had red pigment sprinkled over them. A radiocarbon analysis dated the bench to A.D. 170 +/- 80, in other words, to the Late Preclassic. A special exhibit in the summer of 2002 at the Regional Anthropological Museum Palacio Cantón in Merida displayed a *banco* re-

Figure 3. A Late Preclassic wooden *banco* recovered from Bats'ub/25 Flight Cave (photograph courtesy of Keith Prufer).

covered from the Cenote of Sacrifice at Chichén Itzá by one of the projects conducted in the 1960s (Piña Chan 1970). Thus, there appears to be good evidence that the low *banco* carved from a single piece of wood definitely has pre-Columbian roots that extend back into the Preclassic. Furthermore, while the ethnographic use of the *banco* is noted most frequently in the Maya highlands, the archaeological evidence suggests that, prior to contact, it was used in both the northern and southern lowlands as well.

The evidence for the field table type of *mesa* is more difficult to find because all of the individual pieces tend to be small and the entire structure would be lost as soon as the four supports collapse. Nevertheless, indirect evidence of this type of *mesa* use has been recovered at Naj Tunich. Naj Tunich is a large cave site located in southeastern Peten, Guatemala (Figure 4). The cave's entrance chamber is a huge room running more than 150 m east to west (Figure 5). The eastern third of the chamber contains a natural rise that was modified though filling and leveling behind a series of retaining walls (Figure 6) into a two-tiered balcony structure that rises 14 m above the floor of the cave. A small opening off the upper level of the balcony gives access to the 3.5 km of tunnel passage, most of which is over 15 m in diameter. The tunnels contain the largest corpus of hieroglyphic writing ever found in a Maya cave. I have recently proposed on a number of lines of evidence that Naj Tunich functioned as a major regional pilgrimage center (Brady n.d.).

The balcony was the central ceremonial stage of Naj Tunich with the retaining walls probably serving to restrict access to the upper levels to ritual specialists and those of high status. Strati-

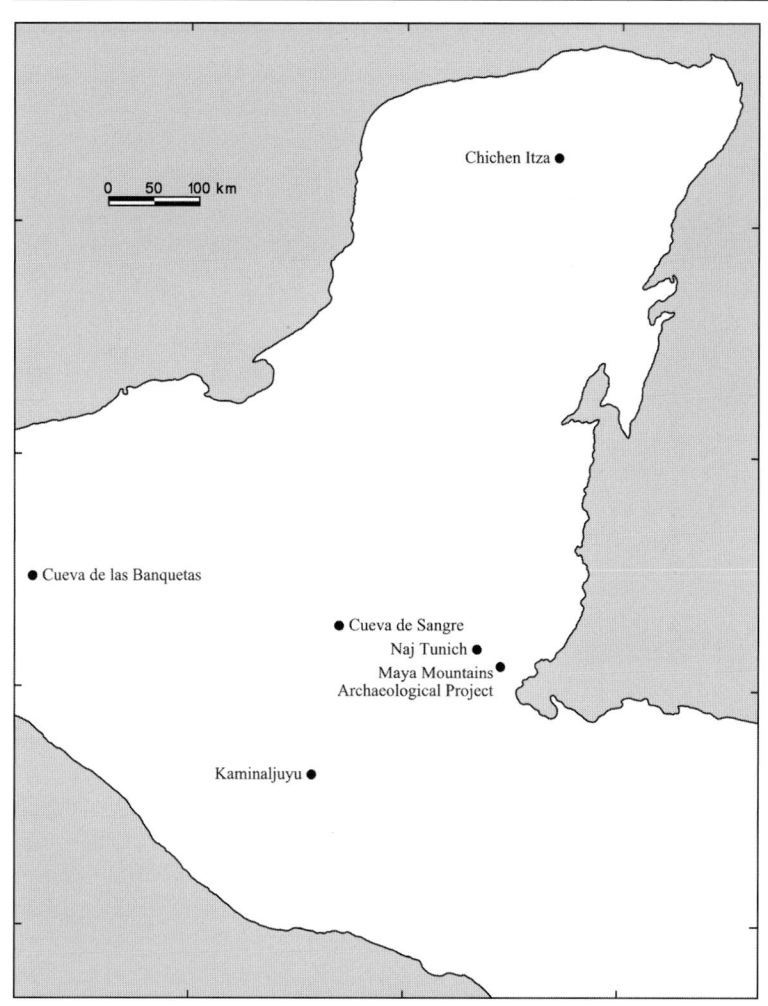

In My Hill, In My Valley: The Importance of Place in Ancient Maya Ritual

Figure 4. Map of the Maya area showing the location of caves.

Figure 5. A view of the entrance chamber at Naj Tunich; note the person standing in the middle of the floor for scale (photograph courtesy of Allan Cobb).

graphic excavations were carried out on the upper level of the balcony. A 2 x 2 m pit was opened along the western cave wall but the western portion of the pit yielded little information because a travertine floor was encountered less than 10 cm below the surface. The eastern half of the pit, however, contained a series of superimposed use-floors that were marked by thin layers of caliche. The floors were stained a dark black by charcoal and perhaps the smoke from copal incense. All of this overlay a layer of heavily compacted sterile yellow clay. The soil characteristics are important because of the dramatic differences in color and compaction between the dark cultural levels as opposed to the yellow non-cultural levels.

In scraping across the surface of the yellow clay, a number of dark circles appeared that resembled post holes (Figure 7). These differed from holes that had been created by dripping water in that the natural holes tended to be shallow and conical in shape. By contrast, the post-holes were deeper and straight-sided. In several cases the post-holes had been plugged by a rock or mud so that when the obstruction was removed, the empty shaft was revealed. Eight of the 11 post-holes had diameters between 6 and 9 cm, much too small to have been supports for anything but small, light constructions. The largest hole was 15 cm in diameter and was equidistant from the cave wall to a similar sized feature (16 cm in diameter and 50 cm deep) just outside of the pit. Because these two holes were similar in size, and so much larger than any of the other holes, they were the only two that could be reasonably paired as having belonged to the same feature. These two holes were separated by about a meter and a half and so probably would have supported a tabletop slightly over 2 m in length.

The large number of post-holes in this one restricted area suggests that literally hundreds, if not thousands, of *mesas* had been set up on the balcony at Naj Tunich during the centuries of uti-

Figure 6. The balcony structure at Naj Tunich showing some of the retaining walls used in construction.

Figure 7. Excavation on the upper level of the balcony at Naj Tunich showing the post holes from mesa construction.

lization of the site. The ceramic chronology documents a utilization from the Late Preclassic to the Late Classic, between 700 and 1000 years from 300 B.C. to A.D. 800. Evidence similar to that reported here from Naj Tunich may have been found at another site in Belize. MacLeod and Puleston (1978:72) state that, "In one cave entrance, excavations this year have yielded large numbers of post holes in otherwise sterile deposits, suggesting the erection of temporary structures perhaps akin to that of the modern Yukatek *ch'a chàak,* a ceremony in which the rain gods are offered maize, *balche* and sacrificial fowls." Although they do not specifically call these *mesas,* it appears to be what they are referring to. Thus the field-table form of *mesa* also appears to have a long pre-contact history. The utilization spans the same period of time as the *bancos* found by Prufer just on the other side of the Belize - Guatemala border from Naj Tunich. This indicates that both forms of *mesas* were in regular use in the southern Maya lowlands.

Once it is established that the *mesa* was a component of pre-Columbian Maya ritual paraphernalia, it is possible to identify other forms. Stone altars are the features that appear to be the most obviously related. While altars are frequently reported in caves, the form is extremely variable. At Naj Tunich, an altar in Operation VII is simply a pile of rough stones topped by a rock that projects vertically from the top at a 45° angle. The necks of two ceramic vessels had been placed on the projecting stone (Brady et al. 1992:78, Stone 1995:128-129). There is, however, no flat surface anywhere on the feature, and I am reluctant to assign the function and cosmological associations of *mesas* to altars that lack a flat, rectangular surface. A flat, rectangular altar has been found and will be discussed below.

In the ethnographic context, very ephemeral *mesas* can be defined by simply laying a blanket on the ground. Little, if any, evidence of this type of *mesa* or the associated ritual would remain for the archaeologist to find. What may have been an analogous behavior was recovered in a muddy trough at the Cueva de Sangre at Dos Pilas. On one occasion, a large flat rock was moved to reveal a prepared surface beneath that had been created by sprinkling a red mineral pigment on the ground. Two bone awls or weaving picks, also covered in red pigment, were lying on the prepared surface. A portion of the surface had been preserved when water-born silts covered the pigment. A second surface was discovered when the sticky clay silt adhered to an archaeologist's boot and was pulled away from the layer of pigment. The accidental discovery of two similar features suggests that this very simple form of *mesa* may have been regularly utilized in the rituals at the Cueva de Sangre.

The Meaning of *Mesas* in Caves

Over the last several decades it has become well established that caves are among the most important features in the sacred landscape (Brady 1997, Brady and Veni 1992, Heyden 1981, Stone 1995, Thompson 1975). Because caves are a focus of Maya ritual and *mesas* play a role in so many ceremonies, it is not surprising to find evidence of *mesas* in this context. Caves, however, are a unique setting that impart a special meaning to rituals and the paraphernalia used in them. This is particularly true of a great site like Naj Tunich. I would like to delve into the special significance of the *mesas* discovered at Naj Tunich.

It is recognized that the *mesa* is a cosmogram that defines the cosmic center and the four quarters that spread out from it. The four quarters are marked very explicitly on the *mesa* by the Ch'orti' Maya who place a stone in each of the directions. The four sacred stones, ideally spherical and all the same size, are gathered from a sacred pool (Girard 1962:23). The center is marked by a fifth stone that is slightly larger than the other four. All space, from the *mesa*, to the house, to the village, to the world, consists of four quarters and a center point (Redfield and Villa Rojas 1962:114). William Hanks (1984:136) says that "There is not a single type of ceremony performed by shamans that does not embody the directional principle."

The center is further seen as the *axis mundi* where the earthly level is connected to a celestial level above and an underworld level below. The problem in interpretation is the tendency to equate caves with the underworld. The association of caves with the underworld received its most explicit elaboration in Barbara MacLeod and Dennis Puleston's (1978) *Pathways into Darkness: The Search for the Road to Xibalba*. Their model of the underworld was constructed from the *Popol Vuh* as well as from Lacandon ethnography. In the *Popol Vuh*, the underworld is portrayed as a place full of dangers and presided over by the malevolent underworld deities. In the absence of serious analysis of caves either ethnographically or archaeologically, the attribution seemed appropriate and so was applied with little question for the next 20 years.

My own reservations about the association of caves with the underworld were aroused by observation of modern Maya cave ceremonies in which the attitude of the participants was very different from what one would expect of a trip to the underworld. The ceremonies were also not dedicated to underworld deities. In modern Q'eqchi' Maya religion, the most important indigenous figure is the *Tzuultaq'a*, often referred to as the "Earth Lord" in English (Adams and Brady 1994). The name literally means "hill-valley" and has counterparts in many Maya languages, suggesting that this represents a pan-Maya concept. The term *tzuultaq'a* also refers to a recognized geographical entity (the hill-valley) so that the Earth Lord is clearly a personification and deification of landscape tied to the Amerindian concept of a sacred, animate Earth. Within a hill-valley the most sacred place is the cave, often referred to as a "stone house" because it is the dwelling place of the *Tzuultaq'a*. But the cave is not important simply as a dwelling of the deity. *Xetish*, an extremely important Ixil Maya cave, literally means "where once there dwelt a god" (Lincoln 1945:95-96). The cave remained important even in the absence of the deity because the power ultimately resided in the earth and the cave was the heart of the earth.

It is also clear in ethnographies that many of the properties MacLeod and Puleston attributed to the underworld are associated with *Earth* in indigenous thought. Thus, it is the Earth Lord that is petitioned for rain and crop fertility. Where ancestors are important, they reside within the sacred mountain, a symbol of the earth, and not of the underworld. Furthermore, I have been impressed with the fact that the underworld and underworld related deities do not appear to play a significant role in day-to-day indigenous life or thinking. For the last five years, I have stressed the role of *Earth* in the interpretation of Mesoamerican caves. In returning to the analysis of the *mesa*, I would note that action revolves around the top of the table, which represents the earthly plain and I would further argue that the cave also represents an intense expression of this level.

As the result of a number of discoveries over the last several years, I have come to believe that *place* was enormously important in Maya cosmology. I have also begun to suspect that many caves carried a far more important and specific meaning beyond their simply being access points to the sacred earth. Let me put this in a larger theoretical framework. Geographer Erich Isaac has proposed that, as ideal polar opposites, there are two basic religious orientations. The first seeks the justification of human existence in the act of creation itself while the second orientation finds it in a divine charter or covenant. Ritual in the second case will repeatedly reference the covenant and landscape modifications will be minimal. In societies that see creation as the central justification of human existence, Isaac (1962:12) says that "the attempt will be made to reproduce the cosmic plan in the landscape with greater or lesser effect upon the land, depending on the elaborateness of reproduction attempted." While the concept of the covenant is not unknown in Mesoamerica, religion definitely focuses on the act of creation. The importance of the concept of world creation has been seriously under-appreciated, especially by archaeologists. Mircea Eliade, however, points to this as one of the fundamental concepts in religion. He says:

> The paramount time of origins is the time of the cosmogony, the instant that saw the appearance of the most immediate of realities, the world. This...is the reason the cosmogony serves as the paradigmatic model for every creation, for every kind of doing. It is for this same reason that cosmogonic time serves as the model for all sacred times (Eliade 1959:81).

Any doubt about the orientation in ancient Mesoamerica around the act of creation should be dispelled by Angel García-Zambrano's discussion of contact period rituals of foundation throughout Mesoamerica. The rituals were performed at the founding of a new settlement and they established the boundaries of that community. He notes that groups attempted to find a spot with certain types of features and that they would often bypass ecologically superior locations that lacked them. He says that:

> Essentially, Mesoamerican migrants searched for an environment with specific characteristics that comprised several symbolic levels.... Such a place had to recall the mythical moment when the earth was created: an aquatic universe framed by four mountains with a fifth elevation protruding in the middle of the water. The mountain at the core had to be dotted with caves and springs, and sometimes surrounded by smaller hills. A setting like this duplicated, and forever would freeze, the primordial scene when the waters and the sky separated and the earth sprouted upwards (García-Zambrano 1994:217-218).

As mentioned above, a number of recent discoveries suggest that many caves were thought to represent the cave of origin. Space does not permit me to detail these here. Several locations that closely resemble García-Zambrano's primordial landscape have been located along with their associated caves. I have also documented two artificial caves, one in Central Mexico (Aguilar et al. n.d.) and the other in the Maya area (Brady 1991) that were built as models of the seven-chambered cave of origin, the Chicomoztoc or the Vucub Pec. Artificial caves are important because their form is the result of decisions of their makers rather than the whim of nature so that elaborate caves provide clues about what caves in general were supposed to mean. I now strongly suspect that a large class of caves was probably understood to have specifically represented the cave of origin in indigenous thought. Did all caves represent the Chicomoztoc or Vucub Pec? At this point, I don't think so! In that case, which ones did?

David Stuart's (Vogt and Stuart n.d.) recent decipherment of the glyph for *ch'en* or cave has

Figure 8. A stalagmite occupies a dramatic position near the center of the chamber at Naj Tunich in which the mesa was found.

provided new insights into the importance of these features in ancient inscriptions. Simon Martin (2001:178) has suggested that, while meaning cave, many times the glyph may actually be referring to a community. If so, *ch'en* may function like the nahuatl word for community, *altépetl*, which literally means "water-filled mountain" (Broda 1996:460). Thus across Mesoamerica, people appear to have been inseparably identified with either the sacred cave or the sacred mountain. I suspect that all of the major caves, the caves that were the focus of group or community identity, were thought to be the cave of origin of that group of people. Given the importance that Isaac and Eliade assign to the act of creation, this has tremendous implications for our understanding the role of caves in defining *place*. The place of creation is the living justification of human existence and defines the center of the cosmos because the great acts of creation always occur at the center. Many of the great caves such as Naj Tunich carry the imagery of the center a step further by containing huge ribbed stalagmitic columns (Figure 8). These formations have been identified by native informants as ceiba trees, the tree of life that stands at the center and holds up the sky (MacLeod and Puleston 1978:74). This fits the *imago mundi*: the place of creation at the heart of the earth where the huge stone trunk of the ceiba reaches from floor to ceiling and perhaps beyond.

The notion of centrality was reinforced at Naj Tunich by virtue of its being a pilgrimage center (Brady n.d.). As Turner and Turner (1978: 22-23) note, for the pilgrim in his hometown, the distant pilgrimage center is seen as being located in the chaotic wilderness. Once the trip commences, however, the perspective changes to a trek through the wilderness to reach the sacred center. As the destination draws near, the pilgrim enters a circuit of secondary sites that builds the drama and anticipation of encountering that which epitomizes the sacred.

Returning to Maya ritual, the *mesa* situates or centers space and re-establishes the cosmic order by defining the four directions. As the place of creation, caves are inseparably linked to the concept of the

cosmic center. *Mesas* erected within such caves would set up their cosmogram as a microcosm of this larger directional symbol, concentrating and accentuating it. The entire cosmos would be seen to emanate from these structures.

This feeling is particularly exemplified by an intact table altar that was discovered in 1989 at the end of the new branch of Naj Tunich. To reach the altar, the pilgrimage must first gain admittance to the balcony. As noted earlier, the balcony was created through the construction of a series of retaining walls, which are thought to have restricted access to the area beyond. The tunnel system can only be entered through a small opening on the upper level of the balcony. The fact that access to the tunnel system was tightly restricted is clearly reflected in the drastic drop in artifact density in the tunnels. From the entrance to the tunnel system, the pilgrim would have had to penetrate over a mile into the earth and would have negotiated a technical climb and a dangerous drop to reach the final chamber. The trip would have been a pilgrimage within a pilgrimage. The pilgrim then entered a circular chamber by crawling through a low opening. A dramatic stalagmite is found near the center of this chamber and a rectangular, flat-topped stone *mesa* was built against a tongue of protruding bedrock (Figure 9). Within the altar on the center-line was a large piece of speleothem with the cortex removed to reveal its crystalline structure (Brady

Figure 9. This unusual rectangular mesa *was found in the most inaccessible part of Naj Tunich, several kilometers from the entrance (photograph courtesy of George Veni).*

and Prufer 1999). Given its location in the deepest, most inaccessible part of Naj Tunich, I believe that this altar represented the most powerful spot in the entire cave. The cosmological model laid out by the *mesa* would have taken on special significance being located at the heart of this extremely sacred site. I have wondered if this chamber was considered within the region to be the very place of creation.

Conclusions

I have attempted to show that archaeologically preserved examples of *mesas* can be dated to at least the Late Preclassic with a wider range dating to the Classic Period. Despite its Spanish name, the *mesa* clearly appears to be part of an indigenous religious tradition. The small body of archaeological evidence that does exist also suggests there were regional patterns of *mesa* forms. Pre-Hispanic *bancos*, associated today with the Maya highlands, have been recovered in both the southern and northern lowlands as well as the highlands. Evidence has also been produced showing that both the bush table and the *banco* were in use in a small area of the Maya Mountains at the same time. A flat-topped, rectangular stone *mesa* has been reported from Naj Tunich and evidence from Dos Pilas suggests that *mesas* may have been laid out by sprinkling red mineral pigment on bare earth.

While ethnography has documented the use of *mesas* in the context of folk religion, the archaeological evidence from Naj Tunich suggests that at least the stone *mesa* was used by the elite as well. The context and associated artifacts of one of the *bancos* recovered by Keith Prufer (n.d.) suggests that it was used by a shaman. Thus, *mesas* appear to have been used at all social levels. This is hardly surprising because the *mesa* embodies the most basic cosmological principals. This allowed *mesas* to be employed by all classes even as the form, function, and message of the rituals conducted on them differed.

Finally, I have suggested that place was extremely important in Mesoamerican cosmology. Caves were important sacred places because they were the dwelling place of the deities and epitomized the heart of the earth. I have suggested that the great caves, the caves that were the focus of community and group identity, may have been thought to have been connected to the fundamentally important acts of world and human creation. Caves, therefore, would have represented the cosmic center and the place of power. The *mesa* carried the same message of centrality. Used within a cave, the *mesa* would have been seen as enhancing by further concentrating, intensifying, and focusing the power inherent in place.

James E. Brady
Department of Anthropology
California State University, Los Angeles
Los Angeles, CA 90032
(323) 343-2440
jbrady@calstatela.edu

References Cited

Adams, Abigail, and James E. Brady
 1994 Etnografía Q'eqchi' de los Ritos en Cuevas: Implicaciones para la Interpretación Arqueológica. In: Juan Pedro Laporte and Héctor L. Escobedo A., eds., *VII Simposio de Arqueología Guatemalteca*, pp. 205-211. Guatemala: Ministerio de Cultura y Deportes, Instituto de Antropología e Historia y Asociación Tikal.

Aguilar, Manuel, Miguel Medina Jaen, Tim M. Tucker, and James E. Brady
 n.d. Constructing Mythic Space: The Significance of a Chicomoztoc Complex at Acatzingo Viejo. In: James E. Brady and Keith M. Prufer, eds., *In the Maw of the Earth Monster: Studies in Mesoamerican Ritual Cave Use*. Manuscript submitted to the University of Texas Press.

Brady, James E.
 1991 Caves and Cosmovision at Utatlán. *California Anthropologist* 18(1):1-10.

 1997 Settlement Configuration and Cosmology: The Role of Caves at Dos Pilas. *American Anthropologist* 99(3):602-618.

 n.d. Caves as Ancient Maya Pilgrimage Centers: Archaeological Evidence of a Multifaceted Role. In: John Carlson, ed., *Pilgrimage and the Ritual Landscape in Pre-Columbian America*. Washington, D.C.: Dumbarton Oaks Research Library and Collection (in press).

Brady, James E., and Keith Prufer
 1999 Caves and Crystalmancy: Evidence for the Use of Crystals in Ancient Maya Religion. *Journal of Anthropological Research* 55:129-144.

Brady, James E., and George Veni
 1992 Man-Made and Pseudo-Karst Caves: The Implications of Sub-Surface Geologic Features Within Maya Centers. *Geoarchaeology* 7(2):149-167.

Brady, James E., George Veni, Andrea Stone, and Allan B. Cobb
 1992 Explorations in the New Branch of Naj Tunich: Implications for Interpretations. *Mexicon* 16(4):74-81.

Broda, Johanna
　1996　Calendários, Cosmovisión y Observación de la Naturaleza. In: Sonia Lombardo and Enrique Nalda, eds., *Temas Mesoamericanos*, pp. 427-469. Mexico: Instituto Nacional de Antropología e Historia,.

Eliade, Mircea
　1959　*The Sacred and the Profane: The Nature of Religion*. Translated by Willard R. Trask. New York: Harcourt Brace Jovanovich.

Gage, Thomas
　1958　*Travels in the New World*. Norman: University of Oklahoma. (Original 1648.)

García-Zambrano, Angel J.
　1994　Early Colonial Evidence of Pre-Columbian Rituals of Foundation. In: Merle Greene Robertson and Virginia Field, eds., *Seventh Palenque Round Table, 1989*, pp. 217-227. San Francisco: Pre-Columbian Art Research Institute.

Girard, Raphael
　1962　*Los Mayas Eternos*. Mexico: Editorial B. Costa-Amic.

Grove, David C.
　1973　Olmec Altars and Myth. *Archaeology* 26(2):128-135.

Hanks, William F.
　1984　Santification, Structure, and Experience in a Yucatec Ritual Event. *Journal of American Folklore* 97:131-166.

Hayden, Brian
　1987　Past to Present: Uses of Stone Tools in the Maya Highlands. In: Brian Hayden, ed., *Lithic Studies Among the Contemporary Highland Maya*, pp. 160-234. Tucson: University of Arizona Press.

Heyden, Doris
　1981　Caves, Gods and Myths: World-View and Planning in Teotihuacan. In: Elizabeth P. Benson, ed., *Mesoamerican Sites and World Views*, pp. 1-39. Washington, D.C.: Dumbarton Oaks Research Library and Collection.

Isaac, Erich
　1962　The Act and the Covenant. *Landscape* 11:12-17.

Kaplan, Jonathan
　1995　The Incienso Throne and Other Thrones from Kaminaljuyu, Guatemala: Late Preclassic Examples of a Mesoamerican Throne Tradition. *Ancient Mesoamerica* 6:185-196.

Lincoln, J. S.
　1945　*An Ethnological Study of the Ixil Indians of the Guatemala Highlands*. University of Chicago Microfilms, Manuscripts on Middle American Cultural Anthropology, No. 1.

MacLeod, Barbara, and Dennis E. Puleston
　1978　Pathways into Darkness: The Search for the Road to Xibalbá. In: Merle Greene Robertson and Donnan Call Jeffers, eds., *Tercera Mesa Redonda de Palenque, Vol. 4*, pp. 71-77. Monterey: Herald Peters.

Martin, Simon
　2001　Under a Deadly Star - Warfare Among the Classic Maya. In: Nikolai Grube, ed., *Maya: Divine Kings of the Rain Forest*, pp. 174-185. Cologne: Könemann.

Piña Chan, Román
　1970　*Informe Preliminar de la Reciente Exploración del Cenote Sagrado de Chichén Itzá*. Investigaciones, No. 24. Mexico: Instituto Nacional de Antropología e Historia.

Prufer, Keith M.
　n.d.　Shamans, Caves and the Roles of Ritual Specialists in Maya Society. In: James E. Brady and Keith M. Prufer, eds., *In the Maw of the Earth Monster: Studies in Mesoamerican Ritual Cave Use*. Manuscript submitted to the University of Texas Press.

Redfield, Robert, and Alfonso Villa Rojas
　1962　*Chan Kom: A Maya Village*. Chicago: University of Chicago Press.

Rodríguez Betancourt, Felipe
　1987　Rescate Arqueológico en la Cueva de "Las Banquetas," Chiapas. In: *Cuaderno de Trabajo 5: Investigaciones en Salvamento Arqueológico I*, pp. 103-139. Mexico: Instituto Nacional de Antropología e Historia.

Stone, Andrea
　1995　*Images from the Underworld: Naj Tunich and the Tradition of Maya Cave Painting*. Austin: University of Texas Press.

Thompson, J. Eric
　1975　Introduction to the Reprint Edition. In: Henry C. Mercer, *The Hill-Caves of Yucatan*, pp. vii-xliv. Norman: University of Oklahoma Press.

Turner, Victor, and Edith L. B. Turner
　1978　*Image and Pilgrimage in Christian Culture: Anthropological Perspectives*. New York: Columbia University Press.

Vogt, Evon Z., and David Stuart
　n.d.　Some Notes on Ritual Caves Among the Ancient and Modern Maya. In: James E. Brady and Keith M. Prufer, eds., *In the Maw of the Earth Monster: Studies in Mesoamerican Ritual Cave Use*. Manuscript submitted to the University of Texas Press.

Southern Mexico and Guatemala

Manipulating the Cosmos: Shamanic Tables Among the Highland Maya

Allen J. Christenson

According to the *Popol Vuh*, a K'iche' Maya text compiled in the highlands of Guatemala soon after the Spanish Conquest in the sixteenth century, the first men created by the gods had the gift of extraordinary vision whereby they could see all things:

> Perfect was their sight, and perfect was their knowledge of everything beneath the sky. If they gazed about them, turning their faces around, they beheld that which was in the sky and that which was upon the earth. Instantly, they were able to behold everything. They didn't have to walk to see all that existed beneath the sky. They merely saw it from wherever they were. Thus their knowledge became full. Their vision passed beyond the trees and rocks, beyond the lakes and the seas, beyond the mountains and the valleys [Folio 33 verso, translation by author].

The ancestors of the K'iche' Maya were described also in the *Título Totonicapán* as being magical and wise, whose "sight reached far into the sky and the earth; there was nothing to equal all that they could see beneath the sky" (Carmack and Mondloch 1983:71; English translation from K'iche' by author). Although the creator gods eventually clouded this vision so that men could only see those things which were "nearby" (Folio 34 recto, translation by author), the progenitors of the Maya and their descendants nevertheless bore within their blood the potential for divine sight, bestowed upon them by their creators. Present-day *ajq'ijab'* (Daykeepers, ritual specialists who utilize the traditional Maya calendar as an aid to reveal the will of ancestral spirits or deities) believe that their divine ancestors, who set the pattern for contemporary rituals, continue to operate through them as conduits at appropriate times and under appropriate circumstances. It is their sacred ancestral vision that allows the *ajq'ij* to "see" beyond the limits of time and distance as the first men once did. Evon Vogt noted that the Tzotzil Maya of Zinacantán believe that anciently their people could see inside sacred mountains where the ancestors live. Today only shamans are recognized to have this ability. Nevertheless, the very word Tzotzil is in part derived from the root -*il* ("to see"), implying not only vision, but insight or sacred knowledge. Thus the Tzotzil term *h'ilol* means "seer," in the sense of one who can "see" things on a supernatural level (Vogt 1993:205).

Figure 1. Maya men from the town of Nahualá, Guatemala (all photos by author).

Douglas Sharon, ed., *Mesas & Cosmologies in Mesoamerica*. San Diego Museum Papers 42, 2003.

Among the Maya, there is no institutional religion to sanction the qualification of a person to become an *ajq'ij*. Every Maya man and woman potentially has this ability because it is inherent in his or her blood. *Ajq'ijab'* are chosen by the ancestors to serve as mediators between this world and that of the spirit not because they are qualitatively different from anyone else in this regard, but because they are called by the spirit world to do so as an obligatory service to the community. Once called, generally through dreams or the discovery of a sign interpreted as an invitation to serve from the ancestors, the prospective *ajq'ij* often enters a period of apprenticeship. The approach that experienced *ajq'ijab'* take in training their apprentices is to teach how to interpret signs and spirit communication, often described as lightning in the blood, that they had always received since childhood but had not the experience to understand properly. Thus Bunzel noted that *ajq'ijab'* have no special relationship with divinity, and their prayers, though perhaps more eloquent, are no more efficacious than those that are voiced by commoners (Bunzel 1952:299).

For this reason, not all *ajq'ijab'* go through a process of apprenticeship. A well-respected *ajq'ij*, named Diego (Figure 2), living in the Tz'utujil Maya community of Santiago Atitlán told me that although he had watched a number of elderly *ajq'ijab'* carry out prayers and ceremonies in his youth, he did not learn how to do his work from them:

> When I was born, I already knew how to do these things. I had no teacher. I speak with the ancestors and ancient kings and they speak with me. They help me to know how to heal and solve problems for people. I ask the ancestors these things in places that are holy where I can be touched by them.

Mendelson was told by an *ajkun* ("Healer," the most prevalent type of ritual specialist in Santiago Atitlán) that sacred knowledge cannot be passed from one person to another. It must come from deity:

> He said that a young man who wished to be an *ajkun* tried to learn the prayers, bit by bit, from another *ajkun* but that there were no direct courses of lessons given by an old man to a pupil and that there could not be since these things came from God. For this reason each *ajkun* had a different way of praying [Mendelson 1957:280-281].

Figure 2. Diego, an ajq'ij from the community of Santiago Atitlán, conducts a divinatory ceremony on the ruins of the old Tz'utujil Maya capital city at Chutinamit.

Apprenticeships, and learning by example, are undoubtedly important methods of passing along knowledge from one generation to another, however, the perception among Maya *ajq'ijab'* is that this is not the principal means by which sacred knowledge is gained. This must come directly from within oneself, directly from one's own blood, or it is powerless. Non-Maya do not necessarily have this kind of ability, because their blood does not originate from the same visionary ancestral source. In my own experience working with *ajq'ijab'* in Momostenango in the late 1970s, my frequent displays of ineptitude in learning divinatory and calendric skills was interpreted as the lack of Maya blood in my veins. I was not able to see with ancestral vision in the same way because I had a different lineage, likely not a very divine one.

Bunzel noted that the K'iche' of Chichicastenango claimed that their formalized speech and ceremonies were attributed to ancient ancestral precedent: "And now this rite and custom belongs to the first people, our mothers and fathers... This belongs to them; we are the embodiment of their rites and ceremonies" (Bunzel 1952:232, 238). To alter the actions of the ancestors would be to change the very fabric of existence in potentially destructive ways. As mediators between this world and that of the sacred, it is the Mayas' obligation to continue the actions of their divine ancestors in as authentic a manner as possible: "It is our name and destiny to repeat and perpetuate these ceremonies before the world" (ibid.: 242). When asking Tz'utujils when certain rituals began, a common response is that they are as old as the world and were first performed by their ancestors who had divine power (Christenson 2001:22-23, 68; Mendelson 1965:91).

At the beginning of shamanistic prayers, *ajq'ijab'* and *ajkuns* in Santiago Atitlán, Guatemala call upon a litany of sacred beings and objects whose power they wish to invoke on behalf of their clients. Prominent in this list are the "Holy Table and Holy Chair" which bear their own souls and influence the outcome of the divination. Possession of a divinatory table implies acceptance of the role of shaman and responsibility to act as a mediator with spirit beings (Mendelson 1957: 281; B. Tedlock 1982:74). This table may be an actual table or altar within the home, or it may be any flat surface utilized for ritual purposes. In 2000 during Easter Week, an *ajq'ij* in Santiago Atitlán went with me to conduct a ceremony at the ruins of the ancient Tz'utujil capital of Chutinamit. He chose this location because there he is "closer to the kings of old and is therefore sacred." Prior to the ceremony he selected 12 flat stones and arranged them into a rough square which he called his "table" before laying out a clean cloth and arranging his ritual paraphernalia for the ceremony (Figure 3). He said that the makeshift altar had the same power as the tables and/or altars on which sacred objects are kept in his home, or in the town's church, or in the various confraternity houses in town. He placed four lit cigars on the north side of this temporary table so that the ancestors who were called to be present at the ceremony could smoke and be content.

The four corners of a shamanic table's surface represent the four corners of the world and the placement of objects upon it suggests the arrangement of specific locations on the earth such as mountains or shrines. The table thus encloses the sacred geography of the universe in a form that becomes intimate, close, and potentially manipulatable. Vogt quoted a highland Maya man from Zinacantán as saying that the universe is "like a house, like a table" representing that which is systematic, and well-ordered (Vogt 1993:11). Wisdom also recorded that the Ch'orti' Maya of Guatemala considered both the squared maize field and the shamanic altar as the world in miniature (Wisdom 1940:430). By laying out the maize field, or setting up a ritual table, the Maya transform secular models into sacred space. With regard to the maize field, this charges the ground with the power of creation to bear new life. In a similar way, the shaman's table provides a stage on which sacred geography may be intimately studied, and even altered. As Mary Helms writes, "to re-create cosmic harmony and governance [is] ultimately to strive to control such powers and to apply them to human affairs" (Helms 1993:27). The possession and authority to manipulate objects on the table gives the shaman the ability to consult, and in some cases, to act in the guise of ancestors who possess divine sight and power.

When the *ajq'ij* sits at his table he places himself in a transcendent role that bridges the three layers of the cosmos (Figure 4). His legs conceptually extend beneath the surface of the earth/ table, his arms manipulate its sacred geography, while his upper body rises into the upperworld.

Figure 3. Divinatory mesa on Chutinamit. The four cigars below are for the ancestors to smoke.

Figure 4. An ajq'ij in Momostenango seated at his divinatory mesa.

In so doing, the *ajq'ij* is able to "see" all places where the spirit beings live and to converse with them. Maude Oakes noted that shamanic tables at Todos Santos bear a cross addressed as *Santo Mundo* (Holy World) which represents the first shaman-priest of the world (Oakes 1951:138). The *ajq'ij* who sits at this table thus acts as the representative of the first ancestral priest who set the precedent for such ceremonies. In a similar way, the *ajkun*-shamans of the Tz'utujil Maya are believed to carry within their blood the power by which they are able to pray "according to the ancient words of god" (Mendelson 1957:281).

At Momostenango, a prominent *chuch-qajaw* (priest-shaman) told me that when he sits at his table, he becomes a living representation of the organization of the world:

> When I am seated at the table, I am *aj nawal mesa* [of or pertaining to the ancestral spirit essence table]. My body is in the form of a cross just like the four sides of the world. This is why I face to the east and behind me is the west. My left arm extends out toward the north, and my right arm points to the south. My heart is the center of myself just as the arms of the cross come together to form its heart. My head extends upward above the horizon so that I can see far away. Because I am seated this way I can speak to *Mundo* [World].

At Momostenango, the shamanic table is called either by the Spanish *Santa Mesa* ("Holy Table") or, as described in the previous quote, with the K'iche' Maya term *Nawal*. The word *nawal* has no English equivalent that embraces all its various meanings. In K'iche' theology everything, both living and inanimate, has a spirit essence or *nawal*. This spirit essence is believed to give humans, animals, and even inanimate objects, the power to communicate on a supernatural plane. Father Thomás de Coto, who compiled a Kaqchikel Maya language dictionary in the early colonial period, ascribed this power to the devil, defining the word *naual* as the magical means whereby the devil spoke to the K'iche through their idols. Thus they would say that the "life of the tree, the life of the stone, of the hill, is its *naual*, because they believed there was life in these objects" (Coto 1983:328, 369). Although originally borrowed from the Central Mexican Nahuat group of languages, modern-day highland Maya associate this word with the verbal root *na'*, meaning "to feel" or "to know." In the *Popol Vuh*, the creator deities brought the first mountains out of the primordial sea at the dawn of creation by means of their *nawal*, their spirit essence or divine knowledge, rather than by physical action. It was by this same power that the first ancestors of the Maya were created by deity (Folio 33 recto):

> xa puz xa *naual* quitzaquic qui bitic rumal ri tzacol bitol alom qaholom, tepeu cucumatz.
>
> . . .
>
> Merely by miraculous power and *spirit essence* was their framing and shaping brought about by the Framer and the Shaper, by She Who Has Borne Children and He Who Has Begotten Sons, by Sovereign and Quetzal Serpent [translation by author].

Nawal may refer to the power of any form of spirit essence which displays miraculous or supernatural qualities, but it may also refer specifically to deified ancestors. Thus the authors of the *Título Totonicapán* described their ancestors as "*Nawal* People" who were the founders of the four great lineages of the K'iche' nation, indicating that their power was similar in kind to deity (Carmack and Mondloch 1983:folio 84, lines 1-2).

In the Tz'utujil Maya understanding of the term *nawal* is most commonly used to describe a great ancestor or priest-shaman of the past who had the power to work miracles (Mendelson

1957:42). When a living *ajq'ij* or *ajkun* repeats the actions of a *nawal* ancestor through ceremony or prayer, he/she becomes a substitute or vessel for sacred power.

In Santiago Atitlán, the world is given life and structure when the *nab'eysil*, a powerful priest-shaman, symbolically dies and resurrects in token of the patron deity of maize, deer, and the fertility of the earth. As part of the ceremony, the *nab'eysil* extracts the garments of the deity from a cloth bundle and wears them as he dances to the four cardinal directions to recreate the limits of the cosmos (Figure 5). Following the performance of this dance in 1998, the *nab'eysil* sought

Figure 5. The nab'eysil *of Santiago Atitlán dances an ancestral bundle.*

me out to ask if I had seen "the ancient *nuwals* giving birth to the world." He explained that they had filled his soul with their presence as he danced, guiding him in his steps, and now everything was new again. In the eyes of the *nab'eysil* the dance was not a symbol of the rebirth of the cosmos, but a genuine creative act in which time folded inward on itself to reveal the actions of deified ancestors at the time of first creation.

In a similar way, the *ajq'ij* in Momostenango functions as a living representative of deity and/ or deified ancestors when he sits at his *Nawal Mesa*. One of the highest titles held by the priest-shaman of Momostenango is *chuch-qajaw* ("mother-father") as he represents the living embodiment of his lineage. As such, he is able to act in the name of his ancestors, whose blood he possesses. It is essential therefore, that he approach the duties of his office with great seriousness and in a state of ritual purity. Prior to laying out the contents of his bundle on the table, the *ajq'ij* calls upon the essential powers of the world as well as his own ancestors to be present for the ceremony. He begins by pleading for them to take away any sin or error that might taint his ability to act in their name and reveal their will. The following is a divinatory prayer I recorded in Momostenango in 1979 given by an *ajq'ij* when he first seated himself at his table on behalf of a sick client:

> We call upon you Earth, we ask you Lord of the day 11 No'j, we ask you Lord 5 No'j, and to you secretary 11 K'at, and you secretary 5 K'at; we ask a favor of you; we ask you a favor because there is sickness among us, there is a sick little girl. Take away my error, King of the World, Savior of the World, so that you may speak—the Seven Skies, the Seven Earths. Take away my error that there may be light, that there may be clarity. Take away my error I ask you, the great mountains, the small mountains; the great plains and the small plains; the great animals who are lords of the mountains and you small animals who are in the mountains. Take away my error you, our people, our mothers and fathers, our grandmothers and our grandfathers. Take away my error and witness us here today at this table. It has its service, to bring out the transformation, to bring out the mothers-fathers. This is its service. Take away my error.

In this litany, the *ajq'ij* asked the powers he wished to have present at the ceremony to take away any flaws in his body or character that would taint the results. Among these powers are: first, the representatives of time in the form of the two principal day lords that preside over that period of the year as well as their two secretaries; second, space or sacred geography as described by the mountains, the plains, as well as their animal inhabitants; and finally lineage, represented by the mothers and fathers, the grandmothers and grandfathers. The Seven Skies and the Seven Earths refer to the organization of the sky and the earth into seven major divisions—the four cardinal directions plus up, down, and center. Thus the shaman positions himself at the center of the cosmos, surrounded on all sides by sacred power.

During ceremonies, the table is covered with a cloth in order to avoid touching its surface directly, in the same way that the Maya drape cloths over their arms and chests when carrying sacred objects to avoid contact with the skin. This symbolically sets the table apart as a liminal object, bridging this world with the next.

There is a carved depiction of a shamanic table on the central altarpiece of the church in Santiago Atitlán (Figure 6). Originally constructed at an

Figure 6. The central altarpiece of the sixteenth-century church in Santiago Atitlán.

unknown date during the early Spanish Colonial Period, the altarpiece fell into severe disrepair and collapsed during an earthquake in 1960. The disarticulated pieces of the fallen altarpiece were left in storage until 1976 when the parish priest, Father Francisco Rother, commissioned a local Maya sculptor named Diego Chávez Petzey to initiate repairs and carve replacement panels for those portions of the altarpiece which were too damaged for reuse. Diego was later joined in this project by his younger brother Nicolás Chávez Sojuel.

Among traditionalist Maya, the collapse of the altarpiece came as a terrible shock. Such sacred objects are considered to be living things, endowed with a *k'u'x* ("heart") and placed there by the ancestors of the community. The shattered wood of the altarpiece was therefore still believed to be animated with the power of the ancient inhabitants of their community. Rather than simply restoring the altarpiece to its original design, the Chávez brothers subtly modified it to give the impression of a sacred mountain with its niches representing caves from which the patron saints of the town emerged. At the base of the altarpiece, the Chávez brothers carved a series of five panels of their own design representing traditional Maya ceremonies meaningful to their community.

According to Diego Chávez, the first panel (Figure 7) represents the revelation of divine will in the life of a Maya child as mediated through an *ajkun*, the Tz'utujil Maya term for shaman:

The scene represents a child's naming and blessing ceremony by an *ajkun*. The *ajkun* is in the center of the panel seated behind his table. The *ajkun* prays to *Ruk'u'x Kaj, Ruk'u'x Uliw* ["Heart of Sky, Heart of Earth"] to determine what blessing the child will receive, whether he will grow well and what he will come to be. The man on the right is the child's father, holding a book containing the count of days. Many years ago, *ajkuns* were much more powerful than now and knew how to read the days, the clouds, and the calls of animals. I've been told by old people that some of them kept books filled with ancient knowledge. So I included one in the panel to show that the ancestors of the Tz'utujils also had writings containing revelations from the spirit world that were equally as powerful as the words in the Bible. All these books are now gone though and *ajkuns* today aren't as powerful as our ancestors once were. The woman on the left is the child's mother. It is a boy child, so he is on the *ajkun's* right-hand side. If it had been female, the child would have been on the other side. On the table are candles, incense, a piece of an old Maya clay

Manipulating the Cosmos: Shamanic Tables Among the Highland Maya

Figure 7. Panel 1 of the Central Altarpiece depicting an ajkun seated at his divinatory mesa.

head like farmers find in their fields, and a quartz crystal. When an *ajkun* looks into the crystal he sees little flashes of light that speak to him. Atop the *ajkun's* house in the panel is a cross. This is not a Christian cross, but represents the four cardinal directions with the house being the center place. The twisted posts in front of the house are like the serpents that guard sacred mountain caves where the saints and ancestors live. The stone blocks of the house represent the mountain itself. The maize canes and thatch above these stones are the maize fields, trees, and vegetation that grow on the mountainside.

For the highland Maya, the day on which a child is born determines to a certain extent the fate he/she will have in life (Schultze Jena 1954:75; B. Tedlock 1982:108-127). Because fate is selected by time itself, there is little that can be done to alter it. As a result, highland Maya who use the traditional calendar are rather obsessive about determining what their fate is and how they can order their lives to make the best of it. Ximénez wrote that highland Maya parents in the early eighteenth century consulted diviners to determine the fate of their newborns during which shamanic rites were performed according to the fates of the days (Ximénez 1967:10). The altarpiece panel thus represents a divinatory ceremony based on the day of the child's birth.

The other items on the *ajkun's* table as depicted on the altarpiece panel are still used in modern Tz'utujil shamanic ceremonies. The small carved head is a fragment from a pre-Columbian figurine. Small stone and terra cotta sculptures are relatively common in the area in and around Santiago Atitlán. Most *atiteco* families, including Diego and Nicolás, keep a collection of them on their personal altars as relics of the ancestors. Each is considered a powerful *rijtaal*, or "sign" of divine communication. *Ajkuns* use them along with quartz crystals, jade, or obsidian flakes as *ilb'al* ("instruments of seeing") whereby mountain or ancestral spirits may be consulted on behalf of clients.

In communities such as Momostenango and Totonicapán, traditionalist K'iche' Maya frequently consult an *ajq'ij* ("Daykeeper" shaman) prior to making important decisions or initiating a significant long-term project in order to ensure a favorable result. This may include building a new house, entering into a business contract, or going on a long journey. If a man and woman plan to be married, each may consult a separate *ajq'ij* to determine if the intended spouse is a deceiver or not. If a man is ill, he may consult an *ajq'ij* in order to determine the proper treatment and likely prognosis.

A prospective *ajq'ij* generally undergoes a period of training under an experienced man who already holds the title. Ideally, this training continues for 260 days, the same number of days in the traditional Maya calendar which the *ajq'ijab'* use as a template for their ritual actions and divination ceremonies (Schultze Jena 1954:75). During this time, the prospective *ajq'ij* often lives with his teacher in his home and observes everything that he does. The period of instruction begins on an evening ruled by a new moon, and ends on an evening with a full moon. Alternatively, instruction begins on the day Batz', esteemed as particularly good for learning and for initiating new projects. After the period of instruction is completed, the apprentice receives the title of *ajq'ij* and is presented with his own bundle by his teacher. In Momostenango the presentation of the bundle takes place on the day 8 Batz', the day on which *ajq'ijab'* gather in the valley of Chuatzak to make offerings of incense, flowers, and candles on behalf of the people (Goubaud Carrera 1935:41).

The bundle is generally made of woven cloth containing approximately 200 seeds, preferably the red seeds of the *tz'ite* or coral tree (*Erythrina corallodendrum*), although some *ajq'ijab'* may use maize kernels, along with a number of pieces of obsidian, jadeite, quartz, and/or fragments of ancient stone or terra cotta artifacts.

Divination using *tz'ite* seeds is closely related to the 260-day traditional Maya calendar and is used extensively throughout the highlands of Guatemala (Ximénez 1977:88; Schultze Jena 1954; Douglas 1969:103, 154-55; B. Tedlock 1982; Watanabe 1992:188). To illustrate how the calendar is incorporated into a typical K'iche' divination ceremony I will describe one such consultation I made with a prominent *ajq'ij* in Momostenango in 1979. At the time, I had contracted a fever and some mild respiratory problems from spending too many hours in smoke-filled Maya homes with too little ventilation. I consulted an *ajq'ij* friend of mine in person, although I could have sent a friend on my behalf if I had been unable to get out of bed. The *ajq'ij* asked a series of questions in order to best plan a ceremony to determine the cause, nature, and severity of the illness. In this case, he asked my name, the day the fever first appeared, my present condition, how I felt living so far from my family, how well I was sleeping, if I had had any unusual dreams, and whether my ancestors had spoken to me more frequently in recent days in the form of twitching muscles or a sensation that the K'iche' refer to as lightning in the blood. Such questions are standard, even if the *ajq'ij* already knows many of the answers. In this case, the *ajq'ij* was a rather close friend of mine and he had been training me in K'iche' ceremonialism for quite some time. He therefore knew my name and a great deal about my dreams and recent communications with ancestors. In most cases, the *ajq'ij* is not asking these questions for his own benefit, but as a way to inform the saints, deities, and ancestors who would be consulted as part of the ceremony.

After obtaining this information, the *ajq'ij* laid a clean cloth over the table specifically dedicated for that purpose and placed his bundle containing the *tz'ite* seeds and other divinatory instruments on top of it. He then opened the bundle and arranged several pieces of obsidian, quartz, jade, and antiquities in a row across the top of the table. He also placed approximately 200 *tz'ite* seeds on the table in one large pile. At this point, the *ajq'ij* prepared himself for the ceremony by asking for forgiveness of his sins and by calling on several representatives of divinity, both Christian and traditional Maya, to attend the ritual. As he prayed, he gently mixed the seeds by passing his right hand in circular motions over them. At length he took one handfull of seeds and placed them to one side. The *ajq'ij* then divided these seeds into smaller groups of four seeds each, arranged across the table in rows of seven groups per row (Figure 8). In most cases, approximately three rows are created in this way:

4	4	4	4	4	4	4
4	4	4	4	4	4	4
4	4	4	1			

After the seeds were arranged on the table, the *ajq'ij* touched each group lightly with his finger tips and successively counted the days of the calendar in order, beginning with the day the fever first appeared—in this case the day 2 Tijax. The order of the count was from from left to right in the first row, right to left in the second row, and finally left to right in the third row, as may be seen in the following diagram:

→	4 2 Tijax	4 3 Kaweq	4 4 Junajpu	4 5 Imox	4 6 Iq'	4 7 Aq'ab'al	↓
↓	4 13 Toj	4 12 Q'anil	4 11 Kej	4 10 Kame	4 9 Qan	4 8 K'at	↵
↪	4 1 Tz'i'	4 2 B'atz	4 3 E	1 4 Aj			

Figure 8. Tz'ite seeds and other objects arranged on a divinatory mesa in Momostenango.

The traditional Maya calendar was further referred to in the interpretation of the ceremony. The *ajq'ij* determined my prognosis by the day name assigned to the last group of seeds as well as by the number of seeds remaining. An odd number of seeds in this group indicated that my fate would be somewhat unfavorable. An even number of seeds in the final group would have indicated that I would improve much more rapidly.

The day name assigned to the last group of seeds also influences the interpretation of the ceremony. The *ajaw*, or "lord," of each named day is believed to influence fate in a specific way. The day name assigned to the last group in the above example was Aj ("ear of maize"), generally a relatively good augury and one particularly associated with families and children. As a result, the *ajq'ij* asked specific questions regarding problems that I might have within my family: Were there any unresolved disagreements with relatives? Did I have unkind feelings toward any of them? Did any of them resent me? Was I homesick? After each question the *ajq'ij* paused briefly to note any sensations he might be having, such as small muscle twitches or lightning in the blood and the severity and location in the body where these sensations manifested themselves. In this case, the *ajq'ij* felt a moderate sensation he identified as lightning in the vein of his right thigh after asking me if I was aware of any errors committed recently by family members. He interpreted this as a fairly certain indication that I was not the problem in this case, but that a male relative (the right side of the body is associated with males, the left side with females) had chosen a path that had brought disgrace on the entire family. Because the sensation was toward the back of his thigh, he knew this to have been an event some-time in the past. After further questioning, the likely candidate turned out to be one of my four brothers, although he didn't attempt to determine which one.

The coefficient day assigned to the final group of seeds was four. On a scale from one to 13 (the number of times that day name occurs during the course of a 260-day period), four is a rather low number. Therefore, the consequences of the disgrace were limited and fairly easy to resolve. He reassured me that it could have been worse. If the seeds had indicated, for example, the day 12 Junajpu, the consequences would have been much more dire. In such a case my illness would perhaps have been the result of a deceased enemy who was calling for my death, since this is the day dedicated to ceremonies related to the dead. Because 12 is a high number, the prognosis of my case would have been nearly hopeless, and he would have expected me to die soon.

After the initial count, the *ajq'ij* took another handful of seeds and repeated the procedure to determine the best day for making offerings to resolve the problem. In this case the day count began with the day I had last received a letter from home. The final grouping of seeds happened to have two left over and the day count assigned to it was 6 Ix. Because the number of seeds turned out to be two, an even number, the augury was a good one and he interpreted this to be a good day to make my offerings. If it had turned out to be one or three, he noted that he would have repeated the procedure until an even number resulted. The *ajq'ij* counseled me that we should go together to the "six shrine" located on a hill in town on the next Ix day (Figure 9). There are 13 such shrines in the mountains in and around Momostenango, corresponding to the number of coefficients used to name days in the 260-day calendric cycle. The nature of the offering I was to give was then determined by yet another arrangement of seeds.

As may be seen from the above example, *ajq'ijab'* are not locked into any one reading of the calendar count during the divination ceremony. The process is fluid enough to allow for a great deal of interpretation according to the circumstances and character of the individual petitioner, as well as communication with ancestral spirits as manifested in the mind and body of the *ajq'ij*. *Ajq'ijab'* often act far more as psychiatrists, marriage and family counselors, and trusted friends

Figure 9. The Waqib'al (Six Place) at Momostenango where offerings are made on days of the ritual calendar that have the coefficient six.

than mere interpreters of inalterable fate. In addition, the power of the *ajq'ij* to actually alter fate is rather limited. Unpleasant things may take place despite offerings and rituals because the world is ordered according to certain outcomes that cannot be changed or postponed indefinitely. Gods, saints, and ancestors may be petitioned for favors, but ultimately they may be helpless to intervene because they are subject to the same cycles of time-based fate that governs the world. Fate, after all, is determined by time itself and cannot be broken.

When I mentioned the results of this consultation to an *ajq'ij* friend of mine in the nearby community of Totonicapán, he was concerned enough to suggest that I also consult one of the mountain shrines there because they were more powerful than those of Momostenango. There is always professional rivalry between practitioners from various communities, and certainly the *ajq'ij* in Momostenango would not have agreed with this assessment. In Totonicapán there are 13 mountains surrounding the community that are recognized by traditionalists as ritually significant. Each has a large altar where offerings of incense, flowers, candles, liquor, etc. are made. Many smaller altars are also located on each mountain. The names of these mountains in the order given to me in 1979 were: María Tekum, Tz'al Awaj, Campana Abaj, Cucaxtun, Chusak Cab, Pa Balam, Tunabaj, Sakmalja, Cux Niq'uel, Sakmachit, Chutamango, Tamborabaj, and Chuxajab Xinul. Because my augury came out to be 6 Ix, my Totonicapán friend suggested that we go to pray on the sixth mountain, Pa Balam on an Ix day. The shrine on the mountain is also referred to as a "table," and during the ceremony there the *ajq'ij* addressed it in prayer in the same way as the wooden table used in his home. The offering in that case consisted of three white *esterina*-type candles, a small bottle of *aguardiente*, and five cents worth of copal incense. All went well with both visits to the mountains and I soon felt much better, although I never did find out which of my wayward brothers had caused me all that trouble.

A characteristic of Maya theology is the tendency to see seemingly ordinary and familiar things as shadows of the sacred. Laying out the boundary stones for a maize field is treated by traditionalists as no less than the delineation of the limits of the world, preparing it to give birth to new life as if it were the dawn of creation. The traditional three-stone Maya hearth replicates the three stones of creation placed by the gods to serve as a foundation for the sky. Caves, or even small clefts in a mountain, are portals to the spirit homes of the ancestors. These are not mere symbolic representations of the sacred, they are divine symmetries—different in scale but not in their essential nature. Shamanic tables are therefore not mere effigy worlds. When used under appropriate circumstances they are "seen" as the cosmos itself writ small. Shamans who manipulate objects on their surfaces thus become vessels for sacred communication, replicating with the same efficacy the actions of their ancestral parents who were created with visionary sight, transcending the limits of their immediate surroundings.

Allen J. Christenson
Department of Humanities, Classics, and
 Comparative Literature 3010 JKHB
Brigham Young University
 Provo, UT 84602-6118
allen_christenson@byu.edu

References Cited

Bunzel, Ruth
 1952 *Chichicastenango: A Guatemalan Village.* Seattle: University of Washington Press.

Carmack, Robert M., and James L. Mondloch
 1983 *El Título de Totonicapán.* México: Universidad Nacional Autónoma de México.

Christenson, Allen J.
  2001 *Art and Society in a Highland Maya Community: The Altarpiece of Santiago Atitlán.* Austin: University of Texas Press.

Coto, Fray Tomás de
  1983 *Thesaurus Verborum: Vocabulario de la Lengua Cakchiquel u [El] Guatemalteca, Nuevamente hecho y Recopilado con Summo Estudio, Travajo y Erudición.* Mexico City: Universidad Nacional Autónoma de México.

Douglas, William
  1969 *Illness and Curing in Santiago Atitlán.* Ph.D. dissertation, Stanford University.

Goubaud Carrera, Antonio
  1935 El "Guajxaquip Bats"—ceremonia calendárica indígena. *Anales de la Sociedad de Geografía e Historia de Guatemala,* Vol. 12, pp. 39-59. Guatemala.

Helms, Mary W.
  1993 *Craft and the Kingly Ideal: Art, Trade, and Power.* Austin: University of Texas Press.

Hill, Robert M. II
  1992 *Colonial Cakchiquels: Highland Maya Adaptation to Spanish Rule 1600-1700.* Fort Worth: Holt, Rinehart and Winston.

Mendelson, E. Michael
  1957 *Religion and World-View in a Guatemalan Village.* Microfilm Collection of Manuscripts on Middle American Cultural Anthropology, no. 52. Chicago: University of Chicago Library.

  1965 *Los escándalos de Maximón.* Seminario de Integración Social Guatemalteca Publicación 19. Guatemala City: Tipografía Nacional.

Oakes, Maud
  1951 *The Two Crosses of Todos Santos.* Princeton: Princeton University Press.

Popol Vuh
  1701 *Popol Vuh.* Manuscript version in Arte de las tres lenguas kaqchiquel, quiche y tz'utuhil. Transcribed by Francisco Ximénez. Ayer Collection at the Newberry Library, Chicago, Illinois.

Schultze Jena, Leonhard
  1954 *La vida y las creencias de los indígenas quiches de Guatemala.* Biblioteca de cultura popular, vol. 49. Tr. Antonio Goubaud Carrera and Herbert D. Sapper. Guatemala City: Ministerio de Educación Pública.

Tedlock, Barbara
  1982 *Time and the Highland Maya.* Albuquerque: University of New Mexico Press.

Vogt, Evon Z.
  1993 *Tortillas for the Gods: A Symbolic Analysis of Zinacanteco Rituals.* Norman: University of Oklahoma Press.

Wisdom, Charles
  1940 *Chorti Indians of Guatemala.* Chicago: University of Chicago Press.

Ximénez, Fray Francisco
  1967 *Escolios a las historias de origen de los indios.* Guatemala City: Sociedad de Geografía e Historia.

  1977 *Historia de la Provincia de San Vicente de Chiapa y Guatemala de la orden de Predicadores.* Vols. 1 and 2. Guatemala City: Sociedad de Geografía e Historia.

Southern Mexico and Guatemala

Altars for Ancestors:
Maya Altars for the Days of the Dead in Yucatán

Judith Green

Introduction

Maya family bonds endure for decades after death. Traditional families in Yucatán express and reinforce these bonds by an annual celebration, a sequence of family feasts lasting nine days, which they call *hanal pixan* (Dinner for Souls). This event takes place around the dates of the Catholic feasts of All Saints and All Souls' Days, November 1 and 2, respectively, including an eight-day extension (octave) to November 8.

In some parts of Central Mexico, the Days of the Dead have become a tourist attraction. This is only beginning to occur in Yucatán, and mainly in a few altar displays in Mérida. My plan was to document all the altar settings for the souls' days in a rural, traditional Maya-speaking home. My choice was Xocen, a pilgrimage village, the home of the Holy Stone Cross and once the owner of a sacred book of predictions, said to have been lost during the Caste Wars (Dzib May 1999, Mújica 1997, Everton 1991:212-215).

Thirty years ago I studied Days of the Dead altars in the Oaxaca Valley (1969, 1995). Their clustered offerings and Baroque appearance (Figure 1) were so different from those I saw at Xocen (Figures 2 and 3) that I had to question why. In fact, the Xocen altar settings looked like diagrams of shamans' altars (*mesas*) that Robert Redfield and Alfonso Villa Rojas (1962:136, 145) published from their 1930s fieldwork in Chan Kom, Yucatán. David Freidel and Linda Schele (1993: Ch.1) provide a convincing argument that the shamans' *mesas* in lowland Yucatán relate directly to Maya pre-Columbian *mesas*. Could the domestic mesa-altars for the dead in Xocen also relate to those the Maya made for their ancestors before the Spanish Conquest?

Since I am describing altars with offerings on them, I use the word *mesa* to avoid confusion. When I refer to a change of some items on the *mesa* to indicate a particular meal, e.g., breakfast on November 1, I call that arrangement a setting. The Maya of X-Cacal use the word *zuhuy-mesa* for both shamans' and Christian altars (Villa Rojas 1945:107). This is a combination of the Maya word for virginal or pure (*suhuy* in Barrera Vasquez 1980:741) and the Spanish one for table. Redfield explains (1962:130-131, 202) the use of *zuhuy*, and refers to the newly made tablecloth on the Chan Kom souls' altar as a *zuhuy-mantel*.

My observations at Xocen and subsequent research indicate that these *hanal pixan mesas*, like those of contemporary shamans, are direct descendants of the altars of the pre-Columbian Maya. Both are based on an underlying belief system that has survived the Conquest. To support this position, I describe the souls' *mesas* I investigated at this pilgrimage village where I was invited to visit the home and record the ceremony of a prayer master (*maestro cantor*) in 1998 and again in 1999. For comparison I use the diagrammed shamans' *mesas* at Chan Kom (Redfield and Villa Rojas 1962:136, 145), X-Cacal in Quintana Roo (Villa Rojas 1945:117), and Becanchen (Love 1984:258), along with material reported by

Douglas Sharon, ed., *Mesas & Cosmologies in Mesoamerica*. San Diego Museum Papers 42, 2003.

Figure 1. Days of the Dead altar, Oaxaca, Oaxaca, 1966.

William Hanks at Oxkutzcab (1990) and John Sosa at Yalcoba (1990). Two of these appear (redrawn) in Figures 8 and 9.

Cosmological Underpinnings of *Hanal Pixan*

The idea of feeding the dead is an ancient concept in Mesoamerica, which is not connected with Christianity. It is based on the belief that the living continue to have a relationship with the dead, and receive protection and help from them (personal communication, Don Lauro of Xocen). The family's generous hospitality to the souls during *hanal pixan* assures their good will. Earle (1986: 163) reports for the K'iche' Maya that they present meals to the dead with candles, liquor, and incense to return the favor of an abundant harvest. Girard goes a step further in stating (1995:338) that the dead themselves help in the farming.

The ritual includes prayers to help the dead on the difficult journey to the afterworld, which for some Maya includes a Christian concept of a fiery purgatory where souls must atone for sin (Redfield and Villa Rojas 1962:199, Villa Rojas 1945:150).

While ideas about the afterlife differ among Maya groups, the annual visit and feast of the dead is widely accepted. Underlying this is a theme of reciprocity with family members and the belief that a soul after death has much the same needs and feelings as a living person. In a self-sustaining agricultural society survival depends on the harvest. The dead are closer to the supernatural forces that control fertility of the land and people. The souls' good will and influence is essential, and neglecting them may lead to retribution, often in the form of sickness or possibly death (Redfield and Villa Rojas 1962:119, 202; Villa Rojas 1945:105). This reciprocity and retribution theme is memorialized in many folk tales (Orilla 1996:41-45).

Origin of the Maya Veneration of the Dead

The journey to the underworld is a theme portrayed in the great K'iche' Maya epic, the *Popul Vuh* (Tedlock 1985). It recounts the trials of the Maya Hero Twins Hunapuh and Xbalanque, who make a harrowing journey through Xibalba (the underworld) and finally jump to their deaths into a stone oven in defiance of the murderous Xibalban Lords. They are reborn as the solar and lunar gods, thereby defeating death (Girard 1995:338-344).

However, before they ascend to the sky, they try to reconstruct their uncle Seven Hunapuh who the Xibalbans had killed in a previous episode. But his flesh had disintegrated, leaving only bones and a talking skull. Therefore, they had to bury him where he died in the ball court. They told him, however, that his name would be remembered, and he would be venerated on his day (the *ahau* days of the Maya calendar). This event is the likely foundation for the veneration of ancestors, according to Andres Xiloj, the K'iche' diviner who trained Barbara and Dennis Tedlock as daykeepers (1985:159-160, 295).

This great epic expresses principles of Mesoamerican thought that Gary Gossen (1986:5-6) presents in his introduction to a collection of scholars' essays on the subject. He identifies five key themes that have continuity in time and space in Mesoamerica, all of which I found to be particularly applicable to the ancestral ritual. One is the basic theme of "cyclical time as a sacred entity." Another two are "supernatural combat and secular conflict as creative and life-sustaining forces" and "complementary dualism." These themes relate to the battle between life and death waged by the Hero Twins against the Xibalban Lords. This dualistic combat between life and death for gods, humans, animals, and plants in endless cycles is a rationale for *hanal pixan*. The festival itself is private, domestic, and primarily maintained by women, who, as Gossen points out, "guard the older order" including ancestor cults even as change is taking place in the male-dominated public arena—an example of complementary dualism.

Another theme identified by Gossen (ibid.) is …a consistent delimitation of sky, earth, and underworld in the spatial layout of the cosmos, with mediation among these realms as a key intellectual, political, and religious activity, for with successful mediation come power, wisdom, even personal health and community survival.

Bringing this belief and resultant activity down to *hanal pixan* at the domestic level, a Maya family's success in getting the good things in life, or avoiding the bad, partly depends on tapping into another level of the cosmos—that of the souls. The last theme, "the extraordinary power of spoken and written language as a symbolic entity," is reflected in the *maestro cantor* calling on the spirits by name—an action that invites their participation—coupled with praying and singing from written material in Spanish and Maya.

The souls' *mesa* is oriented like the saints' permanent altar to the eastern wall (Figure 2). Many scholars have noted this orientation (Redfield and Villa Rojas 1962:131, 205) and a cosmological layout of objects on the *mesa* (Girard 1995:51-52, 216, Fig. 5; Hanks 1990: Ch.7, 8; Sosa 1990; Freidel and Schele 1993:Ch. 1; Paxton 2001:101-104, Ch. 7). Swiss ethnographer Rafael Girard (1995: 67), who studied the Ch'orti', proposed that the cosmogram was the model for the altar, the indigenous temple, the house, the town, the communal territory, the *milpa*, the plaza, and so on.

The Xocen *hanal pixan mesas* I documented all have four candles, one at each corner, with a principal food offering in the center in front of the cross and flowers. The specific foods vary, although the central offering for dinners is corn based, tamales or tortillas (Figures 2 and 3). In the diagram of the dinner setting for the adult souls on November 1 (Figure 4), along both the north and south sides are three clay bowls of *chilmole* (a chili and meat stew). The candles and principal food offering form a simple quincunx pattern: four points and center. Hanks

Figure 2. Hanal pixan mesa for the adult souls' dinner on November 1 (diagrammed in Figure 4).

Figure 3. Hanal pixan mesa for the adult souls' dinner on November 8 (octave); diagrammed in Figure 5.

(1990:Fig. 7.11) illustrates a similar *mesa* for the *hets' lu'um* (Fix Earth) ritual. He demonstrates and explains (1990:Ch.8) more complex patterns in a variety of *mesas* and settings. In my diagrammed *mesas* (Figures 4, 5, 8, and 9), I have used bolder lines for objects that I believe form a quincunx.

For the ancient Maya the veneration of ancestors has been recognized as a basic factor in their view of the cosmos (Freidel and Schele 1993:58) and a "critically important organizing force of all sections of Maya society—among commoners and nobles alike" (McAnany 1995:7-10). Investigations of archaeological, epigraphic, and ethnohistorical sources show that periodic feasting and honoring of the ancestors, long after burial, is a custom that was established early in Maya history (McAnany 1995:xii on the Formative, Masson 2000:Ch.6 for the Postclassic, and Landa 1941:131 for the Conquest Period). However, from the early Colonial Period, the Franciscan friars saw to it that the Maya celebrated their dead annually during the time selected by the Catholic Church. Nutini (1988:77-89) reported that, in Central Mexico, the Tlaxcalans had accepted this change early in the Colonial Period (ca. 1570). Since the Franciscans moved into Yucatán two decades later (1544 compared to 1524), they had already organized their agenda for conversion and control, as Nancy Farriss (1984: 161-162) has observed. They requested legal help from the Crown as discussed in what follows.

Orders to Observe Catholic Feast Days

In 1552, the Spanish Royal Audiencia gave certain orders, the Ordinances of Tomás López (Gates 1937:157-159, Landa 1978:203-219), requiring the Indians in Yucatán to keep all the Catholic holy days "as and in the manner fixed by the religious fathers." This ordinance included the Day of All Saints on November 1 and the Day of All Souls on November 2, established since the 12th century as Church holy days. The same orders forbade the Indians to build temples, oratories, or hermitages, or to possess idols. Naïve rites were also forbidden (including fasting, burning copal incense, and sacrificing animals). The ordinances even prohibited giving any banquet (*convite*) unless for a family occasion such as a wedding, but, even then, for a maximum of 12 guests.

Early in the Colonial Period the Maya adapted their own ancestor celebration to that for All Saints and All Souls, including the Catholic custom of observing the octave of the feast. Counting the first day as October 31, the holy period actually lasted for nine days. Coincidentally, nine was an important number for the Maya. Xbalanque, one of the Hero Twins, is the patron of the number 9, and nine Lords ruled the night hours (Miller and Taube 1993:53, 125).

Thus the Maya were able to retain their veneration of the dead in the domestic setting on the Church-approved days as long as no idols appeared, or copal incense, or other symbols of native religion. As Farriss (1984:289) observed, domestic rites to lesser spirits were not considered as serious a sin as the public ones and were regarded as mere superstition. This was also the case in rural Spain (Green 1995). Assuming the Church did not consider the private veneration of the departed souls as idolatry helps explain the persistence of *hanal pixan*.

Altars and *Mesas*

Hugo Nutini (1988:188-189), in his seminal work on the cult of the dead in Tlaxcala in Central Mexico, speaks of the home altar used for *Todos Santos* as much more than a structure, but as "a sacred precinct complex" and a focus for domestic ritual. Sharon (1976) provides a survey of shamans' *mesas* in Latin America. He identifies these *mesas* in Mesoamerica as "sacred space"(1976:90-91) and further defines the *mesa* as "an altar-like arrangement of power objects" (1976:71). He credits Maude Oakes (1951:180) for suggesting that the drawing of First Father and First Mother of the Aztecs in the Codex Borbonicus, seated in an enclosure, may be the model for the rectangular *mesa* in Mesoamerica.

The cosmogram in the Madrid Codex is another model for the *mesa* of the Maya, as Meredith Paxton has pointed out (2001:102-104) in relation to John Sosa's rendition of the Yalcobá altar (2001:Fig. 5.2) for the *ch'a chàak* rain ceremony. Whether indigenous, Catholic, or a combination, a characterization of sacred space constructed to communicate with supernaturals adequately describes all of these altars, including those for the dead.

The *mesas* of shamans for feeding the demigods and those made for the same purpose for the souls share significant traits that link them in space and time. After an overview of the souls' *mesa* at Xocen, I will discuss similarities in the basic elements of the ritual, orientation of the altar, cosmographic surfaces, and the offerings themselves.

Hanal Pixan in Xocen

The women carefully organize the candles and bowls of food to form a fixed pattern. Counting the objects, Don Lauro tells me, is "not a good thing to do." Earlier, Don Teodoro advised me that the objects on the souls' altar have to be an even number. The women answer my questions about the arrangement with *"cheen beyo"* ("it's just done this way"). Doña Jacinta assures me that this is the way her mother and grandmother always did the *mesa* for the dead.

The celebration lasts for nine days from October 31 through November 8. The schedule is:

• Day 1 (October 31): The family honors the souls of children.
• Day 2 (November 1): They honor the souls of adults.
• Day 3 (November 2): The family goes to the cemetery.
• Days 4 to 7 (November 3 to 6): The family prepares for the octave. The souls are present.

Some Maya exhume relatives who died three to four years previously for a ritual and reburial in a stone box in the cemetery.

• Day 8 (November 7): The family celebrates the octave for children.
• Day 9 (November 8): The family celebrates the octave of the adults and bids farewell to all the spirits.

There are seven separate settings. The dinners for adult ancestors are illustrated (Figures 4 and 5). Only two items are constant throughout the entire ceremony—the table itself and the Maya green-painted cross. The women of the household change the other items on the *mesa*, twice a day. The only exception is the octave day for the children, when they serve only one large meal. The changing offerings fit into fixed categories: flowers, candles, food (cooked and raw), virgin water, embroidered napkins, and tablecloths.

They place certain items under the table—gourds with dry corn "for the chickens the souls bring with them" (Doña Maria). This is the first time I had heard of animal souls being so honored, in Yucatán or Oaxaca. Other items she describes are washing powder and bluing for the souls to

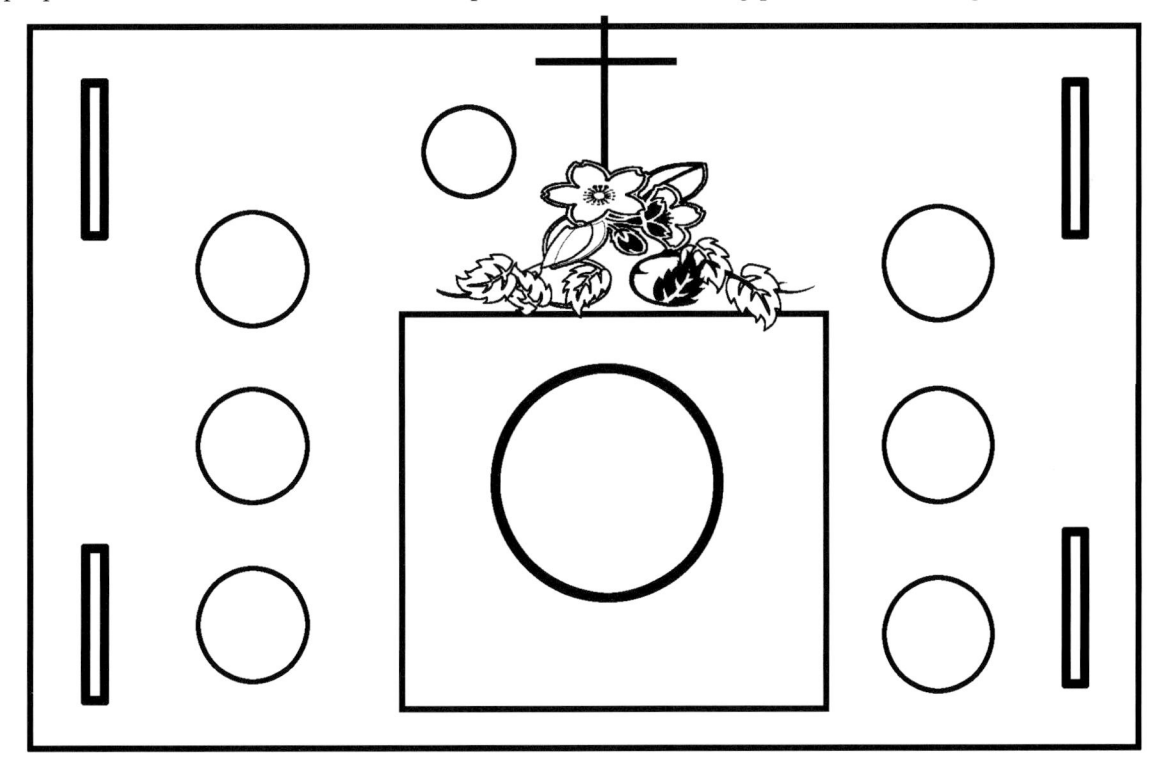

Figure 4. Mesa for the adult souls' dinner on November 1: White candles at the four corners, six pottery dishes of chilmole, one large gourd vessel of tortillas in the center, flowers and leaves at the base of the cross, the Maya cross at center of the east side of the table with a gourd bowl of water with rue next to it. There are two cloths on this table and the one in Figure 5, and a large napkin (latter not shown).

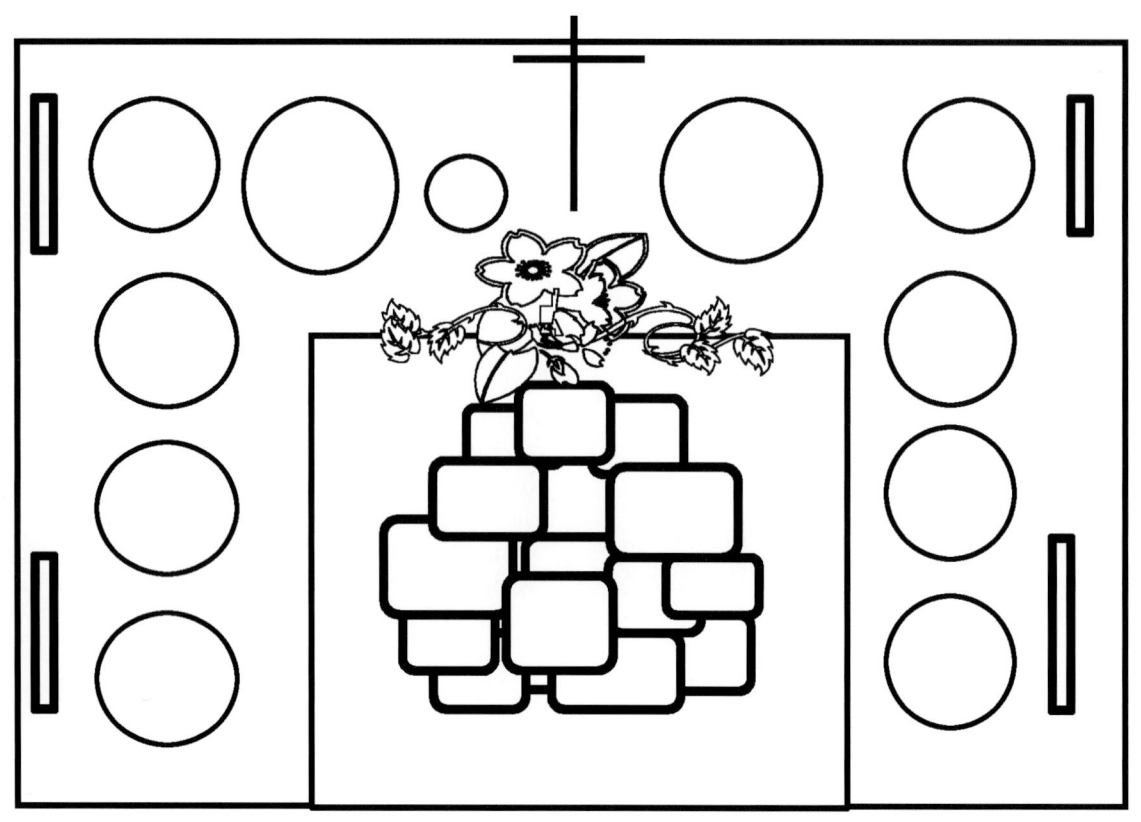

Figure 5. Mesa for the adult souls' dinner on November 8 (octave): White candles at the four corners, eight gourd bowls of atole, a mound of red tamales at center, flowers and leaves in front of the cross with two pails of peeled fruit at each side and one bowl of water with rue.

wash their clothes, Rosa Venus bar soap for bathing, and plain white cloth for the souls to wear while their clothes dry (visible in Figures 2 and 6).

Throughout *hanal pixan* a temporary auxiliary altar hangs in the doorway (Figure 7) over a white candle in a wooden holder on the floor. This hanging altar supports a container with one helping of the food provided at that particular meal. Like table and cross, this small *ch'uyub* (hanging frame for the offering) does not change, although its contents do. Distinct souls, called *las ánimas solas*, the lonely ones who have no one to pray for them, receive this food rather than the spirits of family relatives, who are regaled at the main souls' *mesa*.

Nearly all Maya homes have a permanent saints' altar, and the family I visited is no exception. The women place a portion of the same food offered to the souls for each meal on the saints' altar "so they won't be envious," says Doña Jacinta. On the Xocen permanent altar were images (statues and prints) of Christ as the Sacred Heart, the Virgin of Guadalupe, The Last Supper, and two crosses in a wooden box. The crosses are called saints in Maya (background in Figures 2, 3, and 6).

Figure 6. Doña Jacinta and the adults' breakfast mesa-altar for the octave, November 8.

Figure 7. Lonely soul hanging altar in the doorway.

The lonely souls and certain domestic animals (dogs and chickens) that have spirits also partake. This custom of feeding more than one type of soul with separate *mesas* near the main one has its parallel in today's shamanic ceremonies (Love 1989: Fig. 23.2, Redfield and Villa Rojas 1962:140, Villa Rojas 1945:116).

Comparing Shamans' and Souls' Altars

Given that shamans' altars and souls' altars among the Maya have a common primary goal—communication with the supernatural—one would expect similarities. The two private ceremonies reported in the literature that, in my opinion, most closely resemble the souls' altar in form and content are *u hanli kol/wahil kol* (both mean Dinner of the *Milpa*) and *u hanli kab* (Dinner of the Bees). *Hanal pixan* means Dinner of the Souls.

Redfield describes all three as private ceremonies (1962:134, 144). Individual farmers and beekeepers commission the shamans to lead the rite for the first two. For *hanal pixan* a family contacts the *maestro cantor* to lead the prayers for the souls. Four diagrams (Figures 4, 5, 8, and 9) show the top surfaces of the *mesas*. For a schematic to compare with Redfield's, I chose the most elaborate dinners of the adult souls on the day of arrival, November 1 (Figure 4), and on the day of leaving (octave), November 8 (Figure 5). Photographs of these *mesas* are shown in Figures 2 and 3.

The Dinner of the *Milpa* and Dinner of the Bees

Redfield describes the *u hanli kol* ceremony as only necessary when the cornfield is cut from virgin jungle, although there is another ritual for the used field *(hubche')* diagrammed by Villa Rojas (1945: 117). Figure 8 shows *u hanli kol*. Since the uncultivated jungle belongs to the supernatural beings that guard it, they must be compensated. The *u hanli kab* (diagrammed in Figure 9) fulfills the same obligation to the bee gods for the taking of honey (1962:127). Failure to follow the proper ritual in all cases can result in illness and misfortune (Redfield 1962:128, Villa Rojas 1945:132).

The basic structure of these rituals is almost identical for the gods of the forest, the bees, and the souls. Redfield (1962:128) in Chan Kom, Yucatán, and in X-Cacal in Quintana Roo (1945: 111) described the shaman-led agricultural ceremonies as having the following in common (I use Villa Rojas' categorization verbatim, but Redfield's is consistent with it):

• The careful preparation of certain special foods and drinks to be offered to the gods.
• An invitation to the *yuntzilob* and Christian deities to come and partake of the offerings.
• The formal delivery of the offerings by means of special prayers.
• The actual delivery of the foods and drinks to the gods.
• An interval of 20 to 30 minutes, during which time the gods and spirits are supposed to consume the "grace" or spiritual essence of the food.
• Distribution of the offerings to participants.

Bruce Love (1984) observed and recorded a *wahil kol* ceremony in Becanchen in 1978 that followed this pattern. He included chants for earlier and later stages of the ceremony. Judging by the times foods were served, the liquid (morning) and solids (afternoon) parallel the types of meals (breakfast and dinner) served to the souls in Xocen.

The Maya family at Xocen follows this ritual pattern for the souls. The *maestro cantor* summons

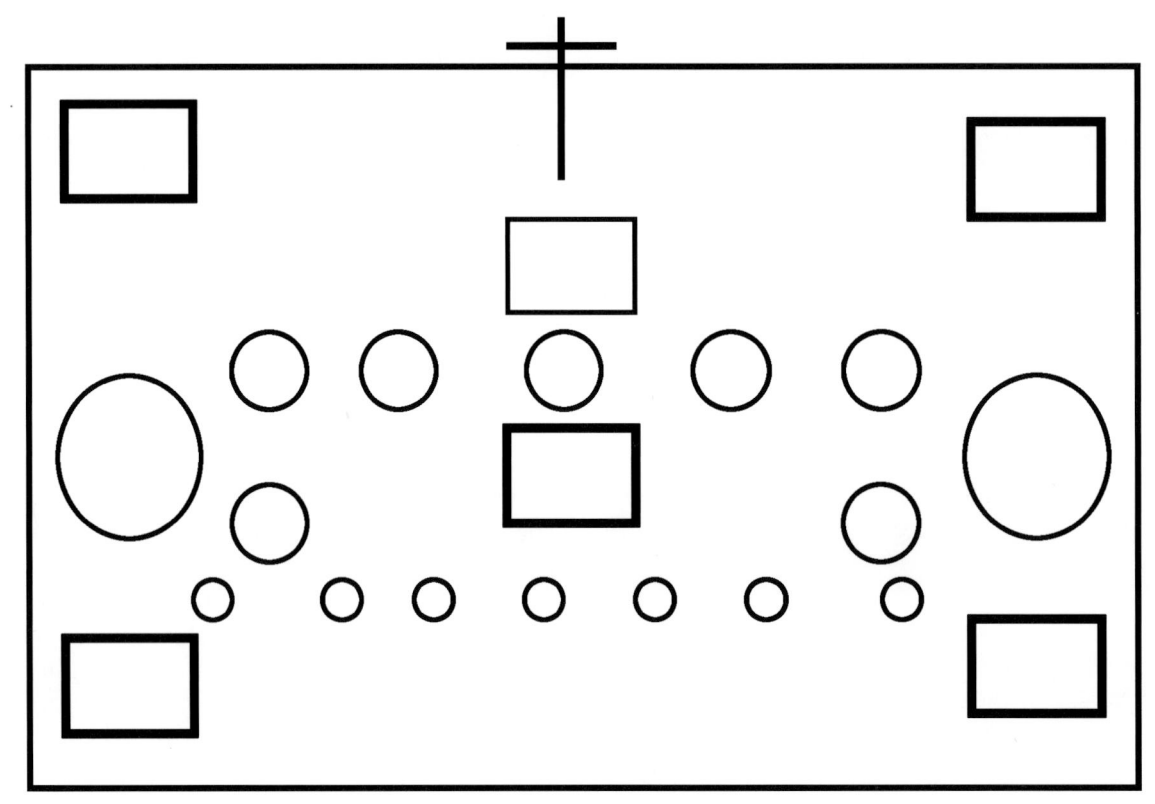

Figure 8. *Mesa* for the Dinner of the *Milpa (u hanli kol)*, redrawn from Villa Rojas (1945:117). A stack of six tamales at each of the four corners and at the center shown as rectangles, each with a gourd bowl on top; one pail of chicken soup between the tamales on each side; seven packages of 13 tortillas; and three tiny gourd bowls of ritual *atole (saka)*.

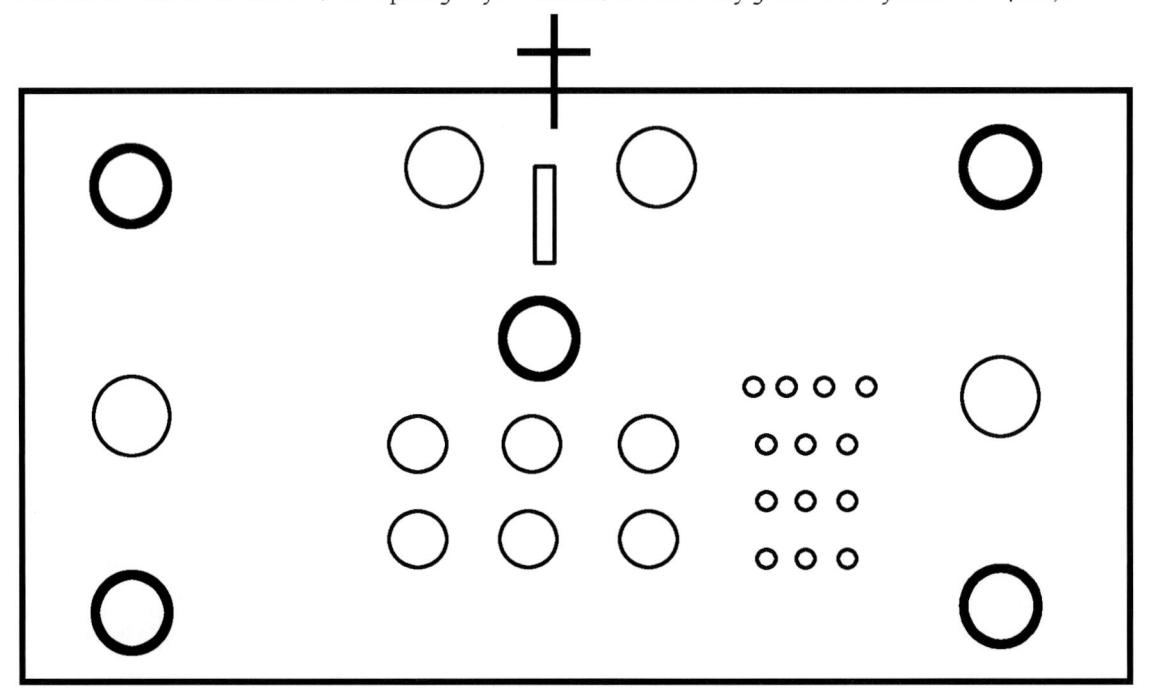

Figure 9. *Mesa* for the Dinner of the Bees, redrawn from Redfield and Villa Rojas (1962:145): Tamales at the four corners and down the sides—two called *bolon tas wah* on the upper corners with dishes of turkey meat on top and four others down the sides and at the lower corners called *yal wah* with turkey meat in dishes; one candle beneath the cross with tamales called *noh wah* next to the cross on either side; one large *cruz wah* (tamale) in the center and below it 6 pails of chicken broth with tamale pieces in it; and finally 13 tiny gourd bowls with a honey liquor called *balche'*.

the souls by name, the prayers and prepared food are offered, and then—following a hiatus for the souls to take the essence—the family eats.

Food and Foliage Offerings on Shamans' *Mesas* Versus the *Hanal Pixan Mesa*

In my opinion, differences in the foods offered reflect the fact that the shamans' *mesa* is dedicated to gods, and the souls' *mesa* to spirits of former humans. Women make the festival foods "consumed" by the deceased family members, just as they do for all the family festivals. In contrast, only men prepare the special tamales for the native gods and *saka'* (atole made without lime) that is used for indigenous rituals, as well as *balche'*, a fermented honey beverage made with strips of *Lonchocarpus* bark. The women do the preliminary preparation of dough and chicken broth at home for the shamans' rituals in the fields, but are not allowed to participate.

As for the altar itself, in all three ceremonies (Dinner of the *Milpa*, Dinner of the Bees, and Dinner of the Souls) the leader, *maestro cantor* or *h-men* (shaman in Maya), uses a rectangular wooden table with four legs for his *mesa*. He sets the Maya cross in the center of the east side. Flowers or leaves decorate the cross or are placed at its base. The principal food offering is placed in front of the cross and foliage in the center of the table. Thus the leader, the *h-men* in the agricultural ceremonies, *maestro cantor* or *rezadora* (female prayer leader) for *hanal pixan*, faces the east and the cross while praying. Along the sides of the table, set in an orderly fashion, are offerings of food or drink in *jícaras* or clay bowls called *lek*. Candles are a part of these ceremonies, but may or may not be set on the table.

In the Dinner of the Bees a single candle is placed on the altar. In Zinacantán, the Maya consider candles as food for the gods because they possess qualities of heat and light and consume themselves in their transformation from solid to gas (Vogt 1993:207).

The foods and drinks are all traditional ones, placed in gourd vessels called *luuch* (*jícara*) or *lek* made of clay. Maize dough is found in the cooked food at the mid-day feasts for the adults and is the main ingredient in the foods at the center of all the *hanal pixan* dinner meals. At breakfast settings the *pan de muerto* (wheat bread of the dead), a Colonial Period Spanish introduction (Green 1995), is served, but it is an obvious substitute for maize bread (Figure 6). For the octave brunch for the little souls both tamales and *pan de muerto* are provided (Figure 10).

The predominant central offerings directly in front of the cross and flowers are maize breads, usually tamales or tortillas, both of which can be called *wah* in Yukatek Maya (depending on the context). In his study of the role of tamales, Taube (1989) provides convincing evidence that they were the main offerings to the gods before and during the Conquest Period. Bruce Love (1989) describes in detail the many types of tamales used in agricultural rituals as well as providing a review of the use of sacred tamales in the ethnohistorical literature.

The *h-men's* table is also decorated with foliage—*habin* leaves (*Piscidia piscipula* in Herrera Castro 1994:Anexo). They are not shown on Redfield's diagrams (1962:136, Fig. 13) but are described in the text (1962:134).

The Xocen family uses amaranth, hibiscus, *op'ol ak'*, and coleus leaves for the souls' altar. Herrera Castro reports the plants used on the saints' altars in the neighboring village of Xuilub as amaranth (*Amaranthus hibridus*), hibiscus (*Hibiscus rosasinensis*), and coleus (*Coleus blumei*); *op'ol ak'* is not identified.

The flowers are important, especially in relation to the cross, which is often foliated with vegetation like the well known Foliated Cross of Palenque (Freidel et al.1993:Fig. 1.9). The Ch'orti'

Figure 10. Praying at the *hanal pixan mesa*-altar.

Maya near Copán (Girard 1995:134-135) cover their crosses and altars with green plants to signify the change of seasons for the Great Winter Opening ceremony. The Tzotzil Maya of Zinacantán adorn theirs with pine branches and red geraniums and refer to this decoration as clothing (Vogt 1993:44-50). Many scholars have studied the *Yaxche'il Kab*, First (Green) Tree of the World, a ceiba tree that intersects heaven, earth, and the underworld in Maya cosmology, and its connection to the Maya cross today (Girard 1995, Farriss 1984, León Portilla 1988, Hanks 1990, and Freidel and Schele 1993).

Pre-Columbian Altars with Offerings for the Dead

All of the *mesas* discussed above correlate with the following pre-Columbian Maya concepts:

• The orientation of the altar/*mesa* on the east side of a house or location so the shaman or *maestro cantor* prays facing east, home of the sun and *Chaks* (rain gods) in the dry season (Redfield and Villa Rojas 1962:116, 131).

• The cosmogram of the universe reflected in a quincunx pattern of altar offerings.

• Reciprocity in presenting food to the ancestors and gods in return for their protection and assistance.

• The centrality of the cross as the image of the First Tree, replacing pre-Conquest idols of deities and ancestors.

• Presence of vegetation on, under, or next to the cross.

• Offerings of prepared foods of pre-Columbian origin.

As for the idols of supernaturals used before the Conquest, archaeologist Marilyn Masson (2000) has found small portable stone sculptures at outlying, non-elite areas of the Postclassic Maya site of Mayapán. She postulates that these may "reflect a small-scale dimension of ancestor commemoration" (ibid.:202). In fact they may be ancestors. Some of the small sculptures she describes as *cuch* (meaning tribute or burden). They are in a diving or crouching position lacking specific iconography of deities and are "individualized" (ibid.:203-205). They may be humbler versions of the larger ceramic and wooden idols that Landa describes for the Maya lords and "people of position" in honoring ancestors on the eve of the Conquest (Landa 1941:131).

Landa writes of pre-Conquest home altars for ancestors described by indigenous informants, but does not describe their structure. He does say that the women made the offerings and maintained them. This reveals that these rituals were probably domestic and private, since only male priests maintained the temple and its altars. Women were excluded.

Richard Leventhal (1983) summarizes what is known about archaeological altars in Postclassic Mayapán. Family shrines are noted at elite residences, but perishable altars that probably existed in smaller, outlying house compounds would not have survived (1983:71).

The description of ancestor idols during the Conquest Period is much clearer than information on the altars. Landa (1941:131) states that

> People of position made for their fathers wooden statues of which the back of the head was left hollow, and they then burned a part of the body and placed its ashes there...They preserved these statues with a great deal of veneration among their idols.

He thus clarifies that idols of both deities and ancestors were kept together.

In the same paragraph he reveals where these idols were kept. Speaking of the deceased lords of the Cocom, Landa states that people kept their cleaned and reconstructed skulls

> ...with the statues, with the ashes, all of which they kept in the oratories of their houses with their idols, holding them in very great reverence and respect. And on all the days of their festivals and rejoicings, they made offerings of foods to them, so that food should not fail them in the other life, where they thought their souls reposed [ibid.].

Masson (2000:202) found miniature temples in outlying areas of Mayapan that suggest that the Maya copied large religious objects in miniature for household ritual. This custom is carried out today. The Tzotzil Maya make house crosses that are copies of the larger ones in the ceremonial center (Earle 1986:171, n. 5). For that matter, the Maya crosses in the Xocen household are painted miniature versions of those at the entrance to Xocen, complete with pedestal and clothing.

Altars and Agricultural Ritual in the pre-Columbian Setting

Landa described an outdoor rite during the month of Mac for which, in Tozzer's opinion, men constructed *mesas* as needed of a "heap of stones" that was decorated with green foliage (Landa 1941:163-164, n. 854, 855). Bishop Landa described the festival as a feast to assure rain, which was held in front of the temple on a temporary stone altar with greenery. The host, an individual sponsor, was the only one to fast beforehand.

The ritual procedure of preparing a *mesa* for the occasion, invoking the gods and perfuming them with incense, making offerings of food, and letting the gods partake before the people is the same pattern followed today for *hanal pixan* and the shamans' ceremonies. Landa stated that Maya

> ...scattered smoke from the incense many times and invoked the *Chaks* and *Itzamna* with their prayers and devotions, and made their offerings. This finished, they comforted themselves, eating and drinking what had been offered, very confident of the good year.

Offerings on the Ancient *Hanal Pixan* Altar

Patricia McAnany points out (1995:33-34) that the care of these domestic altars and idols of gods and ancestors was the women's responsibility. Landa (1941:131), in describing the women as devout and pious, says that they

> ...practiced many acts of devotion before their idols, burning incense before them and offering them presents of cotton stuffs, of food and drink and it was their duty to make the offerings of food and drink, which they offered in the festivals of the Indians.

From this it appears that the women not only maintained the altar, but also made the cloth offerings on their looms and prepared all the food and drink themselves. He makes it clear that the foods offered the souls and gods were festival fare, as they are today. Many of the prepared foods are of pre-Columbian origin. These delicacies are well documented in hieroglyphic inscriptions, iconography, and Conquest Period accounts of foods.

Tamales, chocolate, and *atole* appear as offerings to gods in the codices (Dresden Codex, Schele and Grube 1997), on Postclassic murals at Santa Rita and Tulúm (Masson 2000), and on Classic painted pottery (Reents-Budet 1994). Karl Taube (1989) and Bruce Love (1989) explain the primary role of tamales in ancient and modern ritual. Early chroniclers invariably called tamales *pan* (bread). The Maya called their tamales *"wah."* The hieroglyph for *wah* has been deciphered independently by Love (1989) and Taube (1989). Today the word for tortillas and bread in general is *wah*, although the word is used in special contexts for ritual tamales used in shamans' ceremonies. *Wah* is also used in the name of a special type (*cha'chak wah*, very red tamale) prepared for *hanal pixan*.

In the Dresden Codex alone, the tamales offered to the gods include varieties made of turkey, several kinds of fish, iguana, venison, and beans (Schele and Grube 1997). Landa's report amplifies the variety of tamales with additional information on offerings of tamales made of egg yolks, deer hearts, dissolved pepper *(pimienta)*, quail meat (1978:66), and squash seeds (1978:64). These maize cakes, wrapped in leaves, appear repeatedly as the principal offerings in rituals expressed in Maya art.

Tortillas, made from the same basic corn dough *(sakan)*, may be a close second today as a ritual offering, but are not mentioned in Landa or pictured in the codices. Both tamales and tortillas are pre-Columbian foods, although tortillas apparently came to the Maya area from Central Mexico after the Classic Period (Taube 1989:34)

Pre-Columbian festival food that Maya women prepare for the souls' *mesa* include tamales baked or steamed, tortillas, *atole (sa')*, fresh *atole (is ul)*, chocolate *(chukwa')*, chocolate *atole (tanchukwa')*, and meat stew in a chile and *atole* sauce *(chilmole)*.

Items that appear on the shamans' altar today, but not on the Xocen altar for souls, are specialized tamales made for the gods, the honey liquor *balche'*, *saka'* (the *atole* without lime), and a chicken broth thickened with maize bread. Sophie Coe discusses the pre-Columbian origin and preparation of these foods in her *America's First Cuisines* (1994:especially 120-168).

The *cha'chak wah* is the only *pib*-baked tamale made during the ceremony and the only one colored red with *achiote* (annato). In another paper, I propose that this tamale symbolizes the human body and blood, wrapped in a shroud of leaves and buried in the *pib*, to rise again to join the sun in the east (Green n.d.). This concept is illustrated in a Maya teaching (Dzul Poot, personal communication 1998) and a closely related Lacandón belief (McGee 1990:88-89). It also illustrates the principle of the duality of life and death in the endless cycles of time posited as a basis of Mesoamerican belief (Gossen 1986, Bricker 1981).

Summary

Linda Schele, David Freidel, and Joy Parker (1993:58) summarize the many perspectives scholars have taken towards this complex civilization as paths to understanding Maya reality. They highlight the concept of the quincunx as a "fivefold structure, of material and spiritual space," the belief in the influence of ancestors, the multivalent nature of the deities, and the debt owed to the gods, especially for creating man from maize.

They might as well have been describing the rationale for the *hanal pixan mesa* of the Xocen Maya family. The fivefold structure was represented on their *mesa* with its arrangement of foliage and cross, candles, and banquet foods. The ancestors were the guests at the feasts. As they tell me in Xocen, "It is because of the souls' power to help their descendants that we celebrate *hanal pixan*" (Don Lauro and Fatimo). The Canul family's own ancestors in the Colonial Period must have accepted the cross on their *mesa* as an aspect of the Tree of Life, and they displayed their feelings of obligation by the ceremonies themselves. The life-giving maize, from which humankind was born, was represented on every table setting as food for souls.

Obviously there is much to be done on this subject by students of the Maya, many more *mesas* to visit and study, Maya prayers and stories to translate, sites to excavate, and hieroglyphic texts and iconography to decipher before the fog completely clears. My hope is that this report makes some small contribution to the growing body of knowledge about the framework and cosmological basis for the impressive and reverent ceremony the Maya family of Xocen creates for their ancestors' yearly return.

Acknowledgements. I would like to acknowledge the many people and two organizations that made this fieldwork and resulting paper possible: the San Diego Independent Scholars' Helen Hawkins Fund which supported my research in 1998 and 1999; former Director Doug Sharon and the Collectors Club of the San Diego Museum of Man who sponsored my Maya costume and artifact acquisitions for the Museum's collections and *hanal pixan* exhibit; the Canul family in Xocen, Yucatán: Don Teodoro, Doña María, Don Lauro, Don Tomás, Doña Pascuala, young Fátimo Canul, and especially Doña Jacinta Canul Noh for being the *hanal pixan* organizer; anthropologists Silvia Terán and José Colon for assistance in setting up fieldwork; special thanks to my son, Alex Green, for being my photographer, companion, and driver on the 1998 expedition; and my closest friend and most patient critic, my husband, Willard Wells.

Judith Strupp Green
Research Associate, San Diego Museum of Man
3385 Tulane Court
San Diego, CA 92122
(858) 453-9194
judith.will@prodigy.net

References Cited

Barrera Vasquez, Alfredo
   1995 *Diccionário Maya,* Tercera Edición. México: Editorial Porrua.

Bricker, Victoria
   1981 *The Indian Christ, the Indian King: The Historical Substrate of Maya Myth and Ritual.* Austin: University of Texas Press.

Bricker, Victoria, Eleuterio Po'ot Yah, and Ofelia Dzul de Po'ot
   1998 *A Dictionary of the Maya Language as Spoken in Hocabá, Yucatán.* Salt Lake City: University of Utah Press.

Coe, Sophie
   1994 *America's First Cuisines.* Austin: University of Texas Press.

Dzib May, Andrés
   1999 *Breve Reseña del Pueblo de Xocén "El Centro del Mundo."* Valladolid: Gobierno del Estado de Yucatán.

Earle, Duncan
   1986 The Metaphor of the Day in Quiche: Notes on the Nature of Everyday Life. In: Gary Gossen, ed., *Symbol and Meaning: Beyond the Closed Community,* Volume 1, pp.155-172. Albany: Institute for Mesoamerican Studies.

Everton, Macduff
   1991 *The Modern Maya: A Culture in Transition.* Albuquerque: University of New Mexico Press.

Farriss, Nancy
   1984 *Maya Society under Colonial Rule.* New Jersey: Princeton University Press.

Freidel, David, Linda Schele, and Joy Parker
   1993 *Maya Cosmos: Three Thousand Years on the Shaman's Path.* New York: William Morrow and Company.

Gates, William
   1937 The Ordinances of Tomás López. Of the Royal Audience of the Confines, Promulgated in 1552. In: *Yucatán, Before and After the Conquest*, pp. 157-159. New York: Dover Publications.

Girard, Rafael
   1995 *People of the Chan*. Chino Valley, Arizona: Continuum Foundation

Gossen, Gary, ed.
   1986 *Symbol and Meaning: Beyond the Closed Community*. Essays in Mesoamerican Ideas. Studies on Culture and Society, Volume 1. Albany: Institute for Mesoamerican Studies.

Green, Judith Strupp
   1969 *Laughing Souls: The Days of the Dead in Oaxaca*. San Diego: San Diego Museum of Man.

   1972 The Days of the Dead in Oaxaca, México: An Historical Inquiry. *Omega* 3(3):245-261. (Republished in John B. Williamson and Edwin S. Shneidman, eds., *Death: Current Perspectives*. Mountain View: Mayfield Publishing Company.)

   n.d. Tamales, Souls and Resurrection: The Days of the Dead in Xocen, Yucatán. Ms. submitted for publication.

Hanks, William
   1990 *Referential Practice: Language and Lived Space among the Maya*. Chicago and London: The University of Chicago Press.

Herrera Castro, Natividad
   1994 *Etnoflora Yucatense: Los Huertos Familiares Mayas en el Oriente de Yucatán*. Mérida: Universidad Autónoma de Yucatán.

Landa, Diego de
   1941 *Landa's Relación de las Cosas de Yucatán*. Translated by Alfred Tozzer. Papers of the Peabody Museum of American Archaeology and Ethnology 18. Cambridge: Harvard University. (Reprint edition, Kraus Reprint, Millwood, New York.)

   1959 *Relación de las cosas de Yucatán*. Introduction by Angel Ma.Garibay K. México: Editorial Porrua.

Leventhal, Richard
   1983 Household Groups and Classic Maya Religion. In: Evon Vogt and Richard Leventhal, eds., *Prehistoric Settlement Patterns: Essays in Honor of Gordon R. Willey*, pp. 55-76. Albuquerque: University of New Mexico Press and Cambridge: Peabody Museum of Archaeology and Ethnology, Harvard University Press.

León-Portilla, Miguél
   1988 *Time and Reality in the Thought of the Maya*. Norman and London: University of Oklahoma Press.

Love, Bruce
   1989 Yucatec Sacred Breads through Time. In: William F. Hanks and Don S. Rice, eds., *Word and Image in Maya Culture, Explorations in Language, Writing and Representation*, pp. 336-350. Salt Lake City: University of Utah Press.

   1984 Wahil Kol: A Yucatec Maya Agricultural Ceremony. *Estudios de Cultura Maya* 15:251-300.

McGee, R. Jon
   1998 The Lacandon Incense Burner Renewal Ceremony: Termination and Dedication Ritual Among the Contemporary Maya. In: Shirley Boteler Mock, ed., *The Sowing and the Dawning*, pp. 41-46. Albuquerque: University of New Mexico Press.

McAnany, Patricia
   1995 *Living with the Ancestors: Kinship and Kingship in Ancient Maya Society*. Austin: University of Texas Press.

Masson, Marilyn
   2000 *In the Realm of Nachan Kan: Postclassic Maya Archaeology of Laguna de On, Belize*. Boulder: University Press of Colorado.

Miller, Mary, and Karl Taube
   1993 *The Gods and Symbols of Ancient Mexico and the Maya*. London: Thames and Hudson.

Mújica, Sharon
   n.d. Sacred Books: The Case of Xocen. Unpublished paper in possession of the author, prepared for delivery at the Latin American Studies Association XX International Congress, Guadalajara, 1997.

Nutini, Hugo
   1988 *Todos Santos in Rural Tlaxcala, A Syncretic, Expressive and Symbolic Analysis of the Cult of the Dead*. Princeton: Princeton University Press.

Orilla, Miguel Angel
   1996 *Los Dias de Muertos en Yucatán (Hanal Pixan)*. Merida: Maldonado Editores

Paxton, Merideth
   2001 *The Cosmos of the Yucatec Maya: Cycles and Steps from the Madrid Codex*. Albuquerque: University of New Mexico Press.

Redfield, Robert, and Alfonso Villa Rojas
   1962 *Chan Kom: A Maya Village*. Chicago: The University of Chicago Press.

Reents Budet, Dorie
   1994 *Painting the Maya Universe: Royal Ceramics of the Classic Period*. Durham: Duke University Press.

Schele, Linda, and Nikolai Grube
   1997 Notebook for the XXI Maya Hieroglyphic Forum at Texas. University of Texas at Austin.

Sharon, Douglas
   1976 Distribution of the Mesa in Latin America. *Journal of Latin American Lore* 2(1):71-95.

Sosa, John
   1990 Cosmological, Symbolic and Cultural Complexity among the Contemporary Maya of Yucatán. In: Anthony Aveni, ed, *World Archaeoastronomy*, pp. 130-142. Cambridge: Cambridge University Press.

Taube, Karl
   1989 The Maize Tamale in Classic Maya Diet, Epigraphy, and Art. *American Antiquity* 54(1):31-51.

Tedlock, Dennis
   1985 *Popul Vuh: The Maya Book of the Dawn of Life.* New York: Simon and Schuster.

Villa Rojas, Alfonso
   1945 *The Maya of East Central Quintana Roo.* Washington, D.C.: Carnegie Institute.

Vogt, Evon.
   1993 *Tortillas for the Gods: A Symbolic Analysis of Zinacanteco Rituals.* Norman: University of Oklahoma Press.

Wind, Rain, and Stone: Ancient and Contemporary Maya Meteorology

Matthew G. Looper

The importance of cosmograms in ancient Maya material culture is well known. In a comprehensive treatment of this subject, Freidel, Schele, and Parker (1993) argue that architectural complexes modeled on the fundamental structures of the cosmos served to sanctify the actions performed within their confines. Temple-pyramids represent mountains with caves; stelae embody world-trees; plazas symbolize the primordial sea surrounding the earth; and ballcourts are the passage into the underworld. Although rendered on a monumental scale, these elite structures are still microcosms. Their significance depended upon well-defined notions of an animate, stratified, and geometrically regular universe, as well as knowledge of the ritual procedures required to activate them. Likewise, twentieth-century Maya ethnography provides ample evidence of similar beliefs and practices, well illustrated by the Yukatek rainmaking ceremony called *ch'a chàak* (Freidel, Schele, and Parker 1993:29-33, 51-58; Redfield and Villa Rojas 1934:138-143). Here, a platform laden with offerings is presented to the rain spirits or *Chaks*, who gather above it. An arbor, formed by boughs that arc over the table connecting opposite corners, represents the sky. During the ceremony, a ring suspended by a cord from the apex of the arbor serves as a portal through which the *Chaks* may partake of the offerings. Although separated from the Classic Period monuments by over a millennium, this ritual embodies cosmological principles that are documented in the archaeological record (Looper and Kappelman 2001).

The rainmaking function of the *ch'a chàak* ritual underscores the importance of weather control as a motivation for the contemporary Maya cosmogram. In contrast, the analysis of ancient cosmograms has emphasized geometric, astronomical, geographical, and biological aspects. Meteorology remains an undeveloped domain of cosmology. This is surprising, because *Chak* is commonly represented in all media. For example, two monuments at Quiriguá depict this being in full form, dancing at the mouth of a cave. The image on one of these so-called altars (Altar P') shows bands flowing from the figure's mouth, which twist across the face of the monument, terminating in skeletal heads (Figure 1). Glyphic markings on these bands include *sak* "white, pure," the T533 *ajaw*-face which is a floral icon, and the *ik'* sign, meaning "breath, wind, or spirit." These glyphs suggest that these cords represent the vital forces inherent in the wind that accompanies rainstorms. The prominence of rain imagery on this monument suggests that it may have been functionally analogous to the rainmaking platform used in the *ch'a chàak* ceremony.

This paper proposes that meteorology was a prominent aspect of certain ancient Maya cosmograms. The evidence is drawn primarily from ancient texts and images, but is supported by comparisons with ethnographic information from the Ch'orti', a Maya group that has direct historical connections to the Classic lowland culture. While Altar P' suggests that some of the monuments designated as "altars" are similar functionally to certain present-day Maya rain-

Douglas Sharon, ed., *Mesas & Cosmologies in Mesoamerica*. San Diego Museum Papers 42, 2003.

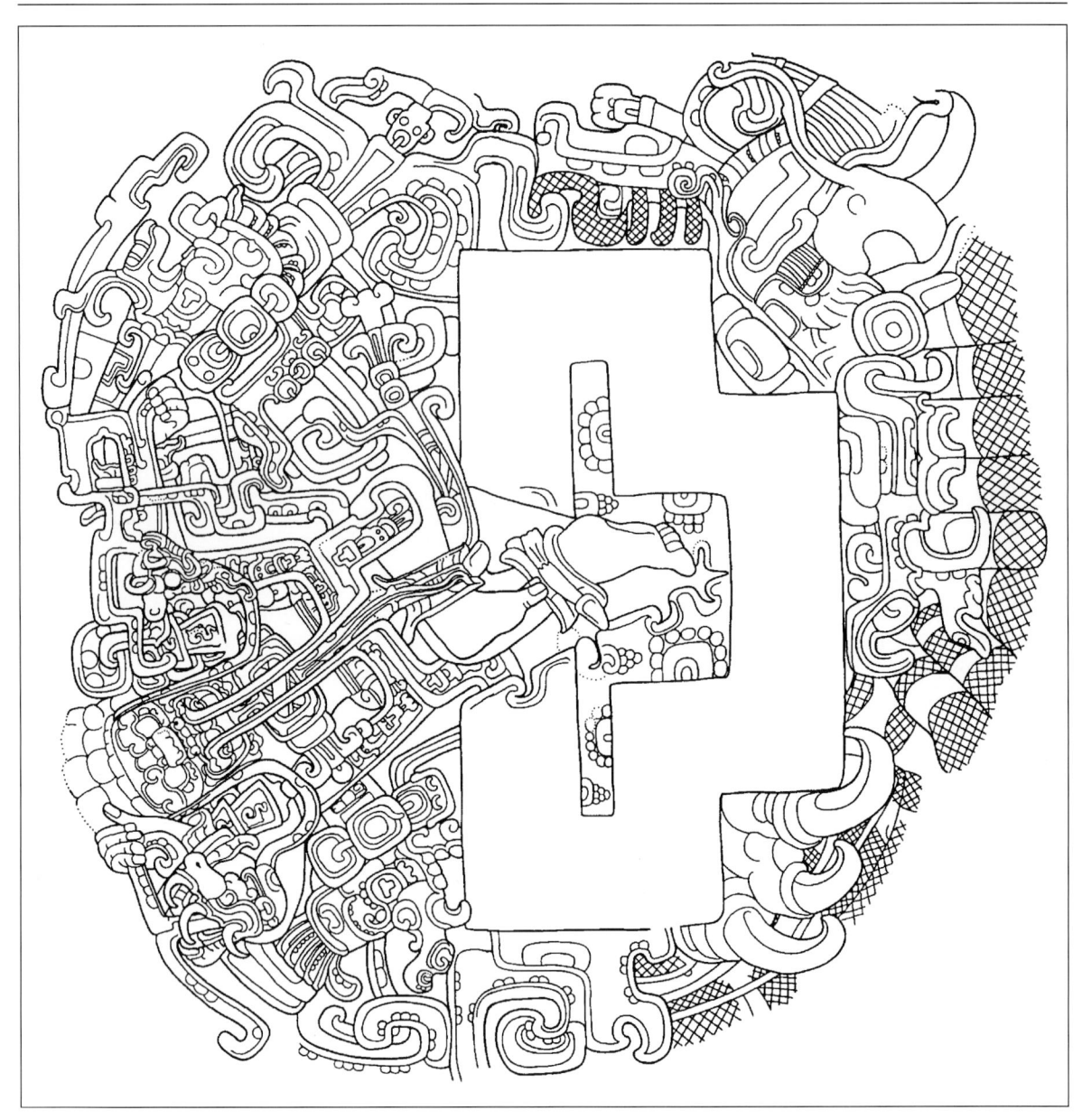

Figure 1. Quiriguá Altar P', upper face (inscription removed).

making cosmograms, I will show that there are other structures that the Maya used to control wind and rain. Indeed, just as the Ch'orti' consider the universe to be miniaturized in diverse patterns, including houses, *milpas,* and the altars upon which the saints are placed (Wisdom 1940:430), I will suggest that the design of an entire architectural and sculptural complex at Late Classic Quiriguá was based on a rainmaking cosmogram. Although this architectural group incorporates chronological and political concepts that are no longer implemented by the Ch'orti', the ritual procedure it commemorates bears a remarkable structural congruence with the main ceremonies that the Ch'orti' conduct to inaugurate the rainy season.

Ch'orti' Meteorology

The information concerning Ch'orti' meteorology is gathered from diverse sources. Undoubtedly the most complete is that of Rafael Girard, based on fieldwork in several communities (especially at Quetzaltepeque) and conducted over several decades (Girard 1949, 1966, 1969, 1995). Additional information was compiled by Wisdom (1940), while the oral histories recorded by Fought (1972) are of great value for their documentation of native terminology. Two aspects of Girard's work need to be mentioned in order to understand the value of his data in relation to the ancient Maya. First, the ceremonies he describes are presented as relating closely to the cycle of slash-and-burn agriculture. Further, Girard claims that the agricultural cycle was structured according to a count of 260 days, starting on February 8 and ending on October 26. Both of these claims have been refuted by other scholars. In fact, Fought (1972:58) questions the association between these ceremonies and the agricultural season, suggesting that many of the rituals described by Girard occur in diverse contexts. These discrepancies, however, do not detract from the relevance of Girard's information for the interpretation of ancient Maya cosmology. As we shall see, the ancient Maya evoked meteorological phenomena in a variety of contexts, even while their calendrical system remained independent of the succession of rainy and dry seasons during the solar year.

In the Ch'orti' area, as in adjacent regions, the year is divided into marked rainy and dry seasons, with the rain, sometimes in the form of violent thunderstorms, beginning around May 1 and lasting through October. This is interrupted by a brief dry spell, or *canícula*, in late July-early August. The remainder of the year is fairly dry, with only occasional and scattered light showers. According to the Ch'orti', this seasonal alternation is caused by movements of the sun, as it departs from its southerly position in December and moves gradually northward. As the strength and heat of the sun increase, displacements in the atmosphere occur, which must be controlled through the release of water to the earth (Girard 1995:49). This is accomplished by the actions of supernaturals called Angels (Fought 1972:377-378), or Working Men (Wisdom 1940:395-396). Normally, the cosmological position of these beings is at the four corners of the earth, where the earth and sky meet at a point, "like the back of a wasp" (Fought 1972:374). Here, they are responsible for holding the pillars that support the sky. *Chihchans*, imagined as great snakes and cloud personifications, serve as the mounts for the Working Men (Wisdom 1940:392-395). To make rain, the *Chihchans* drink from cosmic basins located at the corners of the earth and are then ridden toward the locations where rain is released (Girard 1995:157). The prayer for rain implores these entities: "you towering clouds, rise up, take form in the green lake, the white lake; take form over the green mountains, over the peaks" (Fought 1972:414). To some extent, the Working Men are conflated with wind spirits *(ah yum ikar)*, which are present in every movement of air (see Wisdom 1940:397). Like the Working Men, they are sometimes described as "horsemen" who carry rain over the earth. Girard (1995:66) describes these spirits as bearded and located at the four cosmic corners. Wind may also be caused by the movement of *Chihchans* (Fought 1972:84-85, 122). Using axes (lightning bolts), the Working Men beat the rain out of the clouds (Fought 1972: 436). The same axes are also occasionally flung at the terrestrial *Chihchans* that can cause landslides, or at evil spirits that cause illness (Fought 1972:342).

The purpose of Ch'orti' meteorological ceremonies is to entice these supernaturals with feasting and prayer to move and act in an orderly and beneficial fashion. They are attracted by arrangements of cosmologically-oriented food, images, and ritual objects, presented according to complex ritual procedures performed by elders (*"padrinos"*) and their assistants, called "slaves." Some of these ceremonies occur at sacred sites in the landscape, while others are conducted in the community *cofradía* houses or "agrarian temples," as Girard refers to them (Wisdom 1940:384-385, Girard 1995:245ff). For the purposes of this paper, only the outline of these procedures is presented. As described by Girard (1995:20-54) for Quetzaltepeque, the ceremonies commence on February 8, a date corresponding to cosmic creation. The initial act is a pilgrimage to a sacred pool called El Orégano, located to the west of town. This pool is considered to be a portal to the underworld, as well as a cosmic basin that feeds the clouds. At the pool, a cloth is spread on the ground, and upon it are placed five gourds of *chilate*, a ceremonial drink made of maize and cacao. Arranged in a quincunx, these offerings constitute a "payment" (Fought 1972:416), intended to persuade the spirits of the four directions to withhold the wind and rain until the proper time. Upon return to Quetzaltepeque, the elders perform a ritual in the *cofradía* house in which malevolent winds are captured and sealed in jugs. Otherwise, these winds might escape from the underworld, causing disease and crop failure (see Fought 1972:266-267). These jugs are placed under the altar, a table upon which stands an image of the local saint, along with two containers of virgin water from Esquipulas and a "canoe," or wooden trough (see Wisdom 1940:147). These five containers are arranged in a quincunx, with the canoe in the center, the two vessels of water to the east, and the two jugs of "wind" to the west. A second quincunx, this time of river stones gathered previously at the El Orégano pool, is erected on top of the table, underneath the saint's seat. Finally, a feast is served on an adjacent table.

The purposes of the rites of early February are designed to gather the sacred materials needed for subsequent rituals, and to arrange them in the agricultural temple in preparation for the months ahead. The "creation" rituals inaugurate a period of labor, in which the fields are cleared of vegetation. These conclude by the time of the vernal equinox (March 20), or Holy Week, when "formal invitations" are sent to the spirits (Girard 1995: 72). The peak of this sequence begins on Good Friday, when, following ceremonies in the church, a banquet for the spirits is prepared in the temple, laid on a table. The next day, Saturday, the officiating elder puts out the temple fire and starts a new fire, from which the domestic hearths are relit. Importantly, in Chiquimula, this ritual is conducted using the ancient technique of drilling, in which a stick that is placed in a socket on a board is spun between the hands until sparks appear. This event signals that it is time to burn the fields. Cosmologically, the act of burning serves to feed the clouds which are presently to produce the rain.

The rainy season "officially" commences on April 30-May 1, marked by the zenith passage of the sun. On this date, according to Girard (1995: 58-59) the "fertility god" impregnates the earth when passing through the zenith at noon. This date is announced by astral phenomena, marked by significant positions of Orion, the "Cross of May" and the Pleiades (Fought 1972:59, Girard 1995:100). In addition, a gnomon or the body may be used to verify that the "lord is moving straight" (Girard 1995:183). Even before this date, however, the Ch'orti' elders conduct crucial rainmaking ceremonies both in the *cofradía* house and at certain sacred locations. The first is on April 22, when a cross is planted at the spring that is the source of the La Conquista river, symbolically identified with the underworld (Girard 1995:103-104). This cross, made of the heartwood of the mother cacao *(Gliricidia sepium)* and covered with green *conte* leaves, is inscribed with the name of the elder who made it. It is set in front of the spring, added to the crosses "planted" during previous years. As during the visit to El Orégano, stones are collected at the spring, later to be planted in the corners of the temple or in the lower corners of the saint's table. Shortly thereafter, at midnight on April 24 or 25, a ceremony is held at the La Conquista spring (Girard 1995: 106-117). Here, two ritual structures are prepared, one between the cross and the spring which serves as an offering to celestial spirits, and another near the fire, with a pit for offerings to the earth. Concerning this offering for the Earth, which is termed *"palangana," "convento,"* or *"mesa"* (Fought 1972:525), Fought's informant states:

> They say that there it was put up, the basin of the spirit of the earth. They say that when everything is being set down, *chilate*, chickens, turkeys, incense, they say that it is as if on that table they had placed everything. And the spirit of the earth rises and takes everything which was placed in front of him [Fought 1972:468].

The climax of the ceremony is the sacrifice of *chilate,* and then two turkeys, which have been allowed to copulate:

> After the elder has poured the contents of the five containers of *chilate* into the sacred pit, to "feed" the Earth, he orders the number one slave to perform the sacrifice. The slave then holds the turkey in the air over the pit and with the help of the other slave, with a single slash of his sharp knife cuts off the head of the bird so it falls into the hole. The elder comes to verify that all the blood of the bird falls into the center of the pit, and personally lends his assistance by squeezing the turkey's neck. Then, the same slave opens the breast of the animal and with great dexterity takes out the heart and intestines, which he throws into the cavity; then he does the same with the legs. Next the slaves pluck the turkey completely and fill the pit with the feathers. The same operation is performed on the hen turkey. It is half past two in the morning [Girard 1995:113].

Regarding these opening rites of the rainy season, Girard (1995:199) states that, "everywhere the blood sacrifice of birds is prevalent and indispensable" (see also Wisdom 1940:437-440).

Back in the village, the elders induce the coming of rain using a variety of techniques. First, green leaves gathered from the spring replace the foliage decorations of the saint's altar (Girard 1995:135). Water, frogs, and fish collected from the spring are placed in the canoe, which symbolizes the underworld (Girard 1995:114). In addition, the temple interior is moistened with sacred water (Girard 1995:138). Next, two male and two female elders sit in chairs placed around the table located in front of the saint's altar and stand simultaneously. This ritual, called "raising the sky," is conducted with close attention to simultaneous action so as not to imbalance the cloud layer. Its function is to summon the Working Men to arise into the sky from their position at the corner posts (Girard 1995:141). The spirits are thereby summoned to come to the table to drink *chilate* that is laid out for them. This complex ritual sequence is followed by the planting of the fields, accompanied by additional decapitations and blood sacrifices of turkeys in holes dug in the *milpa* (Wisdom 1940:441-444). Girard (1995:185, 188) states that the seed is consecrated on April 25, and that planting proceeds from this date until May 4, depending on the altitude. Similar ceremonies of rainmaking and offerings to the earth also occur later in the agricultural season, in association with the second planting of the *milpa* which occurs around August 12 or 13, marked by the second zenith passage. However, these ceremonies are held on a smaller scale than those that are held around the first zenith passage (Girard 1995:302).

From the above accounts, it is clear that a variety of cosmograms, created in diverse settings, are used by the Ch'orti' for the invocation of deities of wind, rain, and fertility. Some are placed directly on the ground, others elevated on tables. Some are located in the interior of temples; others at sacred "underworldly" locations in the landscape. However, as emphasized by Girard, the unifying feature of these cosmograms is their conceptual origin as maps of solar movement. The arrangement of offerings in a quincunx is the most basic manifestation of this pattern, in which the four corners correspond to the points of solstitial sunrise and sunset, while the center point represents the sun at zenith. In the shrine at Quetzaltepeque, the local saint is incorporated into this structure, framed by a quincunx of stones arranged on the altar under the image. Perhaps the most complex variant is documented at Chiquimula, in which a feast for the spirits is arranged on the temple floor extending in a long rectangle from the entry on the west to the altar in the east (Girard 1995:200). This arrangement, identified as a diagram of the sun's path, features twelve gourds of *chilate* on the northern edge, reserved for the clouds, and twelve more on the south, assigned to the Angels. A bowl of *chilate* at the center is designated for the "Center God," a personification of the forces of fertility located at the zenith.

In addition, although their forms are extremely diverse, it is clear that the Ch'orti' meteorological cosmograms consist of multiple elements, which are viewed as a symbolic totality. They include a cross and/or saint's image, a pit, and a designated zone, sometimes elevated on a table, for the display of food offerings. With the exceptions of Quetzaltepeque and Chiquimula, most shrines have permanent pits located in front of the altar. At Santa Rosalía, the pit is called the "soul of the world," while at Quetzaltepeque, the canoe substitutes for the pit (Girard 1995:256). Girard notes that the combination of altar, cross, and pit is called "the form" (*la forma*) by the Ch'orti' (Girard 1995:249). While many altars feature arbors of saplings or canes arched over the cross or image, others enclose the entire "form" beneath a celestial arbor, similar to the Yukatek *ch'a chàak* platform. This is documented at Tunucó, where a platform of poles is built over a spring, supported by four forked uprights (Girard 1995:251). A cross clothed in leaves is located in the center, beneath two leaf-covered arches that connect opposite corners of the platform. Underneath is a pit for offerings. This structure is analogous to the ceremonial house at Cayur, in which the entire interior space is encompassed by flexible poles wrapped in foliage that connect the interior posts (Girard 1995:249). In addition to representing the sky, these arbors constitute miniature houses (Fought 1972:525). As such, they emphasize the significance of the "form" as a protective and geometrically ordered cosmographic device that is activated by prayer, sacrifice, and feasting in order to draw beneficent forces from the periphery to the center.

Classic Maya Meteorology

Having outlined the general features of Ch'orti' weather control through cosmographic ritual, we may now turn to the Classic Maya. In fact, Girard (1995:256ff) has already noted the apparent correspondence between the cross-altar-pit complex of the Ch'orti' with the stela-altar-cache complex seen at many ancient sites. While Girard provided little Classic-period data to support his argument, there is some merit to the idea that monumental "altars" such as Altar P' at Quiriguá may have served as sites where spirits gathered to partake of food offerings. Interestingly, the evidence seems strongest from the site of Copán, located within the Ch'orti' territory. For example, one distinctive feature of late Classic "altars" from Copán is the appearance of seated figures on their sides. The most famous example of this is Altar Q, a rectangular stone placed at the base of Structure 10L-16 in 775 CE, which depicts the 16 members of the Classic dynasty of Copán in succession. Similar images depicting what are probably spirit beings or ancestors appear on the sides of Altars T (783 CE) and U (780 CE) as well. Perhaps these images evoke the gathering of supernatural beings that were believed to take place around similar stones.

The proposition that such monuments were similar in function to the altars or feasting tables of the Ch'orti' is supported by the text of Altar U, which contains a reference to drinking. This appears at G5-H5, in which a series of titles and what appear to be deity names is followed by *ti uch'* "with drinking" (Figure 2). The final glyph in this clause, *chih,* is of uncertain interpretation, but may be a term for plant fiber (see Wisdom 1950:700). As such, it may refer to a drink made from steeped plant fibers similar to *balche,* a beverage made of fermented honey to which the bark of the *balche* tree was added (see Thompson 1970:182).[1] In the Yucatán, *balche* is used in *ch'a chàak* ceremonies, as well as in *milpa* ceremonies, when the following prayer is uttered: "To the rising of the clouds in the east, to the ascension to the middle of the heaven, the majesty, to the thirteen layers of clouds in the east, the yellow *Chak,* set in order, the lords of the companions, all the inhabitants, he of the tables placed in order for the holy steeped *balche* drink" (Thompson 1970:193, 259-260). A related glyphic passage may also occur on Copán Altar K, dedicated in 688 CE: *y-a-hiy ch'ok winik i-uch' ti yutal sak sa' chih,* "at that place? was the young person, and now he has drink with his food, the white atol *chih*" (Figure 3). It should be noted, however, that neither of these "altars" have any other specific iconographic reference to drinking, feasting, wind, or

Figure 3. Copán Altar K, M1-N2.

rain, making their relationship to the twentieth-century ceremonies uncertain.

A more convincing argument for the evocation of weather-related ceremonies in Classic Maya visual culture can be found at Quiriguá, where structures other than the stone "altars" document the unfolding of rites that are structurally analogous to Ch'orti' rituals described above. The context for these ceremonies is the conflict of 738 CE, through which Quiriguá, led by the ruler K'ak' Tiliw, achieved independence from Copán. The pivotal event in this ritual sequence was the decapitation of the Copán ruler Waxaklajun Ub'ah K'awil ("18-Rabbit") on May 3, 738—the date of the first zenith passage of the year at Quiriguá (Figure 4). This event recalls the annual turkey decapitation conducted by the Ch'orti' on the zenith passage in order to make the rain fall. In addition, both ancient and contemporary ritu-

Figure 2. Copán Altar U, G5-H5.

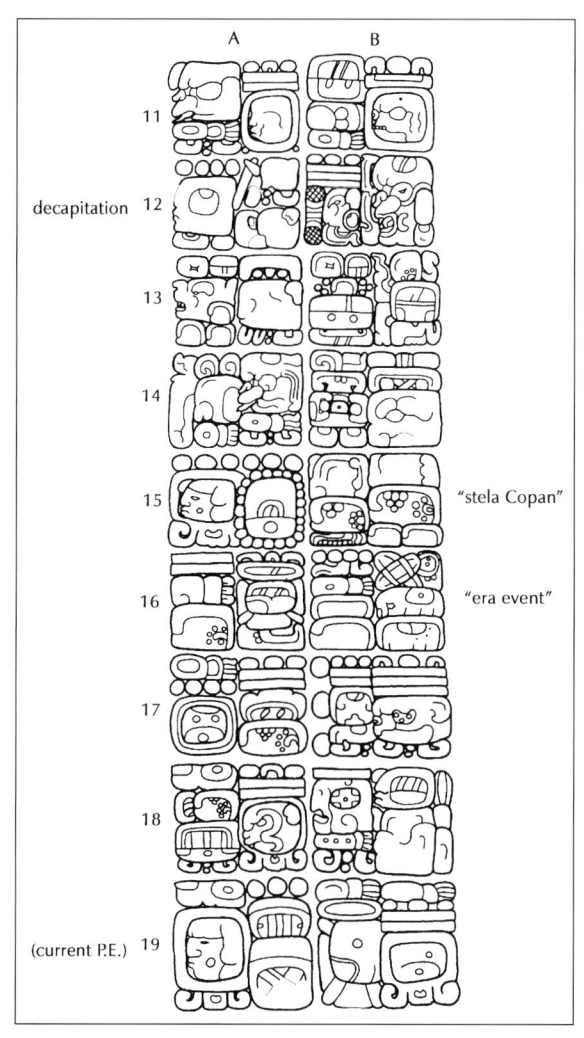

Figure 4. Quiriguá Stela F, west inscription.

als took place at locations associated with the underworld. For the Ch'orti', the place of sacrifice is a sacred spring. At Quiriguá, the place of sacrifice is identified on Stela F as a "black hole place," the glyph for "hole" being identical to the "cenote" glyph in the codices (T591). The same glyph is used on Quiriguá Stela H with reference to the place of monument dedication, suggesting that the Great Plaza itself recreated this particular sacred location. The use of "black" in the name of this place may reflect the Ch'orti' association of rainy season rites with this color. As Girard (1995:160) notes, the principal elder who conducts the rain ceremonies wears a dark (blue) headband.

A second episode recorded in 738 is also structurally analogous to the Ch'orti' ceremony. On April 27, 738, six days prior to the sacrifice of the Copán ruler, the text of Stela I (C8) records a fire-drilling event. The connection of this ceremony to the sacrifice is suggested by the reference to the patron deities of Waxaklajun Ub'ah K'awil which immediately follows it in the text (D8-D10). Although this event occurred shortly before the sacrifice, its position in the ritual sequence is comparable to that of the Ch'orti' of Chiquimula, who perform fire-drilling on Saturday of Holy Week. Overall, both ancient and contemporary Maya ritual sequences include fire-drilling, followed by decapitation events on the zenith passage, performed at an underworld location. It seems highly unlikely that this correspondence of multiple events is due to chance.

The west text of Stela F contains additional support for this thesis. This text includes a series of events that, until now, I have been unable to explain in terms of a coherent ritual structure. As with several other monuments, the text begins with a reference to the accession of K'ak' Tiliw. This is followed by an account of the decapitation of the Copán ruler, as noted above. Next is a reference to a "Copán stela," followed by a reference to the so-called "era event," a verbal phrase

Ch'orti'	Quiriguá
"creation"; setting stones in shrine (February 8)	"era event" (establishment of a stone tripod?) (August 22, 731) (Stela F, B16)
fire drilling (Saturday of Holy Week)	fire drilling (April 27, 738) (Stela I, C8)
erection of inscribed cross (April 22)	"stela Copán" (June 30, 741) (Stela F, B15)
decapitation of turkey at underworld location (April 30-May 1)	decapitation of ruler at underworld location (May 3, 738) (Stela F, A12-B14)

Table 1. Comparison of Ch'orti' rainmaking sequence and the events celebrated at Late Classic Quiriguá.

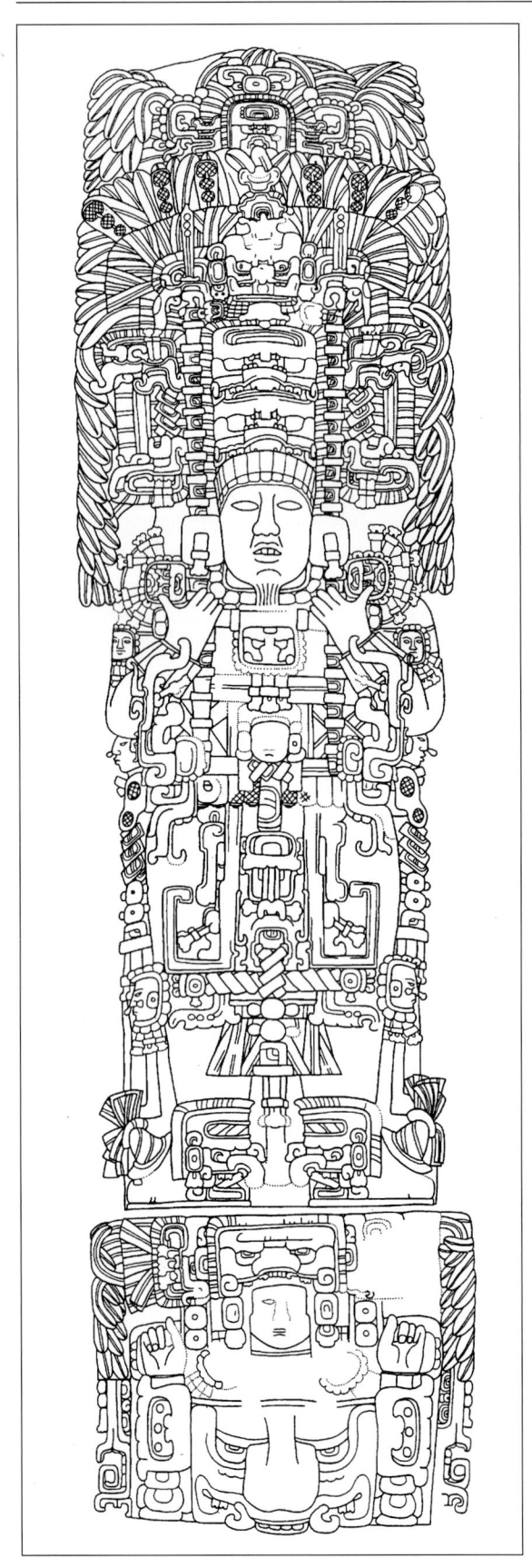

Figure 5. Quiriguá Stela F, south face, unwrapped.

associated with cosmic renewal at several sites. This phrase incorporates a term spelled **k'o-b'a**, which has been interpreted as *k'oob'* "hearth stones," based on a Yukatek word (Freidel and MacLeod 2000:3). In Ch'orti', the cognate of this term, *ch'uhp'* or *ch'uhb'(en)*, refers not only to the three stones of a hearth, but also to the groupings of stones laid at either end of the house as a base for the ridge pole (Fought 1972:336; see also Wisdom 1950:708). Thus, the "era event" may refer to the foundation of the cosmic house in terms of various supporting tripods, not only the hearth. Further, while the "era event" is usually cited in a mythological context, that of Quiriguá Stela F is historical, as are all other events in the west text.

As illustrated in Table 1, the Stela F narrative may be compared to the Ch'orti' ritual sequence of "creation" and the setting of stones on February 8, followed by the erection of an inscribed cross on April 22, and finally the turkey sacrifice on the zenith passage. True, the events at Quiriguá unfolded over a period of several years, and the fire-drilling is cited not on Stela F, but on Stela I. Nevertheless, the similarity in content of the ancient and contemporary narratives suggests that the ceremonies at Quiriguá, like those of the Ch'orti', were based on meteorological models, but performed as royal drama. This significance is reflected in the imagery of the south basal register of Stela F, which is rendered as the face of *Chak* (Figure 5). The prominent place of meteorological rituals and images on the monuments of the Great Plaza, and particularly on Stela F, suggests that this architectural complex was based in part on a meteorological cosmogram, analogous to Ch'orti' ritual platforms.

Several additional aspects of the Great Plaza support this interpretation. First is the arrangement of the stelae on Platform 1A-1, which occupies the northern part of the plaza. Dedicated in a series between 761 and 780 CE, these monuments are arranged roughly at the four intercardinal points (Figure 6). One monument each appears at the southeast, northeast, and southwest corners, while a triad of monuments completes the program in the northwest corner. Zoomorph G, a death memorial, serves to "terminate" the space, by blocking its principal access route from the south. The arrangement of stone monuments at the intercardinal points of the platform suggests a comparison to the Ch'orti' cosmograms which place four stones at the cor-

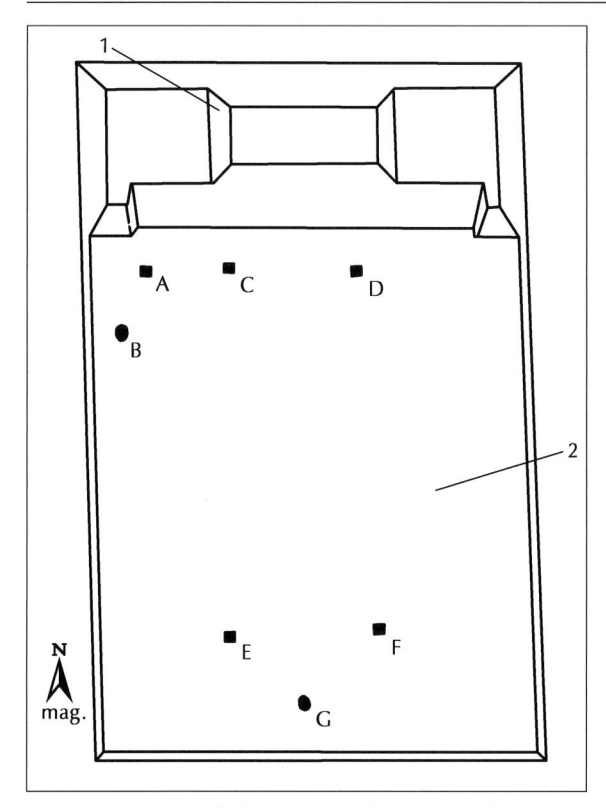

Figure 6. Quiriguá Platform 1A-1. After Jones, Ashmore, and Sharer (1983:28).

conjured by the king's ritual actions. The presence of a "six-cloud" glyph on the head of one of the miniature figures supports this interpretation. In addition, snakes appear repeatedly in the Postclassic Maya codices as rain-bringers, their bodies enclosing streams of rain.[3] On Copán Stela H, twisted cords with occasional snake-head terminations, emerge from *sak* "white, pure" glyphs located behind the ruler's legs. Miniature figures stand within the open cartouches of these glyphs. On Stela N, the snake-cords emerge from the jaws that compose part of the "black hole" location associated with decapitation at Quiriguá. Like the terrestrial bands of Stela D, these portals may be analogous to the cosmic basins that are the sources of rainwater for the Ch'orti'.[4]

Another specific invocation of rain-making ritual at Quiriguá appears on the north faces of Stelae C and A, a pair of monuments located on the northwest corner of Platform 1A-1 (Figure 7). These two monuments, dedicated simultaneously in 775 CE, feature images of dancing supernaturals, holding twisted cords in their hands that descend from a cosmic "house" image located above them. In addition to recalling the image of twisted serpent rain-bringers discussed above, the cords recall events of creation recorded in the K'iche' Maya epic, the *Popol Vuh*, in which the primordial spirits lay out the cosmos by stretching cords in a squared pattern (see Tedlock 1985: 72). Girard (1995:56) explicitly related this text to Ch'orti' notions of perpetual cosmic creation though the measuring of space by solar movement from east to west and north to south and back again. Importantly, Quiriguá Stela C also includes an extensive description of cosmogenesis on its east face, which speaks through this image. In addition, the date recorded in the text below the image of the dancing supernatural on Stela C corresponds to August 11, 775. Not only was this date close to the solar day corresponding to creation in Classic Maya lore, August 13, but it also fell exactly on the date of second zenith passage at Quiriguá. That such a date was commemorated by an image replete with symbolism of cosmic renewal and rainfall, recalls the significance of such dates of zenith passage to the Ch'orti'. Just as the Ch'orti' inaugurate their rainy season ceremonies by a rite symbolizing cosmic creation, so the ancient Maya, at least at some sites, associated cosmogenesis with the rainy season.

ners of the temple to inaugurate the rains. Just as these four points invoke the Working Men who hold the pillars of the sky, so the Quiriguá monuments represent the ruler (sometimes as a double portrait) in the form of a celestial pillar—a stela. It should also be noted that the royal portraits on the Platform 1A-1 monuments all feature beards, while those elsewhere at Quiriguá—even those that represent the same ruler—do not (see Figure 5). This imagery could be compared to the *ah yum ikar*, the Ch'orti' wind spirits at the four corners of the cosmos, who are bearded.[2]

The identification of the Quiriguá stelae with pillars of the winds provides a new perspective on stela imagery from other sites, particularly Copán. Specifically, several of the Copán stelae show rulers holding double-headed serpent bars, surrounded by additional snake imagery. For example, Stela D shows a pair of snakes held by miniature figures above the ruler's head, while additional snakes emerge from stepped terrestrial bands behind the ruler's legs. While these snakes are often interpreted as "vision serpents," or hallucinatory images of the king (e.g., Newsome 2001, Schele and Mathews 1998:133-174), they may instead be metaphors for clouds or wind,

Perhaps no other monument at Quiriguá more

Figure 7a. Quiriguá Stela C, north face.

Figure 7b. Quiriguá Stela A, north face.

explicitly compares rain to cosmogenesis than Quiriguá Altar P', discussed at the beginning of this essay (Figure 1). This monument was dedicated on 4 Ajaw, the same *tzolk'in* calendrical position as cosmogenesis. Accordingly, its text features an account of creation, in this case an event involving *uhub'il chan sak yax chan, uhub'il chan sak yax chan,* "the cord of the snake white first sky, the cord of the snake white first sky" (see Looper and Kappelman 2001:20). This coupleted expression is clearly embodied in the image, which shows the rain deity *Chak* expelling twin strands of wind/breath from his mouth. This image contrasts markedly with that of the adjacent Altar O', dedicated several years before Altar P' on a date that was not 4 Ajaw, and therefore, not as directly evocative of creation. While both monuments show *Chaks* dancing above cave mouths, on the earlier monument, there are no breath strands emerging from the deity's mouth. This contrast underscores the close association between creation and the fertile exhalations of the rain spirit.

The prominence of images and programs related to wind and rain at Quiriguá prompts a consideration of why this might be the case. Indeed, Quiriguá is notoriously wet, with 90-100 inches of precipitation annually, most of it falling from May through December. It is unlikely that meteorological ceremonialism was so elaborated merely to cause rain to fall. Instead, the rituals may have been designed in part as a regulatory mechanism to avoid flooding, to which the site core is particularly prone. In fact, earlier in Quiriguá's history, one of its floodplain settlements, Group 3C-7 was partly destroyed by inundations (possibly resulting from a hurricane) in the sixth or early seventh century (Ashmore 1987:219-221). Perhaps *Chak* was so important at Quiriguá partly in memory of such events. But there were other personal and ritual reasons for such an association. One is that the supernatural constituted an important divine patron of K'ak' Tiliw, which became part of his permanent public persona. In fact, this ruler was named after a manifestation of *Chak*. The first part of his name includes words for "fire" *(K'ak')* and the word *Tiliw*, which is probably a derived form of the root *til*, meaning "burn." The last part of this name, *Chan Yoat* or *Yo'pat*, incorporates the name of a lightning spirit holding a small trefoil or quatrefoil stone. This object symbolizes the caves in which the Classic Maya considered many deities, especially *Chaks*, to reside. Thus, the ruler's name may be translated as "fire-burning celestial lightning god" (see Martin and Grube 2000:218). In addition, when this ruler conducted the ritual sacrifice of his enemy from Copán, he was transformed into another aspect of *Chak*. Recent reconstructions of the inscription from the Copán Hieroglyphic Stairway associate the date of the decapitation, May 3, 738, with the birth of a supernatural called *Yax Ha'al Chak*. According to David Stuart (personal communication, 2002), this remarkable passage explains the supernatural context for the sacrificial event, in which the Quiriguá ruler took on the guise of a "First Rain Chak." Further, this interpretation suggests that the "gods" depicted on Altars O' and P' may in fact be manifestations of the former ruler of Quiriguá, apotheosized as *Chak*. Placed in front of the gigantic Zoomorphs O and P, these images show the deified ruler as predecessor of Sky Xul, the king who commissioned the monuments and whose portrait graces the front face of the zoomorph.[5] The identification of K'ak' Tiliw with the spirit of thunderstorms apparently endured beyond his death, becoming the foundation upon which his successors fashioned their own political images.

In conclusion, there is substantial evidence at Quiriguá for a structural relationship between ancient Maya ritual patterns and Ch'orti' meteorological ceremonies. The Quiriguá Platform 1A-1 program, in particular, may be interpreted as a cosmic house, akin to the temples or meteorological cosmograms of the Ch'orti'. Its portrait-stelae identify the ruler with the movements of the sun as well as the sources of moisture-bearing winds that are released from the four cosmic corners.[6] Certain monuments within this group, specifically Stelae F, C, and A, display images and texts that are especially explicit in this regard. While the Quiriguá program seems to be unique in the Maya corpus in its close correspondence to Ch'orti' ritual sequences, the association of stelae with winds and rain, evoked through imagery of snakes and twisted cords, is more widespread. Such an association may in fact derive from the basic function of stelae as period-ending markers, as monuments that recorded 360-day anniversaries of time elapsed from the base date in the Maya calendar, when the present cosmos was brought into being. As emphasized by Quiriguá Altar P', cosmogenesis occurred during the rainy season, and was therefore accomplished partly through the actions of *Chak*. However, this monument was dedicated on September 15, a date quite late in the rainy season that was strictly determined by the long count calendar. Thus, the period ending commemorated the release of moisture-bearing winds and rain, even though its celebration was not determined by the solar calendar. The general disjunction between meteorological ceremonies and the solar calendar in the Classic period resonates particularly with the observations of Fought, that Ch'orti' meteorological ceremonies have a general purpose of seeking supernatural blessings, without an explicit connection to agriculture. In this light, the timing of events at Quiriguá to correspond to the zenith passages is especially noteworthy. It seems to have been a case in which rituals were timed according to the solar calendar in order to enhance their cosmological importance. Through the assimilation of these events into the rhetoric of period-ending monuments, K'ak' Tiliw and his successor were able to demonstrate the relationship between stone monuments and the meteorological cycles that renewed the cosmos.

End Notes

1. Alternatively, *chih* may be a reference to wine. In Ch'olan, *chi'* is "sweet," while the cognate in Yukatek, *ki'*, is *"vino en general"* (Barrera Vásquez 1980:313).

2. The Yukatek Maya also associated these cosmic corner-posts with the winds, as recorded in the *Chilam Balam of Chumayel* (Roys 1967).

3. E.g., Madrid pp. 3, 4, 5, 6; Dresden p. 35b.

4. This interpretation is also supported by the "Seven-Black-Yellow Place" and "Nine-God Place" names that appear over the terrestrial bands on Stela D. These names also are closely associated with lip-to-lip caches, which usually contain an abundance of aquatic offerings. Buried beneath buildings and monuments, these offerings may evoke the cosmic basins of the oceans, thereby drawing their moisture into the community.

5. Only the portrait on Zoomorph P survives; however, based on a comparison of this monument with the remains of Zoomorph O, it can be assumed that Zoomorph O originally featured a portrait of Sky Xul.

6. Interestingly, the toponyms associated with the intercardinal points on the Río Azul Tomb 12 painting include terms for bodies of water, crocodiles, waterlilies, and the color blue/green. Such associations suggest a comparison with the cosmic basins of the Ch'orti'.

Matthew G. Looper
Department of Art & Art History
California State University, Chico
Chico, CA 95929-0820
mlooper@csuchico.edu

References Cited

Ashmore, Wendy
  1987 Research at Quiriguá, Guatemala: The Site-Periphery Program. In: Gary Pahl, ed., *The Periphery of the Southeastern Maya Realm*, pp. 217-225. Los Angeles: Latin American Center, University of California at Los Angeles.

Barrera Vásquez, Alfredo
  1980 *Diccionario Maya Cordemex: Maya–Español, Español–Maya*. Mérida: Ediciones Cordemex.

Fought, John G.
  1972 *Chorti (Mayan) Texts, 1*. Sarah S. Fought, ed. Philadelphia: University of Pennsylvania Press.

Freidel, David, and Barbara MacLeod
  2000 Creation Redux: New Thoughts on Maya Cosmology from Epigraphy, Iconography, and Archaeology. *The PARI Journal* 1(2):1-8, 18.

Freidel, David, Linda Schele, and Joy Parker
  1993 *Maya Cosmos: Three Thousand Years on the Shaman's Path*. New York: William Morrow.

Girard, Rafael
  1949 *Los Chortis ante el problema maya: Historia de las culturas indígenas de América, desde su origen hasta hoy*. 5 vols. México:Antigua Librería Robredo.

  1962 *Los Mayas eternos*. México:Antigua Librería Robredo.

  1966 *Los Mayas: Su civilización, su historia, sus vinculaciones continentales*. México: Libro Mexicano.

  1995 *People of the Chan*. Bennett Preble, trans. Chino Valley, Arizona: Continuum Foundation.

Jones, Christopher, Wendy Ashmore, and Robert J. Sharer
  1983 The Quiriguá Project: 1977 Season. In: Edward M. Schortman and Patricia A. Urban, eds., *Quiriguá Reports, Vol. 2*, pp. 1-38. Philadelphia: The University Museum, University of Pennsylvania.

Looper, Matthew G., and Julia Guernsey Kappelman
  2001 The Cosmic Umbilicus in Mesoamerica: A Floral Metaphor for the Source of Life. *Journal of Latin American Lore* 21(1):3-53.

Newsome, Elizabeth
  2001 *Trees of Paradise and Pillars of the World: The Serial Stelae Cycle of "18-Rabbit-God K," King of Copan*. Austin: University of Texas Press.

Redfield, Robert, and Alfonso Villa Rojas
  1934 *Chan Kom: A Maya Village*. Chicago: University of Chicago Press.

Roys, Ralph L.
  1967 *The Book of the Chilam Balam of Chumayel*. Norman: University of Oklahoma Press.

Schele, Linda, and Peter Mathews
  1998 *The Code of Kings: The Language of Seven Sacred Maya Temples and Tombs*. New York: Scribner.

Sosa, John R.
  1985 *The Maya Sky, the Maya World: A Symbolic Analysis of Yucatec Maya Cosmology*. Ph.D. Dissertation, State University of New York at Albany.

Tedlock, Dennis
  1985 *Popol Vuh: The Definitive Edition of the Mayan Book of the Dawn of Life and the Glories of Gods and Kings*. New York: Simon and Schuster.

Thompson, J. Eric S.
  1970 *Maya History and Religion*. Norman: University of Oklahoma Press.

Wisdom, Charles
  1940 *The Chorti Indians of Guatemala*. Chicago: University of Chicago.

  1950 Materials on the Chortí Language. *Microfilm Collection of Manuscripts on Cultural Anthropology 28*. Chicago: University of Chicago Library.

Shamanic *Mesas* of Yucatán and Their Historical Roots

Bruce Love

Introduction

Rites and ceremonies conducted by village shamans in Yucatán range from the simple to the complex, from private one-on-one healing and divining rites to village-wide spectacles of exorcism, prayer, and feasting. From the briefest affair of a few minutes to week-long multi-phased community efforts, the range of ceremonies includes the following: the *santiguar* healings using leaves to brush down patients to expel evil winds; divination of various forms using corn kernels and glass objects for "seeing"; *k'eex* rites that pull sickness from a patient and transfer it to the earth; *waajil kool* or *hanli kool* agricultural offerings of thanksgiving; the famous rain ceremony or *ch'a chàak*; and the very complex and elaborate *loj kaajtal* in which an entire village is cleansed of evil winds. For each of these, one or more *mesas* are used, in some cases as simple utilitarian surfaces to hold paraphernalia, in others as symbolic and sacred zones full of ritual meaning.

(The Mayan word for shaman or ritual specialist is *hmeen* [rhymes with ten], with the "h" aspirated but not voiced. The word means "practitioner"; *hmeeno'ob* is the plural form.)

This paper describes numerous *mesas* observed during intermittent periods of fieldwork spanning some 25 years and covering the three states of the Peninsula of Yucatán. As indicated, the range of observations is limited to the author's own, and though not comprehensive, is surely representative.

The content of the current article is twofold. The first part is essentially descriptive, illustrating *mesas* from a number of ritual contexts and in some cases creating composite *mesas* or typical constructions and layouts gleaned from multiple observations. The second part examines the historical origins, not only of the *mesas* themselves but the items and objects of shamanic practice placed on them and used by the *hmeeno'ob* during ritual performance. By noting which elements uniformly appear and which are optional—distinguishing the essential ingredients from the arbitrary items—and by comparing these to the ethnographic and historical record, one may begin to address which components are more deeply rooted in ancient tradition and which parts are more recently introduced and subject to innovation and modification.

The old question of syncretism, the union and fusion of once conflicting beliefs, is hard to avoid when looking at modern ritual practice. Is it possible (some may question whether it is worthwhile) to tease out the differences between pre-Columbian and Catholic elements in present-day ceremonies? The question of the origin of the *mesas* themselves, the wooden structures per se, is a case in point. Are they part of the surviving pre-Columbian substrate of Yukatek Maya religion or do they reflect non-native elements introduced over recent centuries of foreign influence?

Illustrating *mesas* and their objects, describing their details, placing them in their cultural milieu, and summarizing their similarities and differences provides a platform from which to step into anthropological interpretation and theory. The current narrative helps frame that platform, presenting data, basically, which may then be used to facilitate hypothesis and explication.

Mesas Today

An overview of present-day shamanic *mesas* or *mesa*-like apparatuses requires portrayal of many forms of ritual practice. In terms of complexity, expense, numbers of participants, and length of time to perform, the simpler rites do not require formal *mesas*, the mid-level events find *mesas* optional depending on the needs of the presiding *hmeen*, and the high-end performances absolutely require elaborately constructed *mesas* as the central elements around which the entire event revolves.

Utilitarian Tables

The low round table or *banqueta* found in every Maya house, the flat surface of a rustic wooden chair, the permanent family altar at the end of the house, or even an old plank balanced between two rocks, all serve admirably as simple, utilitarian surfaces for many shamanic exercises. To perform *santiguars*, for example, a table is used to hold the ritual objects—the bundle of leaves, the shot glass of *aguardiente* (clear cane liquor), the rattlesnake fang wrapped in black cloth, and the ever-present white candles.

If done on the family altar, the presence of the *santos* in their boxes and picture frames adds power to the cleansing, but the surface itself is not a necessary element. It is utilitarian only, and optional, as observed one evening during preparations for a nighttime healing ceremony.

Seated on the back step of his house, a father holds his sick child in the darkness as Don _____, kneeling, performs *santiguar*. Holding two leaves of *sipiche'* crossways between his thumb and forefinger to form a cross, he dips the leaves in a solution of *aguardiente* and cigarette tobacco that sits in a small ceramic cup on the ground and proceeds to make the sign of the cross at two dozen specific points on the child's head, body, and limbs, all the while praying and exorcising sickness-causing winds.

In the case just cited, there was no *mesa* whatever, but if someone had reached in the house and grabbed the *banqueta*, Don _____ would have put the leaves and *aguardiente* on it.

Divination, on the other hand, absolutely requires a surface to work on by the very nature of the exercise; the shuffling, arranging, and counting of corn kernels to divine the workings of supernatural forces and to read causes and cures. Almost invariably a lit candle accompanies the action. But once again, as with the *santiguars*, these are utilitarian wooden tables or already standing family altars. The tables themselves have no particular meaning or symbolic importance.

The *k'eex* ceremony, generally, involves offering food and drink to the holy sky beings while sickness is drawn out from the patient into eggs or chicken entrails or both, which are then returned to the earth, often by tossing and smashing the eggs in the nearby forest or burying the chicken entrails far from the house. A formal *mesa* is not a requirement, but the food offerings to the sky beings, usually chicken soup and tortillas and sometimes *saka'* (a white corn drink without lime, served cold), may for convenience be set on the house altar or *banqueta*. They may be hung in cups and bowls from nearby trees if the activities are outdoors, or they can be suspended from ropes strung across a path or cleared space, or they may be set on a *k'atal che'*, a simple device of two poles lashed together and set horizontally between tree limbs to create a surface for presenting offerings.

Sky Offerings

The sky beings of Maya religion have myriad names and aspects: *chaaks*, *balams*, *pawatuns* (*papatuns*, *babatuns*), holy beings, cloud beings, waterers, lords, gods, powerful ones, beautiful ones, guardians, and more; not to mention True God, Jesus Christ, Mary, the apostles, and angels. Confusing only to the outsider, the village shaman addresses them individually, en masse, in groups, and at the world directions. He invites them to savor the fresh, aromatic, and sometimes steaming offerings from the earthly plane. Apropos of their nature, offerings to the sky beings may best be suspended in the air, whether from living branches, leafy constructed arches, doorways, eaves, crossbeams over water wells, or wherever else the lords might come to partake.

Rings, suspended by cords or twine, hold the cups of food and drink. For larger offerings, such as baked breads hot from the earth ovens of *ch'a chàak* ceremonies, the Mexican net shopping bag or *sabukan* is hung from branches or arches. In a sense then, there are no *mesas* for these offerings, but the supporting rings themselves, the handmade and sometimes decorated bands of vine or bark that support the cups and bowls of sacred gifts can be made holy by sprinkling them with *baalche'* (a sacred drink of fermented honey and water and bark of the *baalche'* tree) or *saka'* and inserting leaves of *xi'imche'* in their strands.

K'atal Che'

A *k'atal che'*, literally translated as sticks laid crossways, supports offerings to the sky beings in a fashion similar to the suspended vine rings just described. For major ceremonies like the *ch'a chàaks* and the larger *lojs*, they serve as auxiliary *mesas*, long narrow surfaces supporting perhaps a row of 13 small cups, or four cups and an incense burner with a candle at each end, or whatever configuration the presiding *hmeen* prescribes.

Two long narrow sticks bound together are suspended between living tree branches, for example at the edge of the clearing for a rain ceremony or near a cave opening where prayers are made and offerings presented prior to searching for holy water. They are particularly appropriate for the sky gods because of their position up high and their seeming suspension in space. In one instance, at least, this arrangement is referred to as *ka'an che,'* "sky *mesa*."

Three Classes of Ceremony Requiring Large *Mesas*

True *mesas*, large rectangular wooden surfaces on four legs, usually with leafy arches reaching from corner to corner, are erected or placed in forest clearings or in backyards or church yards. They find their greatest elaboration in *waajil kool / hanli kools*, *ch'a chàaks*, and large-scale *lojs* such as the *loj kaajtal*. These three classes of ceremony, all of which involve complex *mesa* construction, are briefly reviewed here in terms of purpose and intent. Physical descriptions of the *mesas* and their offerings follow.

The first are rites of thanksgiving, translated "bread of the corn field / food of the corn field." An individual corn farmer commissions the event, supplies the necessary and very expensive quantities of food and accessory items, hires a *hmeen* to perform, and stages the affair in his own backyard. The offerings are agricultural in nature, derived from field, hive, and yard, and include maize in several liquid and solid forms, squash seed paste, *baalche'*, turkey, chickens, tobacco, and more. The ceremony focuses on presenting gifts of food, drink, and tobacco to the lords or spirit protectors of field and forest, in exchange for good crops and safekeeping. The heart of the event is the shaman's prayers murmured reverently over the sanctified *mesa*.

Ch'a chàaks include essentially the same offerings as the *waajil kool / hanli kools*, with added emphasis on propitiating bringers of rain, the *chaaks*. Ritual performance may include the same prayers as thanksgiving ceremonies, but in addition involves *chaak* impersonators, children croaking like frogs, perhaps *novena* singers from the church, and attendance by the majority of the male population of the town. At the climax, the *hmeen* and his assistants sprinkle *baalche'* over the participants and over the *mesa* itself, creating rain.

Loj kaajtal has been mentioned as one of the major *loj* events, implying there are different degrees of *loj*. At least four are known, from simple to elaborate. The word *loj* means "redeem or take back," and in essence a *loj* retakes a piece of ground from evil and sickness-bearing winds. *Loj corral* redeems a cattle pen; *loj kaab*, beehives; *loj solar*, a house plot; and *loj kaajtal*, an entire village. Simpler expressions of *loj* take a few hours, *loj kaajtal* more than a week. A *loj kaajtal* may employ the same *mesa* arrangement as the *ch'a chàak*, but its purpose is not to bring rain, it is to drive out bad winds and restore health. In one town where it was recently observed, soldiers and musicians encircled the entire town doing battle with winds and capturing worms, snakes, centipedes, and all sorts of creatures of the underground, at the end burning their small mound of dead bodies in an exorcistic fire. Food offerings were distributed to all the town entrances and were suspended over the town water wells. During the days that followed, *novenas* were sung in the village church and after a week a second smaller *loj* was performed at night, completing an eight-day affair.

For these three classes of ritual, large rectangular wooden *mesas*, erected in sacred space, are central to proper execution; the *hmeen* oversees them. Choosing the spot for the clearing, guiding construction of the *mesa*, supervising preparation of food and drink, blessing and cleansing, praying and sprinkling holy liquids, directing ritual performers in their roles, arranging and rearranging the surface of the *mesa*, finally dismantling the *mesa* and exorcising remaining winds before leaving: the village shaman alone has the knowledge and experience to orchestrate the entire operation from start to finish.

At the center of these large-scale ceremonies, the *mesas* take on a symbolic role, expanding beyond their utilitarian natures to become representations of the Maya cosmos itself, the four-sided earth and the arches of the sky. When the presiding shaman carefully places four tiny cups of native-made "*vino*" on the four extreme corners of the *mesa*, he is in fact offering this holiest of beverages to the four-part gods of rain and wind who reside at the edges of the universe.

Mesa Construction

The materials from which the *mesas* are made do not seem to have intrinsic significance in their own right. The basic four-legged wooden table owned by most Maya families can be carried to the yard or forest clearing and used with equal efficacy as the post-and-pole variety cut from wild bush. Their only drawback is their limited size, which is insufficient for the larger community performances where greater surface area is required to hold the multitudinous offerings and artifacts.

A typical large *mesa* consists of four forked posts at the corners imbedded in the ground with cross members between the forks and thinner poles laid between the cross members side-by-side forming a rough rectangular surface sometimes as much as three meters (10 feet) on a side. The orientation is always east-west, that is, the person standing and facing the front side of the *mesa* is facing east. The corners then are northeast, southeast, northwest, and southwest. The sides face the cardinal directions, not the corners.

Arches reach from corner to corner, across the sides and diagonally over the center. Like everything else in Maya shamanic performance, leeway is afforded the individual *hmeen*, who determines the proper configuration. Leafy green branches—usually *jabin*, *xiat* (a small palm), or *xi'imche'*—lashed to the legs at the corners, arc over the sides and center. The four-cornered earth and the four-cornered sky suddenly shrink to a manageably sized model, the invisible becomes manifest on the material plane, the abode of the sky beings comes within reach, and the far limits of the earth compress to human scale. With the central construction complete, the upcoming elaboration of complex ceremony has a framework on which to hang, a focus of activity, an underlying scaffold on which to build holy sacrament. When cups of sacred drink are suspended in the arches and sprinkled over the *mesa* below, the sky is watering the earth.

Food and Drink Offerings

To transform the bare wooden poles of the table surface to a hallowed zone worthy of visitation by the gods, fresh bows of *xi'imche'* are laid across the *mesa* and sprinkled with *saka'* or *baalche'*. Using pointed leaves of *xi'imche'*, the *hmeen* consecrates the *mesa* top by dipping the leaves in the open bowl of sacred drink and tossing droplets to the four directions while reciting formulaic prayers. Lit candles and burning incense accompany the recitations.

Once the *mesa* becomes a sacred space, everything that goes on the *mesa* must also be clean and holy. This holiness requires maintenance. The *hmeen* cannot sprinkle holy liquid and pray one time and expect the space to remain consecrated to the end of the ceremony; it must be repeatedly cleansed and incensed, even to the extent of rising at midnight to offer prayers during the "hour of silence," when prayers go directly to God, when even the birds are quiet.

Always at the center on the east side, one or more holy crosses stand. They may be rustic handmade pieces carved fresh for the occasion, store-bought simple wooden crosses, the *hmeen's* own cross from his house, or one of the crosses from the church in town. As always, variations are myriad, but the underlying theme is constant. The holy cross stands on the east side facing back toward the center of the *mesa*, presiding in a sense over all the land.

Candles—sometimes in holders, sometimes stuck on the wood of the *mesa* itself—have no particular pattern of arrangement, but are always present and must be lit for any prayer or any ritual activity. Also activated are the incense holders, open trays holding hot coals on which incense is burned. Before each round of prayers, the *hmeen's* assistant lights the candles and adds burning embers and stirs the incense.

Next come the cups and bowls. *Baalche'*, usually prepared the day before, is first to be set on the *mesa*, and first to be consumed by ritual participants. This sacred drink, surviving from pre-Columbian times to the present, has the power to purify objects and beings. The presiding *hmeen* sprinkles it over the *mesa*, sets it in cups on the *mesa* in special numerical patterns, distributes it for men to drink who are participating in the ceremony, pours it down the throats of chickens and turkeys prior to their sacrifice, sprinkles it in the form of the cross over the pit oven where sacred breads are baking, dips bundles of leaves in it to perform *santiguar* when participants need special cleansing, tosses it in the sky to fall over the earth during the rain ceremony, and closes the sacred space with it at the very end of the ceremonial activities as the *mesa* is disassembled and the sticks are tossed into the surrounding forest. When set on the *mesa* in arrangements of four, seven, nine or thirteen, for example, or hung from the arches, one on each side, the sky beings will come to partake.

Saka' is also holy drink, and is likewise set out in cups or bowls in patterns based on ancient numerology. Six on one side, seven on the other; nine cups in an arc to complement four cups of *baalche'*—frequently thirteen is key. The cups sit on the green leaves of the table top, sometimes supported by rings. A large bowl may sit at the front of the *mesa* for sprinkling, where the *hmeen* kneels and prays and dips his sprig of leaves to scatter to the four winds.

While *baalche'* and *saka'* are administered to the participants, both human and supernatural, and are arranged in sacred space on the holy *mesa*, food preparations continue in the clearing or house yard. For the larger ceremonies, sacred breads baked in underground ovens constitute the heart of food offerings to the gods.

When the sacred breads come hot and steaming out of the pit oven, the climax of the ceremony is near. The special bread of thirteen layers goes under the cross at the top of the *mesa*. The four breads of twelve layers go to the four corners and nine breads of nine layers go to the center, four on one side and five on the other. A dozen other loaves, each of eight layers, are stacked precariously, temporarily, to be blessed and sanctified prior to their distribution to the hanging rings or the suspended *k'atal che'*. Another two dozen breads—not made of layers, but simply moulded into loaves—do not go on the *mesa* at all, but instead are destined for bread-crumb soup. As the *hmeen* arranges the layered breads on the *mesa* surface, a group of participants busily begins breaking up the other breads, building a pile of crumbs to add to the huge tub of chicken soup simmering on the sidelines.

Bowls of chicken soup with added bread crumbs and flavorings sit also in numerological patterns—fours, sevens, nines, etc.—nestled among the leaves, shoulder to shoulder with bowls of corn drink and cups of fermented honey in the shadows of the sky arches, leaving just enough room for the candles and incense burners. (The foregoing numerical patterns are representative and typical but freely variable within certain bounds, bounds understood by the working shamans.) Topping off the food offerings, literally, pieces of boiled chicken and turkey are balanced on the breads or over the soup bowls.

Non-Food and -Drink Items

A green bed of leaves may cover the entire *mesa* surface, as mentioned, or sprigs of leaves may be placed under each individual offering. During long ceremonies lasting more than a day, the old leaves are changed and replaced with fresh ones at important junctures, like just before the midnight prayers. Tobacco, whether store-bought cigarettes or wild tobacco wrapped in corn husks and tied with bark strips, is required by the *chaaks*, the rain gods. A small pile of thirteen cigarettes may be laid in the center of the *mesa*. Candles, as mentioned, are essential. They must be lit for any prayer to take effect. Incense can be more than one type, collected from the nearby forest or bought at the store. Frequently *santos*, images of Catholic saints, accompany the cross on the *mesa*, perhaps brought to the clearing from the church or maybe from someone's personal home altar.

A green bundle of *sipiche'* leaves may rest on the *mesa*, used when performing *santiguars* on individuals during intervals between main events of the larger ceremonies. Some *hmeeno'ob* place personal sacred items on the *mesa*; an old prayer book, a wrapped archaeological piece such as a figurine, or a fragment of an ancient clay incense burner. Picked flowers set in small glass vases sometimes adorn the altar.

Beneath the *Mesa*

If the *mesa* represents the surface world, it is apropos to place offerings to the creatures of the underworld beneath the table. The *aluxes*, those ever present tricksters who live in caves and archaeological ruins, frequently receive their due: a drink, a piece of bread, and a lit candle on the ground near one of the table legs. As for the rest of the ground surface under the table, it is secular space for temporary storage of pots, or bags, or strips of bark, or stacks of cups, etc.

Beyond the *Mesa*

The main *mesa*, center of ritual activity, may have auxiliary *mesas* around it. The entire clearing, in fact, is sacred space. In some cases a small *mesa*, low to the ground, sits off to one side, near the edge of the clearing, and is dedicated specifically to the *aluxes*, or guardians of the caves and archaeological sites. The *k'atal che'*, of bound poles laid crossways, as mentioned, is suspended in nearby branches, and the vine rings with cups of drink and bowls of food are also hung on surrounding branches.

Another setup, less common, is a flat stone set on smaller stones on the ground, on which the holy cross from the town's church is placed within a framework of small branches arching overhead.

Other constructions include rows of arches leading away from the main *mesa*, rows of flat stone seats for *chaak* impersonators to sit on, or a special space for *chaak* to stand and perform at the edge of the clearing where he may wave his wooden machete and toss *baalche'* to bring rain. The pit oven for the sacred breads may be out of the clearing altogether in a small nearby space in the surrounding forest. The *hmeen* sprinkles *baalche'* in the form of the cross over the fire as the breads are laid among the heated rocks and glowing coals, soon to be covered by green leaves and left to steam.

Sacred space can be extended even beyond the immediate clearing. At the direction of the *hmeen*, net bags with breads, candles, and incense are taken from the *mesa* where they have been sprinkled and prayed over, to the town entrances, to the nearby archaeological site, to the ranch owner's house, or to the church; thereby stretching the reach of ritual performance to encompass the entire village.

Those places beyond physical reach are touched by words in sacred prayer as the *hmeen* addresses outlying caves, cenotes, pilgrimage towns, and all the saints that reside there. If traveling through space is not enough, prayers reach also to previous eras, mythological time when the thirteen holy *hmeeno'ob* lived and when the great ones, the ancestors, built the archaeological sites.

The four-sided *mesa* under the arching leafy sky is the heart of ritual space. From there, prayers accompanied by burning candles and sweet incense go out to the sky beings, inviting them to come and partake of the blessed food and drink. When the *mesa* is constructed with proper care and attention to detail, when all the parts are correctly assembled and reverently blessed, when prayers are recited and food and drink are made strictly according to ritual formulae, then ceremonies work. The gods give protection, the rains fall on the corn fields, evil winds are dispelled, and sickness is averted. The shaman carries an awesome burden, and only a lifetime of practice and accumulation of skills and esoteric knowledge can bring good results. When done right, these long and complex ceremonies with large elaborate *mesas* at their core can successfully restore balance to an entire community and return to the people a sense of well-being and safety.

Historical Antecedents

To analyze the occurrence of offerings, ritual paraphernalia, and the *mesas* themselves, and to compare them across classes of ceremonies as practiced today in the Yucatán Peninsula, and then to seek their ancestral pedigree by reviewing the historical record back to pre-Columbian times, is quite illuminating. A brief summary is presented here examining today's rites in terms of historical antecedents, innovations, borrowings, and emulation. Aware of the pitfalls and difficulties of such an undertaking, a modest effort along these lines is put forth in what follows.

Food and Drink Offerings

Looking across the six categories of shamanic practice as performed by the village *hmeeno'ob* of Yucatán—*santiguar*, divination, *k'eex*, *waajil kool/hanli kool*, *ch'a chàak*, and *loj kaajtal*—and noting the presence or absence of certain offerings, one finds for the latter three types, the so-called major ceremonies, the invariable presence of the following items: baked layered breads of many varieties, *baalche'*, *saka'*, the bread-crumb soup known as *k'ol*, and various sacrificed fowl.

Of these five items, four at least appear integral to religious practice in pre-Columbian times. The breads are depicted in the pre-Contact bark-paper codices, on painted murals showing royal offerings, and on stone monuments and panels at pre-Hispanic archaeological sites. Their names are even spelled phonetically in hieroglyphic writing. *Baalche'* is known not so much from the art and iconography but from the writings of the early Spaniards who witnessed native customs in the 16th century. The antiquity of *saka'* is a little less certain, but references to maize drinks abound in the early Spanish accounts of Maya ritual and, although not specifically named *saka'*, they could well be the same drink so ubiquitous in the modern ethnographic record. The sacrifice of wild turkeys appears in the painted codices and early Spanish accounts, although today domestic chickens and turkeys have replaced the native species as ceremonial foods. Of the main food and drink offerings in modern ceremonies, only the bread soup *k'ol* fails to show up in the historical record.

This core of food and drink offerings seems tenacious indeed, appearing consistently from pre-Contact times to the present, surviving half a millennium of Spanish and then Mexican influence.

Non-Food and -Drink Items

Fresh leaves across the *mesa* and under offering bowls are essential to good performance, and this practice also appears to survive from pre-Columbian times. A mid-16th century eyewitness account of priestly divination recounts that prior to unfolding and reading his sacred codex, the priest laid out a fresh mat of green leaves on the ground, sprinkled it and incensed it, and then laid out his holy book from which he read the omens and prognostications of the upcoming days. Other accounts make abundant reference to boughs of green leaves ornamenting shrines and temples.

Tobacco also has a greater than 500-year history. God L on the Temple of the Cross at Palenque smokes tobacco and smoking gods adorn more than one page of the codices.

Wax candles, more than any other item—food, drink, etc.—always appear in modern shamanic practice. No *hmeen* would consider uttering a prayer without first lighting a candle, whether it be for the simplest of *santiguars* performed at the kitchen table or for the great climactic gathering at the village rain ceremony. Yet candles do not appear in the pre-Columbian record. Beeswax was abundant and used for multiple purposes as described in the early sources, and beeswax lamps may well have been used for lighting. In fact, one of the ancient day names in the series of 20 Maya days is Kib, or beeswax. Torches were used for interior lighting and nighttime illumination and gods bearing torches appear in the codices, but no candles occur. In the 16th century, after candles were introduced by the Spaniards, the Mayan word *kib* is used to refer to candles, as attested in the early dictionaries, but no visual depictions or written descriptions of candles per se appear in a pre-Columbian context. How unusual that the most prevalent item in today's rituals is not also one of the oldest!

Almost as necessary as candles in today's shamanic practice, incense is essential to all the major ceremonies. But unlike the wax candles, ceremonial incense has a clear pre-Columbian presence, appearing in Spanish accounts of native rites, color illustrations in the painted codices, and dramatic carvings of incense scattering on monuments from Classic Maya times in the middle of the first millennium. Although necessary in the major ceremonies today, incense need not be present for the lesser *santiguars*, divining sessions, or *k'eexes*. This element, one of the longest surviving in the historical record, is not as prevalent across classes of modern ceremonies as are wax candles, an element introduced by the Spaniards at the time of contact.

What of the famous arches adorning the *mesas* of the major *lojs*, the *ch'a chaaks*, and some *waajil kool/hanli kools*? The record is not clear. One report from the 1560s describes a procession marching along a path adorned with arches as part of a native celebration, a celebration with no obvious Spanish borrowings, suggesting that the arches are pre-Columbian in nature. But leafy arches do not appear in the painted codices or carved monuments. The question remains unresolved.

Today's *santos* and the holy cross of Christianity have replaced the "pagan" images of the sun gods, the rain gods, the fire gods, etc., which were so prominent in pre-Hispanic religion. This does not represent a break from the past so much as a transformation. Today, Lord Sun can be synonymous with Jesus Christ, the chief of the rain gods is *San Miguel Arcangel* in some communities, and the patron saint of any particular village has its counterpart in the tutelary guardians of ancient eras.

The *Mesa* in History

What of the *mesa* itself—this wooden platform on four legs that is so central to the major ceremonies of today's Yucatán? Although archaeologists have found tantalizing evidence suggesting they perhaps existed in precontact times (see Brady, this volume), neither the 16th-century Spanish accounts nor the richly illustrated codices that depict so much ritual and religious practice make mention of or illustrate the use of any four-legged table-like structure. Offerings are made most frequently in ceramic vessels resting on the ground. The closest thing to tables are the stone benches that the priests, the lords, and the gods sit on, while the burning incense, the bubbling drinks, and the steaming breads are laid out in ceramic jars or bowls set on the floor or on stones. For especially large ceremonies, heaps of stone were piled and adorned on which gods were set, incensed, and fed.

To find the most likely antecedent to today's *mesas*, one has only to observe a modern-day *ch'a chàak* or *waajil kool* and then compare them to performances of the Catholic masses that occur daily in the thousands of churches and cathedrals across the Yucatán Peninsula. The cross on the east side, the rectangular shape, the arrangement of artifacts, the way the priest stands and raises the eucharist and kneels and kisses the altar—these elements appear in the forest clearings and Maya backyards as native ceremony, but they strongly evoke a Catholic origin.

Sixteenth-century reports of Maya mimicry of Catholic rites are plentiful, and what the Spaniards called idolatry in many cases was the sincere appropriation of Catholic performance into a Maya framework. When Maya performers marched in processions with robes and headgear that resembled Catholic vestments and miters, the Spaniards were appalled and outraged when, in fact, the Maya were emulating and honoring the new religion by borrowing and adopting its outward accoutrements.

For a number of historical reasons, many of which are not at all clear, the rural Maya in remote hamlets and villages early on began to hold their own versions of the sacred mass. And the agricultural ceremonies such as *waajil kool*, once held in the corn fields away from prying and disapproving eyes, were referred to by outsiders as early as the 18th century as *misas milperas,* or masses of the corn fields.

Today they are not referred to as cornfield masses, but many Maya *hmeeno'ob*, at the conclusion of agricultural and exorcising ceremonies, conduct an imitative form of holy communion with small cups of *baalche'* as wine and oven-baked breads as host, actually referring to them as *vino* and *hostía*. With these, the *hmeen* administers *k'am*, or communion. Attendees at the *ch'a chàak* or *loj kaajtal* line up and, one at a time, kneel at the front of the *mesa*, now an altar, as the *hmeen* administers the wine and bread. For many ceremonies, perhaps more so in eastern parts of Yucatán, this native communion is integral to the larger village events. This performance of *k'am*, the native version of Catholic communion, reinforces the view that the *mesa* itself is fashioned after the church altar. In both the Catholic church and in the forest clearing, the raised, holy rectangular space between priest and crucifix holds the sacred drink, food, incense, and candles, and is the centerpiece of sacred practice.

Conclusion

A look at shamans' *mesas* across the Peninsula of Yucatán leads to certain general observations. For the lesser shamanic works of individual cleansings and healings and for purposes of divination, a large formally arranged, four-sided *mesa* is not a necessity. Instead, existing house altars, *banquetas*, or any expedient surface will do. This by no means minimizes the sanctity of the performance, as the *hmeen* lights candles and prays fervently and makes the sign of the cross repeatedly during his performance. But the *mesa* itself holds little meaning or import under these conditions.

For the larger ceremonies, however, the ones attended by extended families or entire villages, major four-sided *mesas* are constructed in sanctified space, adorned with arches, covered with fresh boughs of green leaves, and arranged in complex patterns of food and drink offerings as numerous rounds of incensing and prayer invite the spirit beings of sky and earth to partake of holy offerings. The *mesa* functions as a miniaturized cosmos representing the four-sided earth and arching heavens and allows the presiding *hmeen* to present prayers and offerings to the ends of the world. When done correctly, health and well-being result.

The influence of Catholicism is everywhere in these major ceremonies, in both form and substance, but often only in form. The *mesa* itself is imitative of the Catholic altar and the performance of a native version of communion often occurs. However, praying to the four-part sky gods, making rain, presenting offerings of layered breads, corn drink, and fermented honey drink, together with the burning of incense, can all be traced back to their pre-Columbian counterparts.

Perhaps one of the most pervasive outside influences has been the use of candles. No shaman-led ritual in rural Yucatán can be performed without lighting candles, and yet they do not appear in the pre-Columbian record. At the very least, this aspect of Catholic rites has spread thoroughly across the Maya shamanic landscape.

As Maya religion persists and prospers in the rural hinterlands, new effects and influences will bring further change. The village *hmeen* will adapt and adopt new elements of ritual performance as he continues his irreplaceable role in village society, the office of intermediary between mundane and supernatural, secular and holy, civil and religious realms. For the large community performances, he will oversee and orchestrate complex observances of age-old rites. At the center, representing the four-sided earth and the arching sky, abode of spirit beings critical to health and good crops, today stand and will continue to stand the grand ceremonial *mesas* of Yucatán.

Bruce Love
Independent Scholar
crmtech@pe.net

Southern Mexico and Guatemala

Shamanism, Colonialism, and the *Mesa* in Mesoamerican Religious Discourse

John Monaghan

Indigenous groups throughout Mesoamerica make the *mesa* a central element in worship and sacrifice. The notion that the square table constitutes a cosmogram, modeling the Mesoamerican universe with its four sides and center, is widespread in curing, propitiation, and other shamanic rites (Sharon 1976). But why do indigenous people use a Spanish loan word, "*mesa*" for the table, even in communities where few people speak Spanish? Many Spanish words have of course entered Mesoamerican languages, but they are usually associated with items and concepts that were borrowed or introduced after the Conquest. The cosmological significance of the *mesa* predates the Conquest, and it is so deeply embedded in indigenous belief and practice and used by so many different groups that it appears, at least at first glance, to be an ancient component of Mesoamerican religion, like the 260-day calendar or the sacred properties of the Rain. Moreover, most items of shamanic ceremonial use in traditional communities retain names in indigenous languages. So why is a Spanish loan word used for this key element in Mesoamerican religious practice?

The way to address this question is through an historical reading of the role the *mesa* plays in shamanic ceremony and belief. Although shamanism has long been viewed as an archaic and largely homogenous phenomenon, we have come to realize that this view precludes not only in-depth historical analysis, but also an inquiry into origins and an appreciation for regional variation

(see Thomas and Humphrey 1994). What this paper does then is not so much attempt to explain the significance of the *mesa* in terms of the way it functions within ancient indigenous cosmologies (which it does), but examine it in the context of the colonial relations that have left such a profound mark on indigenous society and culture.

It is important to recognize that in most traditional Mesoamerican communities, tables are not used in exactly the same way they are used in non-indigenous and urbanized areas. For one, people do not usually take their meals at tables. They instead sit on low stools or mats, often around the hearth, and place their bowls of food in front of them on the ground. Tables of course are found in many houses, but are used mostly for storage and/or as a kind of household altar. Among the Mixtecs of southern Mexico, where I have carried out most of my ethnographic research, tables also appear in houses on the Days of the Dead, when platforms are built out from the altar table on which meals are placed for those the household wishes to remember. In Santiago Nuyoo these platforms are made by driving posts into the ground, and then setting up a framework of cane. Outside the house, tables are a prominent feature in the municipal hall. If one enters the building one faces a row of tables lined up, facing the doorway, which serve as desks for officials. When the officials are present, they thus form a long row, with the town president sitting in the center. When important outsiders come to visit (such as state officials) the tables may be set

Douglas Sharon, ed., *Mesas & Cosmologies in Mesoamerica.* San Diego Museum Papers 42, 2003.

for meals. In civic ceremonies, if schoolteachers are in charge, meals will also be served on tables. However in the *mayordomias*, where a tremendous amount of food is distributed, people eat the traditional way, squatting or sitting close to the floor.

The ancient Mixtecs developed their own writing system, and the surviving Mixtec codices constitute the largest corpus of pre-Columbian books in existence. Because these sources deal with such a diversity of everyday and elite activities they can provide a baseline for understanding the uses of many elements of material culture, which can then be compared to the corpus of post-Conquest manuscripts written in the native tradition, which is also impressive. Beginning with the pre-Columbian Mixtec codices, it is a fact that there is nothing in these sources that looks like a table. When people are depicted eating or drinking they are shown in precisely the position that modern Mixtecs assume when at meals: sitting on the ground or on low stools, with their bowls and cups in front of them on the ground. When those in positions of power are depicted, they are usually shown seated on mats, thrones or in palaces; never are they sitting behind desks. It should be noted here that in the sixteenth century dictionaries of indigenous languages produced by Spanish missionaries the gloss for *mesa* is usually a description of the activities that take place around a table, such as "the board from which one eats" (Alvarado 1962:249). This is something one often sees in the case of European concepts for which there is no direct equivalent in the indigenous lexicon; if an indigenous item existed that corresponded to something the Europeans brought with them it is more likely that a one-to-one translation is given. At the least, this evidence indicates that tables did not play a significant role in Mixtec everyday life.

In the post-Conquest Mixtec manuscripts, we do see tables depicted. Good examples come from the Codex Sierra, made in the Mixtec town of Texupa (Figures 1 and 2) and the Codex of Yanhuitlan (Figure 3). Both of these manuscripts date from the mid-sixteenth century. In Figure 1, dating to 1558, a group of Spanish officials (the Alcalde Mayor, his scribe, and interpreter) are shown eating a meal that has been served to them by the town. Knives, bread, and cups sit on the table (Leon 1933). Figure 2 depicts the corregidor, Francisco de Melgar, flanked by his scribe, Alejo Linares and probably Francisco de Mesa, his in-

Figure 1. Codex Sierra, Spanish officials eating a meal served by the people of Texupa (drawing by Lee Ann Monaghan, after Leon 1933).

Figure 2. Codex Sierra, the Corregidor, Francisco de Melgar, overseeing the accounts of the town of Texupa (drawing by Lee Ann Monaghan, after Leon 1933).

terpreter. They are overseeing the accounts of the town of Texupa. Their dress and beards identify them as Spaniards, and writing instruments rest on the table. Melgar holds in his right hand the baston, a symbol of authority, and he is counting coins with his left (Leon 1933). Figure 3, from the Codex of Yanhuitlan shows the Dominican Friar Domingo de Santa Maria, who was vicar in Teposcolula from 1541 to 1547. He is using a writing table, with a Mixtec noble looking on (Codex of Yanhuitlan 1994).

The documentary evidence therefore suggests that the uses of tables in consumption, work, administration, and domestic arrangements in pre-Columbian times were minimal at best, and they only took on importance after the Conquest. If this is accepted, then it makes sense that Mesoamerican people would use a Spanish loan word for table. The question for us then becomes: Why were tables, if they only came into extensive use

Shamanism, Colonialism, and the *Mesa* in Mesoamerican Religious Discourse

Figure 3. Codex of Yanhuitlan, the Dominican friar Domingo de Santa Maria and a Mixtec noble (drawing by Lee Ann Monaghan, after Códice de Yanhuitlan 1994).

during the colonial period, incorporated into curing and other rituals, and why in such a central role—even to the point where the concept of *mesa* encompasses the supreme act of social and cosmological synthesis, the offering of sacrifice?

Ethnographic work on shamanic practices, both within Latin America (Feinberg 1997, Taussig 1991) and elsewhere (Tsing 1993), indicates that, in discourse and practice, shamans seek to exert and respond to power, authority, command, and mastery. After all, shamans are "warriors" (Dow 1986). Thus Feinberg (1997) argues that when Mazatec religious leaders, or "persons of knowledge," perform their well known mushroom ceremonies, they enact the way power is perceived to operate in their area of Oaxaca. He argues that many of the images in the mushroom ceremonies that have received so much attention over the years are not ancient pre-Columbian symbols, but have to do with Mazatec interactions with officials, wealthy merchants, and foreign tourists, and the practices and imagery in the ceremony draw upon features of these actors that Mazatec associate with their power. Can the *mesa* be seen in a similar way?

The first thing to note is that in the post-Conquest sources the people who the scribe depicts using tables are all Spaniards. Moreover, in almost every instance of post-Conquest table use in the Mixtec sources the individuals and activities portrayed are linked to colonial control and administration. In the examples from the Codex Sierra and the Codex of Yanhuitlan, we see depicted the bureaucracy put in place by the Spanish crown, the system of tribute that underwrote the colonial government, the policy of conversion and surveillance associated with the Catholic Church, and the ethnic differences and sumptuary codes of the colonial caste system. The scribes who produced these manuscripts portray indigenous actors standing in a subservient position before the table. The clearest example is from the Codex of Yanhuitlan, where the Fray Domingo de Santa Maria is shown twice the size of the indigenous nobles, a device still employed by Mixtecs today to indicate hierarchy and relative differences in power (e.g., see Monaghan 1995:322). Indeed Domingo de Santa Maria was one of the instigators of the infamous Inquisition trial of Yanhuitlan, where native lords were persecuted for continuing to perform non-Christian ceremonies. In the few examples of indigenous people using tables in the sixteenth century pictorial sources, they are not depicted sitting at meals or in a position of power and authority. Rather, they use the tables in work-related activities, usually involving technologies imported from Europe. In the example from the Florentine Codex (Figure 4), the man is shown using metal shears to cut cloth.

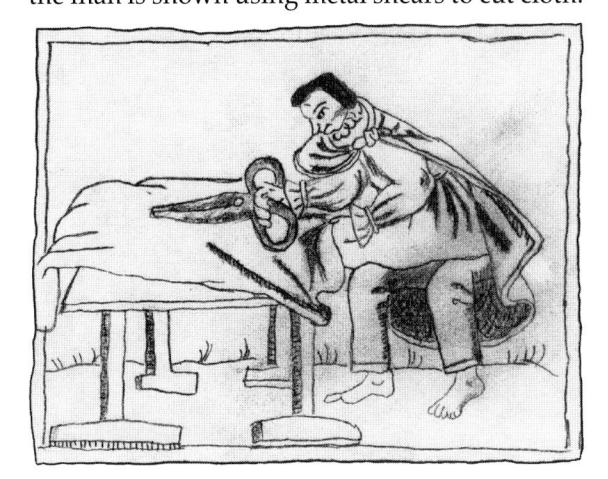

Figure 4. Florentine Codex, an indigenous man using a metal shear to cut cloth (drawing by Lee Ann Monaghan, after Sahagún).

Thus in the sixteenth-century sources, tables tend to be associated with powerful officials, colonial government, religious authority, bureaucracy, European technologies, and Spanish eating habits. The link drawn between colonialism and food by the indigenous authors of the codices is not purely symbolic—in the Codex Sierra, which is an account of town expenditures from 1550 to 1564, one of the largest categories of debits the town incurs is what they needed to pay for the special foods townspeople served to visiting Spanish and Church administrators. (The food served to the Spanish officials in Figure 1 cost the town 15 pesos, at a time when a good horse cost about 35 pesos.)

The idea that the *mesa* incorporates an indigenous perspective on governmentality can be demonstrated in the uses and imagery of the *mesa* in contemporary shamanic discourse. In some Mixtec towns prayers and offerings that involve the *mesa* are made before the *ndoso*, important figures in contemporary Mixtec cosmology. One example is a prayer by Florentino Velasco, where he asked for the return of a client's soul. The following is a relevant excerpt (the full text is reproduced in Monaghan 1990):

> Where is the one who wants to eat?
> Where is the one who wants to drink?
>
> Because the angry *nu'un* is seated here.
> The *nu'un* that eats is seated here.
>
> The one who was born in the cloud
> The one who was born in the wind.
>
> Those who gave
>   Breath of your mouth you gave
>   Breath of your face you gave
>
> At the center of his bones
> At the center of his muscles
>
> At the center of his mouth
> At the center of his veins
>
> And now we are falling again
>   Seven tables
>   Seven adornments
>
> We are falling
>   We will introduce the tables (*mesas*)
>   We will introduce the adornments
>
> And I am going to introduce
>   Seven tables
>   Seven adornments
>
> We are going to introduce
>   Underneath this
>   Underneath this now
>
> I am going to stick it in
>   To the angry *nu'un*
>   To the *nu'un* of the air.
>
> The god *San Atatya*
> The god *San Ishumu*
> The god *San Kisencio*
>
> You, *Juana*
> You, *Tiresa*
> You, *Tifania*
> You, *Masave*
> You, *Masalu*
>
> All the holies that exist
> And I am going to shout your name
>
> So that you come together again
> So that you come together again
>
> Where will I place the table?
> Where will I place the table?

While the *ndoso* in Florentino Velasco's town is located on a hill above the town center, in many places *ndoso* are associated with caves, in which they have stored great wealth. They are often said to take the form of a luminous ball of fire that can be seen flying through the air at night. *Ndoso* have individual personalities, and are associated with specific locales, often mountains, where they occupy caves that contain wealth items (Jansen 1982; for another account see Monaghan 1995). They are closely connected with saints, and often the terms saint and *ndoso* are used interchangeably. Stories about the *ndoso* portray them as heroic figures. In Santiago Nuyoo a *ndoso* defended a mountain from the attack of another *ndoso*, who attempted to carry it off. They also enter into competitions with one another, seeing, for example, who can best endure heat and cold, who can eat the most, who has the most money. These same kinds of general stories are also told about *caciques*, the ancient Mixtec nobility. Indeed in San Miguel el Grande *ndoso* are referred to as *caciques* (Jansen 1982:310). The sixteenth-century *Relación Geografica* for Juxtlahuaca calls the *ndoso* a valiant warrior, sacrificed to the sun, and the Alvarado dictionary translates it as war captain (Jansen 1982:311). In the Mixteca Baja people tell the same general kinds of heroic stories about the *ndoso* that they do in the Alta and on the coast, but they refer to them as *iya*, using the old Mixtec term for royalty.

Ndosos, then, are clearly associated with the ancient noble and warrior class. They are strong, heroic, wealthy, and divine figures, who often have prickly personalities. In the coastal region of the Mixteca they are associated with ancient kingdoms, and take the form of large boulders or standing slabs of stone that look like blank stela. Mixtec people on the coast of Oaxaca come to these places to pray and make sacrifices.

In praying for the return of his client's soul Florentino Velasco created a cosmogram, and invoked the presence of the gods, calling them forth. He then named them. The closest term for shaman I could find in the Mixtec of Santiago Nuyoo was *tee* (or *naa*) *ca'a shini nu'un* "he (or she) who speaks the name of the holy," highlighting the Native American proposition that uttering something makes its existence manifest. The curer thus creates a setting or forum for interaction with the gods, who then can be appeased and manipulated on behalf of clients. In the case of the prayer he offered before the *ndoso*, Don Florentino made offerings of food of some sort (candles, incense, and flowers are foods the gods eat). He fed the gods because they were "angry." His hope was that the offerings would substitute for the client and they would release the client's soul.

In Mesoamerican theology gods are distinguished not by being absolutely good or pure, but by their power. This is one of the reasons some of the imagery of the gods is drawn from locally powerful figures who may have roots in the indigenous nobility. However, features of landlords, Spaniards, other Europeans, *mestizos*, government officials, and others whom the indigenous people may have been in contact with are included. In this theology, gods and humans are not bound to one another through a project of salvation. Rather, the gods are vital because they control fertility, health, and life here and now. The gods, at the same time, are aloof, and can easily be made angry. Mixtec religiosity requires one to be humble, to beg forgiveness, even to weep. In other parts of Mesoamerica people have to work hard to get the gods to notice them, making elaborate offerings, playing music, shooting off fireworks, and making other loud noises. In the prayer cited above, Florentino Velasco "shouts" the names of the gods, to gain their attention (for a review see Monaghan 2000).

Part of the significance of the *mesa* in Mesoamerican belief and ceremony is—as the above example and other accounts in the ethnographic literature (Sharon 1976) suggest—that it underpins the meeting of humans and the gods. The roots of this can be seen in sixteenth-century depictions, where the *mesa* is portrayed as a place of mediation between Spanish colonists and indigenous subjects. Note that in Figures 1 and 2 from the Codex Sierra, the indigenous artists (and indigenous readers) look on the table as something one approaches, not something that one sits at in a position of power. We would even be able to see the Mixtec officials of Texupa standing before the table of the *corregidor* in Figure 2 if the page did not have a hole in the place where they were drawn; we know they were there because the accompanying text lists them: the governor, the *alcaldes*, the *escribano*, the *alguaciles* and the *tequitlato*. As I pointed out, in government offices throughout rural Mexico (which are descended from the colonial *cabildo*), the tables of officials are lined up in the municipal building, with the highest official in the center. Those who enter the building are thus immediately confronted by this row of figures behind tables and desks, who one must approach to make a petition or to answer a summons. In contemporary religious discourse, the gods are often depicted sitting behind tables like officials. For example, Maria Sabina, in an interview with Alvaro Estrada, spoke of a vision that the mushrooms ("the saint children") gave her: "Some people appeared who inspired me with respect. I knew they were the Principal Ones of whom my ancestors spoke. They were seated behind a table on which there were many written papers…I knew it was a revelation the saint children were giving me" (Estrada 1981:47-50). For the Mixe, the calendar "is visualized as a set of stairs or a ladder leading up and down a mountain from a celestial table where the divine elders hold their reunions" (Lipp 1991:152; see also Sharon this volume for Tepehua and Totonac examples).

In the Mixteca, as in many other places, rights and resources have long been allocated through patron/client ties, so that power accrues to those who are able to act as intermediaries between officials in high positions and local people. To be successful as a mediator, one has to be able to deliver resources to clients (e.g., jobs on road construction, development loans for housing construction, a favorable judgment in a legal proceeding) and keep one's clients convinced that one has the ability to successfully interact with the powerful. At the same time the mediator must be able to show those in power that he or she can mobilize clients on their behalf (such as getting everyone in town to travel to a distinct capital dressed in traditional costumes to attend a political rally), and he or she must be unstintingly hospitable to those in power when they come to visit by providing elaborate meals, handing out gifts, bribes, and kickbacks, all accompanied by special pleading, flattery, and servility. Another example of the correlation between the way people interact with the gods and the way they interact with the powerful concerns the Otomi saint *Santa Catarina*. James Dow tells us that *Santa Catarina* is an evil god, whose church is compared to the municipal building, and the Otomi bribe *Santa Catarina* to get out of trouble, just as they do with officials (Dow 1986:87-88). Indeed, early Spanish observers sometimes glossed the offerings they observed Mixtec people making to the gods as "tribute."

Saying simply that the person of knowledge making offerings functions as a kind of mediator leaves a lot unsaid. There are, for example, many possible relationships among the mediator and the parties to the transaction. But the main point here is that *mesas* are central to religious discourse and ceremonial practice precisely because they are associated with officialdom, the state, the church, and European food habits and the fact that the power of the *mesa* in ceremony and belief is derived from the role it initially played as a place of mediation between Spanish colonists and indigenous subjects. In the specific case of the *mesa*, the person who sets the table and serves those sitting at it positions himself or herself as an intermediary—be it a shaman attempting to free a client's soul from the grasp of an earth deity, or a broker in a district capital office trying to get judicial police to release a client's son from jail. Shamans in the Mixteca, by setting up a *mesa* for curing, propitiation, and other rites, create the conditions—dictated by their historically situated and regional reality—whereby they can function as intermediaries, pleasing and pacifying the powerful on behalf of needy clients. The *mesa* thus functions not only as a prop in the staging of a ceremonial performance, but also as a kind of technology for dealing with capricious, distant, and powerful beings.

It is important not to fall into an extreme reductionism by viewing Mesoamerican discourse surrounding *mesas* as an eccentric version of government policy and European culture (see Feinberg 1997:432-433), or that, in treating religious practices historically, we only look at them as the product of conquest and colonization, forgetting that people like the Mixtec are also the heirs of one of the great world civilizations. More specifically, while the concept of the *mesa* can be seen as part of a complex surrounding the making of a gift, bribe, tribute, or payment to a powerful being, this does not account for the full range of meanings associated with it or why the *mesa*, rather than some other item associated with European culture and power (the chair, for one) should be the object of such complex symbolic elaboration and widespread ceremonial use. Part of the answer has to do with the way the shape of the table, with its four sides and center, expresses Mesoamerican cosmological principles (Sharon 1976). But the significance of the table must also take into account the way it expresses and enacts basic moral propositions articulated in Mesoamerican theology.

In the *circa* 1650 dictionary by the Friar Tomás de Coto, he tells us that the Maya at this time already used the Spanish loan word "*mesa*" for table. But he also adds that in the past they had a "table of stone," upon which they would make sacrifices, which they called *cemet abah* (Coto 1983:346). Other examples can be presented, such as the use of tables for offerings in Days of the Dead rites; even a casual search of the pre-Columbian sources or review of the archaeological record (see Brady this volume) reveals the altar as the nearest equivalent to a Spanish table. It thus appears that in many traditions, Spanish tables have been synthesized with Mesoamerican altars.

The connection between tables and altars goes beyond similarities in their appearance. Both the Spanish table and the Mesoamerican altar have close links to food, especially prepared food. The offerings religious specialists make throughout the Mesoamerican region are primarily, if not exclusively, food of some sort. There is the food that humans conventionally consume (eggs, tortillas, meat, and broth) as well as the foods that the gods consume, such as the smoke of incense, the tallow of candles (in Zinacantán, candles given to the gods must be made from tallow because they want to eat meat [Vogt 1976:56]), rubber, and so on. The Nahua linguist Hernandez Cuellar (1982:53) even uses the compound term "*comida-*

ofrenda" to characterize the essential nature of sacrificial offerings made in his town. Furthermore, throughout the region, offerings are related metonymically and metaphorically to the human body. For example, in the Mixteca, flowers may be rubbed all over a client's body before they are offered to the gods—the plants then carry some of the substance of the person. The foods may also stand for organ parts, or even be shaped in the form of the human body, such as Lacandon rubber offerings (for a discussion, see Monaghan 2000:36-39).

Elsewhere I have argued that the offerings Mesoamerican people make are predicated upon a covenant of mutual obligation made between humans and the gods. This is recorded in many Mesoamerican traditions (see Monaghan 2000:37-38). In essence, this covenant specifies that the two sides have suffered to make possible one another's continued existence. In the Mixtec version it is the Earth which suffers as humans till it; and humans are consumed by the Earth at death so that human life can be transformed and enlarged by agriculture and a civilized existence. As they put it, "We eat the Earth and the Earth eats us." The gods, then, through their self-sacrifice, merit the continued obeisance of humans, who are thereby obligated to the gods and need to do what is necessary to continue to merit the gods' attention. The covenant thus links humans and the gods through a relationship of debt and merit, which is tied to all sorts of desired processes, from good crops to health for family members. The offering, or more concretely, the self-sacrifice, repeatedly invokes the ultimate act of merit and the cancellation of debt, when humans are themselves consumed by the gods.

Sharon's work on the importance of the church altar in the concept of the *mesa* should also be cited in this context (Sharon 1978). The point I wish to make here is simply that long before the Spanish arrived, Mesoamerican peoples used an alimentary idiom to describe their relationships with the gods. It thus appears that the *mesa* has come to play a central role in contemporary Mesoamerican religion not only because it is a kind of technology for dealing with the powerful, or that it conforms to basic cosmological orientations, or that it references the transformations worked by the Catholic priest on the church altar, but also because of a longstanding Mesoamerican proposition that the relationships of debt and merit, which are so important in structuring the moral universe, are articulated through self-sacrifice and expressed in acts of consumption. So the food offerings—once set out on the altar to merit the attention of powerful, distant, and perhaps angry gods—are now set out for them on the *mesa*. Sacrificial activity and the *mesa* are now so closely tied that in some traditions the *mesa* can no longer be translated as "table." In the prayer Florentino Velasco shared with me in which he asked for the return of a client's soul, he describes the series of offerings he made (in the couplet "adornments and *mesas*") which were a chicken, flowers, candles, and copal set on the ground to one side of him. What is important to note is that he called each of these a "*mesa*." That is, each chicken, each bunch of flowers, each candle, and each piece of copal that he placed on the earth is a "*mesa*," so that the *mesa* is conceptually indistinguishable from the sacrificial offering. In this discourse, the *mesa* has been so thoroughly reinterpreted through the lens of the altar that it is no longer a piece of furniture. Similarly, the beings seated behind the shaman's *mesa* are not colonial officials, but ancestors, principle ones, *ndosos*, and other gods. What may have begun as a quintessential symbol of Spanish food habits and power has become a distinct Mesoamerican phenomenon.

References Cited

Alvarado, Francisco de
   1962 *Vocabulario en lengua mixteca*. Mexico City: Instituto Nacional de Antropología e Historia.

Codice de Yanhuitlan
   1994 *Codice de Yanhuitlan*. Facsimile edition. Mexico City: Instituto Nacional de Antropología e Historia y Benemerita Universidad Autonoma de Puebla.

Dow, James
   1986 *The Shaman's Touch. Otomi Indian Symbolic Healing*. Salt Lake City: University of Utah Press.

Estrada, Alvaro
   1981 *Maria Sabina: Her Life and Chants*. Translated by Henry Munn. Santa Barbara: Ross-Erikson.

Feinberg, Benjamin
   1997 Three Mazatec Wise Ones and Their Books. *Critique of Anthropology* 17:411-437.

Hernandez Cuellar, Rosendo
   1982 *La religion nahua en Texoloc, municipio de Xochiatipan, Hgo*. Cuadernos de Información y Divulgación para Maestros Bilingues, no. 51. Mexico City: Instituto Nacional Indigenista y Secretaria de Educación Pública, Programa de Formación Profesional de Etnolinguistas.

Jansen, Maarten
  1982 *Huisi Tacu: Estudio interpretativo de un libro mixteco antiguo: Codex Vindobonensis Mexicanus I.* Amsterdam: Centrum voor Studie en Documentatie van Latijns Amerika.

Leon, Nicolas, ed.
  1933 *Codice Sierra: Traducción al español de su texto nahuatl y explicación de sus pinturas jeoglíficas.* Mexico City: Museo Nacional de Antropología.

Lipp, Frank
  1991 *The Mixes of Oaxaca: Religion, Ritual and Healing.* Austin: University of Texas Press.

Monaghan, John
  1990 Performance and the Structure of the Mixtec Codices. *Ancient Mesoamerica* 1:133-140.

  1995 *The Covenants with Earth and Rain: Exchange, Sacrifice and Revelation in Mixtec Sociality.* Norman: University of Oklahoma Press.

  2000 Theology and History in the Study of Mesoamerican Religions. In: John Monaghan (volume editor) and Victoria Bricker (general editor), *Handbook of Middle American Indians, Ethnology Supplement.* Austin: University of Texas Press.

Sahagún, Fray Bernardino de
  1950-1982 *Florentine Codex: General History of the Things of New Spain, by Fray Bernardino de Sahagún.* Translated from the Aztec into English, with notes and illustrations, by Arthur J. O. Anderson and Charles E. Dibble. In 13 parts. Monographs of the School of American Research, no. 14, parts I-XIII. Santa Fe: The School of American Research and the University of Utah Press.

  1982 *Historia general de las cosas de Nueva España: Primera version integra del texto castellano del manuscrito conocido como Códice Florentino.* Introducción, paleografía, glosario y notas por Alfredo López Austin y Josefina García Quintana. 2 vols. Mexico City: Fomento Cultural Banamex.

Sharon, Douglas
  1976 Distribution of the Mesa in Latin America. *Journal of Latin American Lore* 2(1):71-95.

  1978 *Wizard of the Four Winds: A Shaman's Story.* New York: Free Press.

Taussig, Michael
  1981 *Shamanism, Colonialism and the Wild Man: A Study in Terror and Healing.* Chicago: University of Chicago Press.

Tsing, Anna Lowenhaupt
  1993 *In the Realm of the Diamond Queen: Marginality in an Out-of-the-Way Place.* Princeton: Princeton University Press.

Thomas, Nicolas, and Caroline Humphrey, eds.
  1994 *Shamanism, History and the State.* Ann Arbor: University of Michigan Press.

Vogt, Evon
  1976 *Tortillas for the Gods: A Symbolic Analysis of Zinacanteco Rituals.* Cambridge, Mass.: Harvard University Press.